Roseann Adams

Adults and the Changing Workplace

1985 Yearbook
of the
American Vocational Association

American Vocational Association, Inc.
2020 North Fourteenth Street
Arlington, Virginia 22201

1985 Yearbook Advisory Committee
William Ashley
Project Director
National Center for Research in Vocational Education
Columbus, Ohio

Gene Callahan
Deputy Superintendent of Instruction and Personnel
Francis Tuttle Vo-Tech Center
Oklahoma City, Oklahoma

Arnold Loomis
State Director
Vocational-Technical Education Service
Michigan State Department of Education
Lansing, Michigan

Bruce Merrifield
Assistant Secretary
Productivity, Technology and Innovation
U.S. Department of Commerce
Washington, DC

Gloria Pursell
Economic Development Coordinator
Fox Valley Technical Institute
Outagamie County
Appleton, Wisconsin

Kenneth Jamison
President
Ashtabule County Joint Vocational School
Jefferson, Ohio

Richard Guantone
Assistant Dean
Industrial Technologies
Kirkwood Community College
Cedar Rapids, Iowa

Editor
Carol Herrnstadt Shulman

ISBN-0-89514-047-0 (cloth)
ISBN-0-89514-048-9 (paper)

Contents

INTRODUCTION

Adults are a growing and important population in postsecondary education. And, most adults turn to education for job-related reasons: to upgrade skills, to advance in a career, or to change careers. Concurrent with the growth of the adult student market, rapid technological developments and structural changes in the economy have made the need and the demand for vocational education even more imperative among the adult population.

These developments means that lifelong learning is becoming a familiar concept. No longer can Americans assume that a high school diploma or the postsecondary education and training they received as recent high school graduates will be sufficient for a lifetime. Experience in the job market teaches them otherwise.

Given these trends, the 1985 American Vocational Association Yearbook, *Adults and the Changing Workplace: Vocational Educators' Challenge*, presents, in 31 chapters, information about adults, the economy, and the workforce that lead to several strong conclusions about what vocational educators should be thinking about and acting on in the coming years:

- Vocational educators must focus on adult workers as much as, if not more than, on those just entering the job market.
- Vocational educators must consider the technological and structural changes at work in the nation's economy so that they can prepare their students to adapt to them.
- Vocational educators must be sensitive to and know how to utilize adult education theory.
- Vocational educators must seek new and creative approaches to training adults for employment, especially in partnership with the private sector.

This Yearbook is organized in five sections, each one focusing on a major issue concerning the adult worker's educational needs and vocational education's role in meeting those needs.

Section I reviews and analyzes the changes that are occurring in the labor force. Morgan V. Lewis, Senior Research Specialist at the National Center for Research in Vocational Education, projects labor market needs to the year 2000. He examines both the view that high technology will create new jobs and the opposing position that high technology means a decline in new job opportunities. And, William L. Ashley and Frank C. Pratzner, Research Specialist II and Senior Program Specialist, respectively, at the National Center for Research in Vocational Education, identify the general rather than specific skills that adult workers must have if they are to adapt successfully to changing job requirements.

Section II looks at the universe of adult education, first in broad terms and then at specific organizations and programs that offer adult education. Wendell Smith, Dean of Continuing Education at the University of Missouri-St. Louis, discusses the term "adult education" in both its narrow and broad interpretations. He examines changes in delivery systems that promise to improve participation rates for adult learners. Robert M. Worthington, Assistant Secretary for Vocational and Adult Education, the United States Department of Education, takes a close look at the issues involved in adult vocational education. He focuses particularly on the vocational training needs of special groups in the population, such as those with limited proficiency in English, and on building working adults' productive capacity. Carol B. Aslanian, Director of the Office of Adult Learning Services, The College Board, describes the conditions under which adults are likely to seek out further education, arguing that certain changes in adults' lives compel them to get more education.

Patrick R. Penland, Professor, School of Library and Information Science, University of Pittsburgh, describes adult learning styles, pointing out that adults learn best when educators can match learning styles with the instructional approach. Paul E. Barton, President, National Institute for Work and Learning, examines funding and resources for adult education, especially state-supported training for unemployed workers. Beverly Copeland, Associate Executive Director, the American Association of Adult and Continuing Education, and Meredyth A. Leahy, Director, Continuing Education, Cabrini College (Pennsylvania), talk about recruiting and employing adult educators, paying particular attention to how to evaluate applicants for employment and how to supervise them once they are hired.

Opportunities for adult vocational education are incredibly diversified. Nine chapters of Section II describe some of this diversity as it occurs in formal settings. Lee R. Kerschner, Executive Director, and Christopher Davis, Assistant for State Relations, both with the National Association of Trade and Technical Schools, discuss enrollments, curriculum, and training in private and proprietary schools. Dr. Kerschner is also Secretary of the Association's Accrediting Commission. Robert Craig, Executive Vice President for Government Affairs, the American Society for Training and Development, describes training efforts in industry, a growing sector of the postsecondary adult education market. Approximately $30 million is spent annually for employee education and training. Edgar Czarnecki, Assistant Education Director, the AFL-CIO, talks about unions' efforts at educating their members. Their work focuses on union-related issues, such as shop management and labor union history. Michael Crawford, Chancellor, Eastern Iowa Community College, discusses community colleges generally, and their efforts in vocational education in particular. Lt. Col. (Ret.)

Clinton L. Anderson examines the special training efforts the armed forces make to ensure that their servicemen and women can accomplish their tasks. Lee Transier, Dean, Continuing Education, University of Houston-Central Campus, describes the organization, the structure and the market for continuing education. Mary Nell Greenwood, Administrator, Extension Services, United States Department of Agriculture, provides a briefing on the organization, structure, program content and delivery systems for cooperative and extension services. Paul V. Delker, Director, Division of Adult Education Services, discusses the continuing need for adult high school education opportunities and describes the avenues open to adults who seek to get their high school diploma. And, Thomas N. Daymont, Assistant Professor, Department of Industrial Relations, Temple University, analyzes federal job training program efforts, with special attention to the Job Training Partnership Act of 1982.

Section III deals with special issues that surround the education and training of adults. Mary Ellen Kiss, Director, Institutional Development Programs, and Margaret A. Taibi, Program Director, Career Assessment Planning System, both with Prince George's Community College, examine adults' need for support services and present a model for assessment and counseling now in use at their institution. Yvonne Ferguson, Assistant Director for Adult Education, the Bureau of Vocational-Technical Adult Education, West Virginia, discusses creative approaches adult educators can take to recruit and retain adult learners. David L. Goetsch, Director of Educational Services and Director of Institutional Research, Okalossa-Walton Junior College (Florida) looks at the implications of high technology for vocational education curricula and delivery systems, pointing to a promising model for curriculum development. And, Alan B. Knox, Professor of Continuing and Vocational Education, the University of Wisconsin, discusses the factors educators should consider in deciding to form or not to form collaborative arrangements.

Section IV considers groups with special needs and interests in the adult learner population. The National Council for the Future of Women in the Workplace of the National Federation of Business and Professional Women's Clubs, analyzes the problems of women in the workforce. Roy G. Phillips, Campus Vice President, Miami-Dade Community College-North Campus, discusses minority groups' attrition as they move up the educational ladder. William P. Reich, Training Director, United States Catholic Conference, describes issues facing refugees and immigrants. George Travis, Systematic Human Resource Development Coordinator, Ohio Developmental Disability Planning Council, looks at the problems facing disabled adults. And, Robert G. Wegmann, Professor, Behavioral Sciences, University of Houston, Clearlake, examines the changing mix of employment opportunities and how these changes affect workers, particularly those employed in factories.

Section V offers examples of how to put theory into practice. Its authors describe successful adult education programs. Robert E.Scarborough, President, Greater Cincinnati Industrial Training Corporation, describes that organization's partnership with industry, government and education. Robert W. Rupert, Assistant Superintendant, Adult/Regional Occupational Centers/Programs, Education Division, the Los Angeles Unified School District, analyzes the predominantly minority population served in that District, the District's programs, and its delivery systems. Gale King, Training Director, Fisher Body Division, General Motors Corporation, and William Weisgerber, Chief, Program Planning and Development, Michigan State Department of Education, explain how changes in the automotive industry have resulted in new collaborative efforts to train workers among industry, unions, and government. Barry L. Reece, Professor of Marketing Education, Virginia Polytechnic Institute, describes the short-term adult vocational education programs recently developed for the State of Virginia. And, Rosemary F. Kolde, Administrative Specialist, Great Oaks Vocational Joint School District, Cincinnati, discusses the District's Center for Employment Resources Development that makes available one-stop job counseling services for adult workers.

This 1985 Yearbook promises to be only the beginning of a continuing focus for the association on vocational education for adult workers. How we respond to the challenges presented here may well determine the future vitality of our field.

Gary D. Meers
President

American Vocational Assocation

YEARBOOK CONTRIBUTORS

CLINTON L. ANDERSON is Lieutenant Colonel, Retired, Lexington, Virginia.

WILLIAM L. ASHLEY is Research Specialist II, the National Center for Research in Vocational Education, Columbus, Ohio.

CAROL B. ASLANIAN is Director, the Office of Adult Learning Services, The College Board, New York, New York.

PAUL E. BARTON is President, National Institute for Work and Learning, Washington, D.C.

BEVERLY COPELAND is Associate Executive Director, American Association of Adult and Continuing Education, Washington, D.C.

ROBERT CRAIG is Executive Vice President for Government Affairs, the American Society for Training and Development, Washington, D.C.

MICHAEL CRAWFORD is Chancellor, Eastern Iowa Community College, Davenport, Iowa.

EDGAR CZARNECKI is Assistant Education Director, AFL-CIO, Washington, D.C.

CHRISTOPHER DAVIS is Assistant for State Relations, the National Association of Trade and Technical Schools, Washington, D.C.

THOMAS N. DAYMONT is Assistant Professor, Department of Industrial Relations, Temple University, Philadelphia, Pennsylvania.

PAUL V. DELKER is Director, Division of Adult Education Services, United States Department of Education, Washington, D.C.

YVONNE FERGUSON is Assistant Director for Adult Education, Bureau of Vocational-Technical Adult Education, Charleston, West Virginia.

DAVID L. GOETSCH is Director of Educational Services and Director of Institutional Research, Okalossa-Walton Junior College, Niceville, Florida.

MARY NELL GREENWOOD is Administrator, Extension Services, United States Department of Agriculture, Washington, D.C.

LEE R. KERSCHNER is Executive Director, National Association of Trade and Technical Schools, Washington, D.C.; and, Secretary of that association's Accrediting Commission.

GALE KING is Training Director, Fisher Body Division, General Motors Corporation, Warren, Michigan.

MARY ELLEN KISS is Director, Institutional Development Programs, Prince George's Community College, Largo, Maryland.

ALAN B. KNOX is Professor of Continuing and Vocational Education, University of Wisconsin, Madison, Wisconsin.

ROSEMARY F. KOLDE is Administrative Specialist, Great Oaks Vocational Joint School District, Cincinnati, Ohio.

MEREDYTH A. LEAHY is Director, Continuing Education, Cabrini College, Radnor, Pennsylvania.

MORGAN V. LEWIS is Senior Research Specialist, the National Center for Research in Vocational Education, Columbus, Ohio.

NATIONAL COUNCIL ON THE FUTURE OF WOMEN IN THE WORKPLACE is a project of the National Federation of Business and Professional Women's Clubs, Inc., Washington, D.C.

PATRICK R. PENLAND is Professor, School of Library and Information Science, University of Pittsburgh, Pittsburgh, Pennsylvania.

ROY G. PHILLIPS is Campus Vice President, Miami-Dade Community College, North Miami, Florida.

FRANK C. PRATZNER is Senior Program Specialist, the National Center for Research in Vocational Education, Columbus, Ohio.

BARRY L. REECE is Professor of Marketing Education, Virginia Polytechnic Institute, Blacksburg, Virginia.

WILLIAM P. REICH is Training Director, United States Catholic Conference, Washington, D.C.

ROBERT W. RUPERT is Assistant Superintendent, Adult/Regional Occupational Centers/Programs, Education Division, Los Angeles Unified School District, Los Angeles, California.

ROBERT SCARBOROUGH is President, Greater Cincinnati Industrial Training Corporation, Cincinnati, Ohio.

WENDELL SMITH is Dean of Continuing Education, University of Missouri, St. Louis, Missouri.

MARGARET A. TAIBI is Program Director, Career Assessment Planning System, Prince George's Community College, Largo, Maryland.

LEE TRANSIER is Dean, Continuing Education, University Houston-Central Campus, Houston, Texas.

GEORGE TRAVIS is Systematic Human Resource Development Coordinator, Ohio Development Disability Council, Columbus, Ohio.

ROBERT G. WEGMANN is Professor, Behavioral Sciences, University of Houston-Clearlake, Houston, Texas.

WILLIAM WEISGERBER is Chief, Program Planning and Development, Vocational-Technical Education Services, State Department of Education, Lansing, Michigan.

ROBERT M. WORTHINGTON is Assistant Secretary, Vocational and Adult Education, United States Department of Education, Washington, D.C.

SECTION I

CHANGES IN THE LABOR FORCE

Vocational educators have always had to prepare their students to enter the workforce and to be competitive in the job market. Today, this imperative means that vocational educators need to know about demographics which define the characteristics of their students, and about changes in the labor market and in the workplace—both technological and by occupational sector—that determine job opportunities and employment mobility.

This first section describes the demographic and industrial context in which vocational education must function through the end of the century. One fact is quite clear: adults already in the workforce will not be lost to vocational education. Technological change and worker displacement will send these workers back for more training so that they can once again become competitive in the marketplace. At the same time, changing demographics will mean that there will be fewer new entrants into the workforce. Without a large supply of recently trained young workers, older employees, and their training needs, become even more important to them and their employees.

By the year 2005, most of the babies born in 1984 will be employed. Morgan V. Lewis looks at the needs of the labor market into which these infants will enter. He presents both sides of the argument about the implications of technological development for workers—whether it will require a more or a less highly skilled workforce. And, he provides a prospective for viewing the unfolding changes in the nation's labor market.

Frank C. Pratzner and William L. Ashley discuss the critical importance of occupational adaptability and transferable skills in today's and tomorrow's labor market. They argue that vocational education has an essential role to play in developing those skills, and they provide guidance on how educators can plan for teaching their students so that they can sustain their careers.

1

Together, these authors make a powerful argument that vocational educators would be doing an incomplete job if they did not prepare their students to expect that their careers will involve considerable change and, often, more education to be competitive in the labor market.

LABOR MARKET NEEDS TO THE YEAR 2000

*Morgan V. Lewis**

Many of the babies born in 1984 will enter the labor force in some type of regular, paid employment when they are 16 years old in the year 2000. By 2005, most of 1984's infants will be members of the labor force. What kind of skills will they need? And, how should our society's education and training institutions prepare these new babies, as well as millions of older children and adult workers, with the skills this nation will need?

This is the dominant educational question of our time. It is the focus of a debate between those who believe the rapid technological and economic changes this nation is experiencing will require higher skill levels throughout the work force and those who believe the net effect of technology is to lower, not raise, the skills workers need.

This chapter provides a perspective for viewing the technological and structural changes acting on the economy and the effects of these changes on the skills needed in the labor force. It summarizes the main arguments on both sides of this debate and presents some projections on the general distribution of occupations during the next ten years. This chapter does not attempt to describe new jobs that will appear in forthcoming years. That task has been performed by others.

Arguments in the Debate

Will forthcoming technological changes raise or lower the level of skills workers need to use these technologies? Two major positions on this question dominate the debate and command public attention.

Technology Requires Higher Skills

Among those who assume that higher skill levels will be needed are the various commissions and task forces that issued reports on the condition of secondary

*The material in this chapter is based on research conducted at the National Center for Research in Vocational Education with support from the Office of Vocational and Adult Education, U.S. Department of Education. Jeannette Fraser and Paul Unger have assisted in this research.

3

education in 1983. The most prominent of these reports, *A Nation at Risk* by the National Commission on Excellence in Education, provides a good example of this viewpoint. The Commission presents indicators that show a decline in the basic skill levels of students and warns: "These deficiencies come at a time when the demand for highly skilled workers in new fields is accelerating rapidly." As evidence of the need for higher skill levels, the Commission cites:

- the penetration of computers and computer-controlled equipment into every aspect of American life;
- an estimate that by the turn of the century millions of jobs will involve laser technology and robotics (the source for this estimate is not reported);
- the technological transformation of occupations in health, medical science, energy production, food processing, construction, and the building, repair and maintenance of sophisticated equipment.

Technology Lowers Skill Requirements

There are, on the other hand, many researchers who have examined labor market trends and concluded that the overall effect of most technological advances is to lower skill levels. The most prominent of those who argue this position are Henry Levin and Russell Rumberger, coauthor of papers analyzing the effects of technology on skills, particularly the so-called "high technology."

Levin and Rumberger concede that advanced technology will increase employment in some scientific and technical occupations. In total, however, these increases constitute few of the new jobs to be created in coming years and an even smaller portion of the total work force.

Most of the new jobs, they observe, will be in low-skill service, sales and clerical occupations, and even in these occupations, Levin and Rumburger see technology lowering skill levels. The counter clerk in a fast food restaurant is a good example of this phenomenon. Before the introduction of more sophisticated cash registers, a clerk needed to be able to write a customer's order on a note pad, add the cost of the separate items ordered, add in the sales tax, total the bill, and calculate the amount of change due. With the new registers, the clerk merely pushes buttons which have small replicas of the items ordered and enters the amount paid. The machine calculates the total cost, including tax, and the amount of change to be returned to the customer, thereby eliminating the need for even low levels of reading, writing, and calculating skills. Such an example offers compelling evidence that advanced technology can lower skill levels.

Arguing by example is risky, however, for contrary examples can often be offered. Either side of this issue can use the effects of word processing equipment on the skills required by typists to support their view. The claim is sometimes made that word processors lower the skill requirements for a typist. The equipment makes it very easy to correct key stroke errors, automatically hyphenates words at the end of lines, and can even check and correct spelling errors. Understanding the manner in which word processors work, however, the transfer of material from temporary to permanent storage, the use of various command keys and so forth, appears to require higher level conceptual skills than those involved in straight typing. Supervisors of word processing operators find that there are some good typists who cannot make the transition to word processing.

An Unresolved Issue

The effects of advanced technology vary so much by occupational area, and data on these effects are so sparse, that no overall conclusions are warranted. New technology will undoubtedly require some well-trained, highly skilled individuals to design, manufacture, maintain, and repair the new equipment. It will also undoubtedly displace some workers and make their skills obsolete.

For most workers though, the major influence of new technology will be on how they do their jobs, not on what they do. Office workers will use personal computers and electronic storage rather than typewriters, paper, and file cabinets. But they will still create and transmit information. Machinists may use lasers rather than drill presses and lathes, but they will still shape metal. In most cases technological development neither creates new jobs nor destroys old ones; it primarily changes existing jobs.

Projected Demand for Workers

Despite the rapid pace of technological change, major changes in the overall composition of the labor force appear unlikely. Table 1 presents four widely accepted myths about the effects of technology and counters these myths with the actual evidence. Furthermore, the most recent projections on industry and occupational trends available from the U.S. Bureau of Labor Statistics also indicate that overall composition will remain relatively stable. These projections cover the period 1982 to 1995.

Labor Force

Total civilian employment is projected to increase 25 percent from 1982 to 1995, from 102 million to 128 million. Mainly contributing to this increase will be growth in employment in service-producing industries, namely transportation, utilities, trade, finance, insurance, real estate, other services, and government.

Within this broad clustering, the fastest growing category is the one labeled

TABLE 1

Selected Myths and Realities About the Effects of Technology on Occupations

Myth	Reality
Virtually all businesses use computers to keep their financial records	In 1982, there are almost twice as many bookkeepers who kept records by hand (957,000) as there were computer specialists in the total work force (521,000 programmers and systems analysts)[a]
Automatic teller machines are replacing human tellers in banks	Between 1979 and 1982, the number of automatic tellers in use increased over 19,000.[b] In that same period, the number of human tellers increased by 73,000.[c]
The automation of manufacturing will create a major demand for robotics technicians	Maintenance and repair of robots is primarily done by industrial mechanics who receive a few weeks of training from the robot manufacturers.[d]
High technology will be the major source of new jobs in the future	High technology industries (even when defined quite broadly) are projected to account for only 17 percent of the new jobs created between 1982 and 1995.[e]

Sources: [a] Silvestri, Lukasiewicz, and Einstein
[b] Nilson Report
[c] Silvestri, Lukasiewicz, and Einstein
[d] Fraser, Unger, and Lewis
[e] Riche, Hecker, and Burgan

"other services." This includes such diverse industry classifications as medical care, business services, recreation, and personal services. This "other services" classification is expected to account for one out of every three new jobs over the period 1982 to 1995 and to employ about one-fourth of the total work force by 1995.

With the movement away from manufacturing and toward services, vocational educators should understand that service industries are not synonymous with service occupations. Service industries employ the full range of occupations. In some service industries, such as medical and professional services, large proportions of the work force are professionals and technicians and are classified as such. In other service industries, such as protective services, most of the workers are in actual service occupations and are classified as such. Even in protective services, however, there are workers who are classified as managers, technicians, sercretaries, etc.

Moreover, the proportion of the work force expected to be employed in manufacturing industries in 1995 (18.4 percent) is virtually the same as was employed in 1982 (18.8 percent). If this projection holds, it means that the steady decline in the proportion of the work force in manufacturing since World War II will not continue in the coming decade. Since the total labor force will be growing, manufacturing should provide about 17 percent of the new jobs expected between 1982 and 1995.

The recent attention that high technology industries have received seems to suggest that they will be the prime sources of economic growth, productivity improvement, and employment in the coming years. While these industries will probably stimulate growth and productivity throughout the economy, their direct effect on employment will be more limited. The U.S. Bureau of Labor Statistics has developed three definitions of high-technology industries to project three different levels of employment. All three projections indicate that employment in these industries should increase faster than total employment between 1982 and 1995.

Nevertheless, even the broadest definition projects that high-technology industries will provide only 17 percent of the new jobs during this period. The middle definition suggests high-technology will provide eight percent, and the narrowest definition yields slightly more than three percent. These projections should be a warning to those states and localities attempting to deal with unemployment by focusing their economic development efforts on high technology. High technology is unlikely to mean many new jobs.

Job Growth and Openings
Industrial trends provide the context for employment, but vocational educators train for occupations, not industries. Employment opportunities for students completing vocational programs depend on growth in the total number of jobs in the economy and turnover rates in the existing jobs. For most jobs, turnover is a far more significant source of openings than is growth.

To highlight these differences, Table 2 provides two sets of projections from the Bureau of Labor Statistics. The first column contains projections of *average annual* job openings for 20 selected occupations for the period 1980 to 1990. (These 20 represent the top 10 and bottom 10 from a list of 40 developed by BLS.) These projections allow for replacement as well as growth. The second column provides projections of the growth in these occupations from 1982 to 1995. These projections do not include openings due to turnover of workers; they reflect only growth over a thirteen year period.

Clearly, worker turnover is a far more significant source of employment

Table 2

Projected Average Annual Job Openings 1980-1990 and Total Employment Change 1982-1995, by Occupation

Occupation	Projected Average Annual Openings 1980-1990 (thousands)[a]	1982-1995 Change in Total Employment (thousands)[b]
Retail trade sale workers	1,999	685
Waiters and waitresses	788	562
Cashiers	648	744
Secretaries	575	719
Cooks and chefs	399	402
Bookkeepers and accounting clerks	373	152
Assemblers	364	333
Typists	299	155
Kindergarten and elementary school teachers	217	511
Carpenters	180	247
Dental assistants	44	65
All-round machinists	43	58
Bricklayers and stonemasons	38	39
Programmers	36	205
Lawyers	34	159
Air-conditioning, heating, and refrigeration mechanics	33	55
Systems analysts	28	217[c]
Buyers	26	75
Printing press operators and	26	[d]
Automobile body repairers	25	41

Source: [a] Hecker
  [b] Silvestri, Lukasiewicz, and Einstein
  [c] This increase represents an average of 16,700 new jobs per year over the 13 year period. Since average annual openings during the period 1980 to 1990 are expected to be 28,000, replacement needs are expected to account for 11,300 jobs per year, the difference between projected annual openings and estimated annual growth.
  [d] Projections for this specific occupation not available.

opportunities than is growth for all but one of the occupations listed in the table. Growth plays an important role in many occupations. But only for systems analysts will growth account for more job opportunities than will replacement needs.

Occupations that already have large numbers of workers and that experience fairly high rates of worker turnover will in the future—just as they have in the past—provide the most employment opportunities.

Expected Technological Displacement

Robotics is one area in which the displacement of workers by machines has become an important issue. The manufacturing sector will experience the largest displacement effects of this technology. Some regions of the country will be affected far more than others. The Great Lakes states particularly, with their heavy concentrations of steel and automobile manufacturing, where the workers receive high wages, are likely to experience considerable technological displacement.

The automotive industry will experience worker displacement in four major application areas, namely, welding, assembly, painting, and machine loading and unloading. Projections of expected worker displacement range from a low of five to ten percent of the total 1980 automotive employment in assembly operations, to a high of 27 to 37 percent of total 1980 automotive employment in painting operations.

Other occupations, including checkers, examiners, packers, and machine operators are projected to experience displacement effects due to robotics by 1995, ranging from 10 to 15 percent of all workers employed within these groups.

Historically, the service industry sector experiences less fluctuation as the economy changes than does the manufacturing sector. Even during the 1979-1982 recessionary period these industries, especially the "other services" category, added workers. The increase in other services was 2.4 million workers from 1979 to 1982, a greater increase than the 2.2 million drop experienced in manufacturing during that time. Thus, employment within the service industries is not likely to be affected by automation as much as manufacturing within the next decade.

These occupation projections assume moderate rates of growth in the economy. If growth is not maintained, the rate at which corporations will invest in new equipment will decline, and technological changes will affect jobs more slowly. Conversely, higher rates of economic growth could accelerate the rate of change. The Bureau of Labor Statistics' projection methods have been criticized for not explicitly allowing for differing rates of technological change. A model has recently been developed that makes such allowances by stating differing basic assumptions about the diffusion of technology and testing the impact of these differing assumptions. If this approach improves the accuracy of projections, it is likely these features will be included in the Bureau's methods.

Evolutionary Change

This chapter presents an optimistic perspective about forthcoming technological and economic changes. The optimism is warranted despite the fundamental shift in this economy from the production and distribution of goods to the provision of information and services. The majority of the labor force is already employed in service industries, and all projections indicate that is where most new jobs will be. This is not to say that the United States will not remain a major manufacturing nation. Although only about three percent of the labor force is directly involved in farming, the United States is the world's major agricultural exporter. This three percent provides employment for a considerable proportion of the work force involved in the service industries that transport, warehouse, and market the products this sector produces. Similarly, as the productivity of our manufacturers increases, fewer workers will be able to produce more goods, and employment in industries that service these goods will increase.

Although the change this country is experiencing is revolutionary, day-to-day reality is evolutionary. No organization, public or private, can replace all its equipment and retrain all of its workers at one time. It takes time to affect the skills of the 100 million workers in the labor force. Change occurs machine-by-machine, worker-by-worker. Electric typewriters replaced manual ones and in time the electrics will be replaced by word processors. Numerically controlled lathes are replacing manually controlled ones and may themselves eventually be integrated into flexible manufacturing systems. In most cases, the secretaries and machinists who used the old equipment learn to use the new; rarely is it necessary to replace existing workers with newly hired ones. The massive displacements experienced during the past recession, primarily among steel and automobile workers, were caused far more by poor sales and international competition than they were by technology.

Optimism, however, is not an excuse for complacency or preservation of the status quo. Vocational educators have an obligation to keep their programs attuned to the needs of the workplace, and this requires a continuing effort.

The message of this chapter is that the forthcoming changes can be managed. It takes time for a new technology to move through the economy and affect the skills of any significant number of the 100 million workers in the labor force. The time required for this diffusion process allows the most likely influences of the technology to be anticipated. The best way for training institutions to identify such influences is to maintain close contact with the employers they serve. In this revolutionary period, the challenges are many, and vocational educators can play a major role in meeting them.

References

Cetron, Marvin J. "Jobs with a Future" in American Vocational Association, *Collaboration: Vocational Education and the Private Sector*, 1984 Yearbook. Arlington, VA: AVA, 1983.

Feingold, S. Norman and Miller, Norma R. *Emerging Careers: New Occupations for the Year 2000 and Beyond.* Garrett Park, MD: Garrett Park Press, 1983.

Fraser, Jeannette L.; Unger, Paul V.; and Lewis, Morgan V. *Robotics and Office Automation: Implications for Vocational Education.* Columbus: The National Center for Research in Vocational Education, the Ohio State University, 1984.

Hecker, Daniel E. "A Fresh Look at Job Openings," *Occupational Outlook Quarterly* 27 (Spring 1983): 27-29.

Hunt, H. Allan and Hunt, Timothy L. *Human Resource Implications of Robotics.* Kalamazoo, MI: W. E. Upjohn Institute for Employment Research, 1983.

Leontief, Wassily and Duchin, Faye. *The Impact of Automation on Employment 1963-2000.* New York: Institute for Economic Analysis, 1983.

Levin, Henry M. and Rumberger, Russell W. *The Educational Implications of High Technology.* Stanford, CA: Institute for Research on Educational Finance and Governance, Stanford University, February 1983.

Masuda, Yoneji. *The Information Society as Post-Industrial Society.* Washington, DC: World Future Society, 1981.

National Commission on Excellence in Education. *A Nation at Risk: The Imperative for Educational Reform.* Washington, DC: Government Printing Office, April 1983.

The Nilson Report, Number 296, (November 1982): 1, 4-5.

Personick, Valeria A. "The Job Outlook Through 1995: Industry Output and Employment Projections." *Monthly Labor Review* 106 (November 1983): 24-36.

Riche, Richard, Hecker, Daniel, and Burgan, John. "High Technology Today and Tomorrow: A Small Slice of the Employment Pie.'"*Monthly Labor Review* 106 (November 1983): 50-58.

Rumberger, Russell W. and Levin, Henry M. *Forecasting the Impact of New Technologies on the Future Job Market.* Stanford, CA: Institute for Research on Educational Finance and Governance, Stanford University, 1984.

Russell, Jill Frymier. *Implications of New and Changing Occupations for Instructional Development.* Columbus: The National Center for Research in Vocational Education, The Ohio State University, 1981.

Silvestri, George T., Lukasiewicz, John M., and Einstein, Marcus. "Occupational Employment Projections Through 1995," *Monthly Labor Review* (November 1983): 37-49.

OCCUPATIONAL ADAPTABILITY AND TRANSFERABLE SKILLS: PREPARING TODAY'S ADULTS FOR TOMORROW'S CAREERS

Frank C. Pratzner and William L. Ashley

Talk with vocational educators about the nature and importance of occupational adaptability and transferable skills, and several responses are almost inevitable. They usually agree about the fundamental importance of adaptability and such basic and transferable skills as: communications, computation, problem solving, decisionmaking, planning, reasoning, and interpersonal skills. They have experienced the importance of these skills in their own lives, and they have heard about their importance from employers.

Often their next response is that the development of these skills is someone else's responsibility. Their responsibility is to teach students the specialized skills and knowledge of their trade or occupation so that they can enter and succeed in that occupation or in closely related jobs. Moreover, vocational educators will claim that such preparation is what their students want and expect to get from their programs. Their students want to get into the shop or laboratory to develop and practice the skills of their occupation. Students do not want to listen to time-consuming discussions of such abstract things as problem solving, planning, and interpersonal skills. In such discussions, vocational educators make many assumptions based on popular misconceptions that confuse the meaning and importance of the concepts of adaptability and transferable skills, and what vocational education should do and not do about their development. Except for the first assumption listed below, these assumptions are false.

- Occupational adaptability, basic, and transferable skills are all important skills and abilities;
- There is little, if any, relationship between basic, transferable skills and occupationally specific skills and training;
- Basic and transferable skills are general or abstract skills taught through lecture and listening;
- Transferable skills and adaptability are essentially someone else's responsibility; they are not the focus or responsibility of vocational education programs and little is or can be done to develop them in vocational programs without major changes in the programs.

Vocational educators need a better understanding of the concepts of adapta-

13

bility and transferable skills and of the conditions that require their development in vocational education programs. This chapter examines both types of skills in the context of vocational education.

Adaptability and Transferable Skills

Adaptability usually refers to the ability to adjust one's behavior in response to external conditions or requirements. It also refers to the ability to change one's environment. In occupational terms, adaptability refers to the ability to adapt to job requirements, and to the ability to change jobs so that they are more suited to individual needs.

Adaptability is perhaps an unfortunate word to use for both types of changes because it is often taken narrowly to mean only individual *conformity* to fixed conditions. The meaning and use of the concept is broader in this chapter and is summed up in Arthur Wirth's definition of *integration*:

> Integration results from the capacity to adapt oneself to reality plus the critical capacity to make choices and to transform that reality. When we lose our ability to make choices and are subjected to the choices of others; when decisions are no longer our own because they are imposed by external prescriptions, we are no longer integrated. We have "adjusted" or "adapted." We have become *objects* instead of integrated active, human *subjects*.

Transferable skills are important to the development of adaptability. They are broadly applicable, widely useful, and durable skills in which relatively high levels of proficiency have been attained. A list of transferable skills would have to include such broad skills categories as: communications, computation, problem solving, decisionmaking, planning, reasoning, and interpersonal skills. It is the development of skills in these broadly defined categories that can prepare individuals to deal with life's challenges.

The Need for Occupational Adaptability

The accelerating rate of change is the single characteristic of work in America that is experienced by most adults. Among the many forces that have and will continue to reshape adults' work lives well into the next century are the shift from an industrial to a service and information based economy; the internationalization of that economy; and, the increasing use of technology in the workplace.

Moreover, even as, occupations continue to change, many Americans will continue to change their occupations. Occupational mobility, once exceptional, now helps to characterize the American labor force. In a recent update of previous mobility studies, January 1981 census data indicated a 10.5 percent occupational mobility rate for employed workers 18 years of age and over and not in school; a total of 8.4 million workers had changed occupations in January 1980. The 1981 mobility rate was about the same as the rate reported for 1966, 1973, and 1978. As might be expected, the rate of change tends to decrease as workers become older, and the rate is lower for occupations requiring high levels of education or specialized training.

Future changes in the workplace will require individuals to be occupationally adaptable and prepared to cope with the stresses of an unpredictable career progression, as the demands for skills and roles at work evolve. Additionally, many workers will make one or more changes to new occupations, prompted either by choice or by circumstances.

Vocational educators should anticipate the need to prepare their students to face the challenges of rapid and somewhat unpredictable occupational changes. Vocational programs can be used to develop students' transferable skills as well as more specific skills so that students have the skills and knowledge they need for advancement as well as entry in an occupation. Programs and learning experiences that emphasize and develop transferable skills and occupational adaptability can and should be the responsibility of vocational education, given its ties to the workplace. The content of vocational education is based on and reflects the demands of the workplace. Therefore, the instructional practices of vocational education are not fixed. They change as the skills, tools, and practices of occupations change.

However, vocational education programs' potential for developing transferable skills and adaptability is obscured because of the false assumptions discussed earlier. The following section addresses these assumptions.

General Versus Specific Skills

The first assumption that confuses the meaning and importance of adaptability and transferable skills is that some skills are "general" skills and some are "specific" skills. Second, and closely related, is the notion that some skills are "saleable" and other, presumably more general skills, are not. Third, there is an idea that transferable skills are abstract skills taught best through lectures. Finally, there is a whole set of questionable assumptions about the nature of specialized occupational skill training and vocational education's responsibility for developing broadly applicable skills.

There is nothing inherent in the nature of skills that makes some skills general and others specific. What usually passes for a general skill is a skill that can be used in many different settings. Therefore, it is the range of potential applications that characterizes some skills as general and some as specific. In this concept, it is more accurate to characterize skills as generally applicable or as specialized, rather than using the short, but misleading, labels of general and specific skills.

It is also worth noting that a skill is characterized as general not only because of its potential range of applications and use, but also because of the level of proficiency that has developed. A skill brought to a high level of proficiency is potentially more transferable and useful than one that has only been developed to a minimum level. The potential transferability of a skill is a function of both applicability and proficiency.

Saleable Skills versus General Skills

It is completely misleading and useless to say that some skills are saleable and others are not. Saleability, like specificity, is not inherent in the nature of skills. All skills are saleable skills to some degree. Value or saleability is an attributed characteristic of skills, not an inherent characteristic. It is based upon the range of applications a skill has. Those skills that are the most widely applicable and durable are those that are more highly valued by society. Skills that have limited applications generally are less highly valued.

Therefore, the most saleable and most valued skills are those that have many potential uses. That is, those usually referred to as general, or more appropriately, as generally applicable skills. Ironically, when vocational educators apply the term "saleable" to occupationally specific skills, they misunderstand what skills really sell in the job market. General skills are the really saleable skills.

Teaching Through Lecturing and Listening

Two widely held assumptions about the teaching of transferable skills are false. The first is that transferable, broadly applicable skills are most effectively taught through the combined lecture—listening method. The second is that vocational education can do little to develop transferable skills in individuals.

There is no basis for the belief that transferable skills such as problem solving, decisionmaking, or interpersonal skills are learned best through lecturing. In fact, most learning theory and practical experience suggest that extracting the general processes or procedures from these skills and lecturing about them is probably the *least* effective means of presenting them. Instead, students must be provided with a wide range of opportunities to apply and practice these kinds of skills. Indeed, the more opportunities given to individuals to practice these skills, and the more realistic these opportunities are, the more effective the teaching will be. Also, given such instruction, individuals are far more likely to exhibit sustained interest and involvement.

A Role for Vocational Education

The potential and relevance of the vocational education approach to teaching and learning is routinely overlooked or ignored in the pursuit of specialized occupational skill development. Vocational education has a shared responsibility with other educational and training programs to contribute to the development of occupational adaptability and broadly transferable skills. It is unique among educational programs in its potential for doing so because it provides many opportunities for hands-on, experiential approaches to learning and for the extensive practice of skills.

Many vocational educators seem convinced of the value of these arguments and approaches at the high school level, but their acceptance, relevance, and implications are in doubt at the adult and postsecondary level. Moreover, there are questions on what can be done about the development of transferable skills at either the secondary or postsecondary levels.

Many adults in postsecondary and adult vocational programs are there because of, and can benefit from, highly specialized occupational skill training. However, the alternative program and approaches are clearly as necessary and appropriate at this level as they are at the secondary school level, and for many of the same reasons. One of the alternatives most needed at the postsecondary level is the development of programs and approaches that emphasize occupational adaptability and transferable skills.

Identifying Program Content

Assuming that vocational educators choose to incorporate occupational adaptability and transferable skills as an objective of their programs, they are likely to ask at least two critical questions. First, "what would the content of such a program look like?" And second, "what instructional strategy should be employed to teach it?"

In response to the first question, it is unlikely that an entire and separate curriculum for transferable skills and occupational adaptability will be forthcoming in the immediate future, nor is it likely to be necessary. However, it is necessary to have a sample portfolio of transferable skills and to have them defined at a level of specificity that will enable instructors to integrate them into the curriculum. The presentation of a complete portfolio is beyond the scope of this discussion but the following example (Table 1) is offered as a representation of what such a portfolio might contain.

It should be obvious from the example that it is somewhat misleading to limit the domain of such skills by the term occupationally transferable skills. They are skills that have applicability in many aspects and stages of life. As such, they are not unique to any one vocational program or occupational area. At the same time, they can be defined specifically enough to be organized and related

Table 1

Selected Examples of Occupationally Transferable Skills

Cognitive	Affective	Psychomotor
• Communications	• Attitudes toward work	• Measure distances
Read and evaluate	Responsibility	• Draw graphs
Write technical reports	Diligence	• Operate calculator
Speak fluently	Determination/	• Uses senses
• Mathematics	perserverance	
Read graphs	Reliability	
Determine equivalents	• Attitudes toward others	
Compute ratios	Converses pleasantly	
Solve work problems	Reacts to others	
• Reasoning	Manages others	
Develop	Gives praise	
classifications	• Attitudes toward self	
Make decisions	Self-confidence	
Outline plans	Self-discipline	
Priorities	Self-actualization	
	Assertiveness	

Source: Brickell and Paul, 1978, Table 2, p. 22

to learning outcomes and instructional objectives. Consider, for example, the way transferable skills were defined and related to the requirements of technical management jobs within AT&T for the purpose of facilitating the movement of women into nontraditional areas. The list (Table 2) represents commonly referenced categories of transferable skills compared to a set of skills, identified through tasks/skill analysis, that are generalizable across several management levels and functional areas within AT&T.

Clearly, the two examples presented here represent only a brief glimpse of what a full inventory and categorization of all transferable skills might include. Indeed, it is unreasonable to imagine that all students would master all of the skills in the inventory, just as it is unreasonable to expect all people to master the complete domain of knowledge in a discipline. However, individuals should master the transferable skills that are applicable to the occupational area in which they are employed or are preparing to enter. By doing so, they will be better able to deal with changes in the specific content of the occupation and to make occupational changes when necessary or desirable. Transferable skills will not guarantee successful adaptability, although they should facilitate it.

Individuals must also develop competency in adaptive skills. Adaptive skills are also referred to as coping skills, occupational employability, or survival skills, or, sometimes, career development skills. Such skills go beyond performing tasks or getting the job done. Adaptive skills, as used here, refer to

Table 2

Comparison of Skills Lists

Employer Sample (Wiant, 1977)	Bell System (Youngblook, 1978)
1. Communicating	Maintaining upward communications
	Maintaining downward communications
	Maintaining peer communications
	Providing written communications
2. Working with others	Involvement with meetings
	Community relations
3. Problem solving	Problem solving
4. Planning/layout	Planning the job
	Managing time
5. Organizing	Controlling the job
6. Managing others	Developing subordinates
	Providing performance feedback
7. Decision making	Decision making
8. Positive work attitude	Creating a motivational atmosphere

Source: Peterson, R. O. 1979, Table 1, p. 23

those skills used to deal effectively with changes in the worker-work inter-relationship and to effect change to meet one's own needs.

The adaptive skill areas include: transfer skills, learning-to-learn skills, change skills, energizing skills, coping skills (affective), self-assessment skills, special mobility skills, anticipatory skills, and cognitive skills (which overlap with basic transferable skills).

Transfer skills enable a person to draw upon prior learning and previous experience for application to new and different situations. Abilities that illustrate transfer skills are: generalizing; synthesizing; discriminating important from unimportant information; and dealing with ambiguity or complex or multiple rules.

Learning-to-learn skills include the notion of learning as a lifelong process and the ability to attack learning problems with different approaches and learning strategies.

Change skills are those involving changes of attitude, values, or behaviors through unlearning, mental or behavioral experimentation, reevaluation, and relearning.

Energizing skills are related to change skills and may be a component of them. They enable a person to respond to a situation and to initiate appropriate and positive action, despite ambiguities or lack of structure in a situation.

Coping skills enable a person to stabilize internal emotional conditions and to manage stress effectively. Brammer and Abnego list coping skill categories as "mobilizing a personal style of responding to change; assessing, developing, and utilizing external symptoms and internal support systems; skills for reducing emotional and physiological distress; and skills for planning and implementing change."

Self-assessment skills involve periodically analyzing one's strengths and weaknesses and recognizing areas in need of improvement or growth in anticipation of problem changes.

Mobility skills are used to make career or job changes and include job-seeking and job-getting abilities such as interviewing skills, resume preparation, and carrying out alternative job search strategies.

The boundaries and content of some of the areas may overlap and should be expected to do so, as behavior involves the whole person in interaction with the environment.

Attempting to teach all of the adaptive skill areas in any one program or at any one time is impractical. Selected areas should be addressed by various programs in concert with ongoing life experiences and individual needs. The development of transferable and adaptive skills in adult vocational education should complement the teaching of essential occupational knowledge and job skills, not replace them. Accomplishing both purposes calls for a change in instructional strategies along with a refocusing of the content. The following suggestions are offered as practical examples of appropriate instructional techniques.

Teaching for Transfer and Adaptability

Five aspects of instructional practice lend themselves as areas for implementing effective teaching strategies.

Awareness. Increasing learners' awareness and understanding of the skills that are transferable will influence their potential to transfer effectively learned behaviors to new situations. Providing instruction and practice in various learning techniques will enhance the learners' capacity to learn different types of skills and content in different ways. Identifying and building upon prior knowledge and experience will enhance learning and transfers. Teaching learners to evaluate their own performance and establish their own standards will enable them to be receptive to feedback suggesting that they improve, change or acquire new knowledge and skills.

Sequencing. Transfer occurs more readily when learning tasks are arranged according to their similarity. Sequences can be based on similarity of concepts, elements, principles, or learning strategies. Arrange learning tasks along a range of similarity but avoid unnecessary repetition. Emphasize and teach the transferable skills inherent in a sequence of learning tasks, such as problem solving skills and techniques, or oral communication skills.

Practice. Only the knowledge and skills that are mastered and remembered can be transferred. Skills that are transferable should be developed to mastery and then practiced for application under new and varying conditions. Provide guidance in practicing for transfer with prompting that will lead to correct reasoning and transfer approaches.

Reinforcement. To optimize positive transfer, reinforce correct applications of skills and knowledge. Provide adequate feedback by rewarding successful attempts and correcting inappropriate ones. Once mastery of a skill or technique is achieved, reinforce those applications or thought processes that facilitate skill transfer to new and different situations.

Cues. An important aspect of the ability to transfer skills successfully involves the ability to recognize the proper cues. Cue recognition should be taught so learners can associate what is common in a new task or situation and in prior learning or experience. Providing practice in cue recognition in different perceptual modes will enhance transfer and strengthen retention of knowledge and skills for future recall.

These suggestions are intended to provide a perspective on various instructional strategies that can help individuals learn to transfer skills and knowledge. Their ability to do so can contribute to their capacity to be adaptable and effective adults, both in the workplace and in other life activities.

Valuable Skills

There are several major reasons for emphasizing occupational adaptability and transferable skills in both secondary and adult vocational education. Broadly applicable skills, learned well, are highly valued skills. They are also important ingredients of adaptability, the ability to adjust oneself to changes in work and the capacity to change the conditions of work. Vocational education can offer a viable alternative approach to the development of such skills and abilities, and in so doing, contribute to achievement of a more flexible and productive work force.

All educators who serve adults, and vocational educators in particular, should recognize the need to emphasize occupational adaptability and transferable skills in their programs and should seek opportunities to do so. Our society and our work force is changing. Our educational system at all levels must also change to accommodate new circumstances and serve the needs of today's adults who must work and succeed in tomorrow's careers.

References

Brammer, Lawrence M., & Abvego, Philip J. "Intervention Strategies for Coping with Transitions." *The Counseling Psychologist* 9, no. 2, (1981): 19-35.

Brickell, Henry M., & Paul, Regina H. *Minimum Competencies and Transferable Skills: What Can Be Learned from the Two Movements* (Information Series No. 142). Columbus: Ohio State University, National Center for Research in Vocational Education, 1978.

Faddis, Constance R. *The Worker as Proteus: Understanding Occupational Adaptability*. Columbus: Ohio State University, National Center for Research in Vocational Education, 1979.

Fraser, Berna S. *The Structure of Adult Learning, Education, and Training Opportunity in the United States*. Washington, DC: National Institute for Work and Learning, 1980.

Peterson, Richard O. "An Employer's Concern for Occupational Adaptability" in *Occupational Adaptability: Perspectives on Tomorrows Careers. A Symposium* (Information Series No. 189). Columbus: Ohio State University, National Center for Research in Vocational Education, 1979.

Rytina, Nancy. "Occupational Changes and Tenure, 1981," *Monthly Labor Review*, 105 No. 7 (September 1982): 29-33.

Selz, Nina & Ashley, William L. *Teaching for Transfer: A Perspective* (Information Series No. 141). Columbus: Ohio State University, National Center for Research in Vocational Education, 1978.

Wirth, Arthur G. *Productive Work in Industry and Schools: Becoming Persons Again*. Lanham, MD: University Press of America, 1983.

SECTION II

EDUCATING ADULT STUDENTS

Adults are becoming the nation's most important student population. October, 1982, census data analyzed by the National Center for Educational Statistics show that there are just over nine million adults, defined as those 25 years of age or older, enrolled in postsecondary education. Of this total, nearly one-third are enrolled in vocationally-related programs: almost two million adults are seeking a credential in a vocational education program, a figure that does not include those in vocational programs who do not seek a credential; and, approximately 1.5 million people are enrolled in non-credential programs to improve their job skills. Most of this group are adult students.

The large percentage enrolled in vocationally-related programs is not surprising. Adults' reasons for getting more education are, more often than not, job-related: to upgrade skills, move up a career ladder, change careers. Consequently, their particular needs, their choice of courses and programs, and their educational providers are likely to differ from those of traditional postsecondary students.

This section looks at the adult education universe, describing its scope, its population and their needs, and the wide variety of educational providers which serve adults.

Wendell Smith defines adult education and provides a context for the discussions that follow. He observes that definitions for adult education can be fairly narrow or rather broad, thereby giving differing statistical pictures of adult education. In either case, however, he finds that adult education is growing in importance and opening new opportunities for current education providers as well as encouraging the growth of new, private sector providers.

Vocational education is critically important to many adults as they prepare to enter the workforce or adapt to the many technological changes that are occurring in the workplace. Robert M. Worthington describes the scope of adult vocational education and discusses the particular adult populations that are likely to seek vocational education. He examines adult vocational education's response to these populations, especially from the federal perspective, but also cites exemplary programs offered in the private sector or in public postsecondary education.

Carol B. Aslanian profiles adult learners. She reports on the findings of a College Board study that investigated why adults learn. Most often, life transitions cause adults to return to school, often for job-related reasons.

Adults learn differently from children, Patrick R. Penland observes, and these differences must be respected and used to ensure effective learning. He describes adult learning styles and how to incorporate those styles into teaching situations.

Most adults do not qualify for federal financial assistance, which has become the financial foundation for many younger students in postsecondary education. Instead, Paul E. Barton points out that adults and their educational providers must find other ways to pay for education. He talks about innovative approaches to financing workers' education, particularly in state-education cooperative efforts.

Beverly Copeland and Meredyth A. Leahy describe the ingredients that need to go into adult education programs. They focus on instruction—training, recruitment, selection, and supervision of the adult education teacher.

Instructional Settings

There are at least nine different formal instructional settings for adults, most of which are not in traditional postsecondary institutions.

Lee R. Kerschner and Christopher Davis describe the purposes and organization of proprietary vocational schools, which account for nearly three-fourths of all postsecondary vocational school enrollments.

Robert Craig discusses the vast enterprise that is industry training of its workforce. Employers spend about $30 billion annually for employee education and training.

Edgar Czarnecki discusses labor unions' involvement in educating workers about the labor movement and providing them with information and skills they can use to redress shop and office problems.

Michael Crawford describes the size and scope of the nation's community colleges—a comprehensive delivery system of education for the adult learner. He urges that the community college reflect and respond to community needs.

Clinton L. Anderson reports on how military training efforts are designed to give service members the skills and knowledge they need to carry out military goals. In fiscal year 1983, the Department of Defense spent $10.5 billion on individual training.

Lee Transier discusses the goals, populations, funding sources, and programs of continuing education. "Continuing education" includes several concepts:

credit courses, summer school, evening school, non-credit offerings, and conference programs.

Mary Nell Greenwood describes the work of the Department of Agriculture's Extension Service and the cooperative extension services at the state and county levels. Together, they are the "educational agency of the Department of Agriculture," with local offices in most of the nation's 3500 counties.

Paul V. Delker outlines the comprehensive high school adult education programs. Even today, they are of continuing importance: the 1980 Census showed that nearly 48 percent of the population 25 years older and over had not completed high school.

Thomas N. Daymont provides a history and analysis of the Job Training Partnership Act of 1983 and its predecessors in federal legislation. He finds that measured performance has improved compared to the Comprehensive Employment and Training Act.

These chapters, together, demonstrate how different the education of adults is from that of younger students. It is highly job-oriented, meeting the real concerns of adults who seek a secure economic footing in changing workplaces and industries.

ADULT EDUCATION DEFINED

Wendell Smith

Adult education today occurs in many settings, involves numerous providers and meets a variety of individual, corporate and societal, vocational and avocational needs. This chapter provides an overview of adult education in America and offers general insights regarding the scope and diversity of the numerous programs which are provided.

Terminology

Since adults pursue education for a variety of reasons and there are a number of private and public sector providers, a number of overlapping terms and definitions have evolved.

"Adult education" and "lifelong learning" have become the two generic terms which cover the educational programs and pursuits that are generally available beyond compulsory education, or as opportunities supplemental to the education required for initial entry into a given vocation.

Numerous additional terms which involve the education of adults refer more to specific types of program purposes, objectives, philosophies or specific educational delivery systems. These terms include: human resource development (HRD), community education, vocational education, continuing education, extension education, independent study, correspondence study and apprenticeship education.

Increasing Participation

The scope of participation in lifelong learning is defined narrowly or broadly, resulting in very different statistical pictures of adult participation in lifelong learning. On the conservative end of the continuum, the National Center for Educational Statistics (NCES) restricts its reporting of adult education to the United States population that is twenty-five years of age or older and involved in a formal learning experience leading to a diploma or certificate.

Allen Tough of the Ontario Institute of Studies, on the other end, has a much broader definition, which also includes all informal self-directed and avocational learning projects, such as systematic reading, self-directed improvement of work, educational travel and both credit and noncredit class participation.

Tough's research, encompassing formal as well as informal self-directed learning, found that 700-800 hours of individualized learning is undertaken annually by the average adult in the North American population.

Variance among researchers' statistical reporting represents differing interpretations of the extent of instructional formality and length of instruction which should be considered an adult learning experience. However, all of the studies support the fact that the rate of participation in adult education has grown in the past and will continue to grow in the future.

The United States Census Bureau reports that there are 120 million persons in the United States who are 25 years of age or older. NCES, recently reported that 20 percent, or 24 million adults, are annually enrolled in classes offering course work leading to a certificate or diploma.

The College Board conducted a national study in 1982 which indicated that 60 million persons (or approximately one-half of the adult population) had studied one or more topics during the preceding year in a classroom setting; this study encompassed noncredit courses as well as courses for credit leading toward degrees and certificates.

Other data suggest how and why labor market changes will occur. Daniel Yankelovich in *New Rules: Search for Fulfillment in a World Turned Upside Down*, indicates that 73 percent of the population likes cultural diversity, freedom of choice, and opportunities for creative individualism. According to the College Board, as many as 40 million adults are in transition today regarding their jobs or careers and 60 percent of this number will require education and specialization to achieve their goals.

NCES reports that participation in lifelong learning has increased 12 percent per year in each of their three most recent years of analysis. Futurists project that the need for adult education will continue to increase as society moves from an industrial to a technological information and communication era. John Naisbitt notes that in 1950 only 17 percent of the workforce was employed in information-related or communication jobs. Within the next ten years, he projects that 75 percent of the workforce will be involved in such jobs. Naisbitt stresses that information jobs are not limited to computer programmers. They also include the entire educational community, doctors, lawyers, governmental workers and a host of other professions.

According to the U.S. Department of Labor, 75 percent of the workforce in the year 2000 is already in place. Peter Drucker, a leading management theorist, predicts that 15 million jobs in manufacturing will become obsolete in the next decade. Those who are successful in remaining employed will have to retrain and update their job skills.

The number of women working in the United States has risen by 21 million, or 95 percent, in the last two decades. The Department of Labor predicts that two-thirds of future entrants to the workforce will be women. The workforce is also growing older. In 1975, the average worker was 28 years old. The Census Bureau estimates that by the year 2000, approximately 60 percent of the population will be over 30 years of age. While the number of adults in the population will increase, the traditional 18-to-21-year-old college population will decline 29 percent in the next ten years.

Providers of Adult Education

As the interest and demand for adult education has increased in society, so too have the number of educational providers. Traditional educational establishments, such as secondary schools, vocational schools, and colleges and universities, are increasing their offerings to adult learners; however, the most significant increases have occurred in the private sector in programs provided by community agencies, such as the American Red Cross; professional associations, such as the American Banking Association; and, in the HRD programs of business and industry.

Tables 1 and 2 show the nature and scope of the agencies which are primarily involved in adult and continuing education today. The table is not intended to be inclusive, but it does reflect the typical situations for the provider and their programs.

In addition, it should be pointed out that, for most persons, more adult learning occurs in the domain of unintentional learning, which is not reflected in the table. Sources such as family members, friends, mass media, travel and hobbies are major learning sources throughout one's life.

Projections for the Future

In a society oriented to information and high technology, adult education will become increasingly important. Enormous opportunities will exist for providers that: offer relevant quality resources at convenient times and locations and at affordable prices.

Unfortunately, I do not presently see many of the traditional adult education providers making strategic plans to serve the increasing needs of the adult learner. Many administrators are caught up in the task of managing declining enrollments, which are associated with the declining youth population and in retrenchment, which is associated with reduced levels of state and federal financial support. I am fearful that many of our institutions, when facing financial exigency, will

Table 1

Major Adult Education Providers/Programs—Public Sector

	MAJOR SOURCES OF FINANCIAL SUPPORT				MISSIONS		
Provider	**Governmental**	**Student Fees**	**Other**	**ADMINISTRATIVE Unit**	**Job Related**	**Avocational**	**PURPOSE/PHILOSOPHY**
Adult Basic Education/ Adult Secondary Education	X			Secondary Schools	X		Provide basic skills and prepare persons to take high school equivalency exam (GED)
Community Education	X	X	X (Philanthropy)	School Districts	X	X	Match educational needs of the community with its education resources
Continuing Education	X	X		Postsecondary Colleges, Universities and Junior Colleges	X	X	Extending academic resources of the institution by providing non-credit conference and workshops
Cooperative Extension	X			Land-Grant Universities	X		Extend the expertise of universities statewide (primarily agriculturally related)
Junior Colleges, College and Universities	X	X		Governing Boards	X	X	Provide certificate and degree programs
Libraries	X			Local Government	X	X	Provide a resource base for self-directed learning
Vocational Technical Education	X			School Districts	X		Provide pre- and in-service skills

not make the often difficult decision to place resources in line with opportunities—adult education opportunities.

The effect of supply and demand, one of the basic concepts from the business world, will become pronounced. As the demand for adult education increases enormously, other educational providers will emerge.

Influx of New Providers

In recent years, there has been a rapid expansion of business- and industry-sponsored human resource development activities. These programs have often

Table 2

Major Adult Education Providers/Programs–Private Sector

Provider	MAJOR SOURCES OF FINANCIAL SUPPORT Governmental	Student Fees	Other	ADMINISTRATIVE Unit	MISSIONS Job Related	Avocational	PURPOSE/PHILOSOPHY
Apprenticeship Programs			X	Labor Unions	X		Provide entry level job skill
Community Agencies	X	X	(Dues)	Local Agencies		X	Provide personal interest programs. Examples: YMCA/YWCA, American Red Cross
Human Resource Development			X	Business and Industry	X		Provide in-service education opportunities for employees
Professional Association		X	(Employer)	Non-Profit Corporations	X		Provide in-service reinlicensure. Examples: American Medical Association, American Optometric Association
Trade Schools		X		Proprietary Organizations	X		Provide entry level job skill

been characterized as ''shadow educational systems.'' However, in terms of size and expenditure, these programs cast quite a long shadow.

In 1983, according to the American Society of Training and Development, business and industry's expenditure for educational programs was $30 billion. This is the same amount as the combined budget of all postsecondary institutions each year.

The Fall 1981 continuing education supplement to the *New York Times* cited companies such as McDonald's, which offers its own curriculum of 18 courses to 614,000 franchisers and company managers. It was reported that McDonald's students from 29 countries do not learn how to fry hamburgers. They learn human relations skills and other management concepts that higher education would find academically very respectable.

Although it is not yet commonplace, a number of corporations are even offering degree programs to their employees and to persons living in the communities surrounding their training centers. The American Council on Education has listed over 1,000 courses worthy of academic credit offered by more than 100 corporations.

Complete degree programs are now available at many corporations. Arthur D. Little offers a master's in business administration that is accredited by both a regional accrediting agency and the American Association of Collegiate Schools of Business, the professional business school accrediting agency. Wang Computer Laboratories offers a master's degree in Software Engineering and the Xerox Corporation, R.J. Reynolds, the American Institute of Banking, and General Motors are among the many corporations which have their own bachelor's degree programs. A total of 5.8 million students were enrolled in industry-sponsored degree programs in 1983.

In addition to the rapid growth in business and industry-sponsored adult education programs, adult educators are beginning to see many new programs emerge from proprietary and consulting organizations, professional associations, and community agencies. The American Banking Association provided in-service programs for 230,000 bank employees in 1983, and more than 200,000 adults learned cardio-pulmonary resuscitation and other life saving skills from the American Red Cross.

Increased Use of Media
Media technology, including home computers, teleconferencing, electronic mail, electronic banking, video fixed disc and satellite signal relaying, will have a significant impact on this nation's educational system. This impact will likely be more significant than newspapers, radio and television were in the past.

With video and audio signals relayed via satellite, opportunities exist for worldwide programming. In Fall 1983, a new company called Tele Learning was announced. This "electronic university," as the company calls itself, provides a private instructor, through the student's own personal computer at home or office, 24 hours a day. The former chief executive officer of Atari, Inc. is the new company's founder and chief executive officer. The company presently offers 150 noncredit programs and has plans for rapid expansion.

Most computer relay systems, such as Tele Learning, use the telephone as the connecting medium. Recently, it was announced, however, that software radio stations, termed "Radioware" will likely be the next primary medium of delivery. Unlike teledelivery or telephone downloading services, there will be no charge to the user for the radio service. To offset costs, commercial advertising will be interspersed between the radio software transmissions.

Many of the new providers of adult education programs will be utilizing electronic media in the delivery of programs. The traditional providers of adult education programs should move aggressively into this new medium of program delivery. There will always be a need and demand for the traditional classroom with "live" instructors; however, the information age will provide many promising mediums of educational delivery which can serve to augment programs and in many instances, reduce instructional costs.

Increased Collaboration Among the Providers

It is fairly clear that the next decade will bring an influx of new educational providers and that a variety of new technologies will be employed to deliver adult education programs. *A Nation at Risk* recognizes the confusion that can result for the adult learner in tomorrow's environment and has called for a "coherent continuum of learning" with linkages among the educational providers.

A major conference in 1983, which was attended by leaders of twenty national lifelong learning associations, identified fragmentation as a major obstacle to delivering adult education. There has been, for example, too much educational jargon, too many independent programs attempting to serve the same audience, and too little dialogue between the providers.

If the adult learning profession is to grow to its optimal level, it is imperative that collaboration among the providers occur at the local, state and regional levels as well as on the national scene.

References

Aslanian, Carol S. *Proceedings of 1981 National Adult Education Conference*, New York: The College Board, 1982.

Bureau of Census. *1980 Census of Population*. Volume 1: *Characteristics of the Population*, Chapter A: *Number of Inhabitants*, Part 1, pp. 117-118, Washington, D.C.: U.S. Department of Commerce.

Dearman, Nancy B. and Plisko, Valena White (eds.) *The Condition of Education*, Washington, D.C.: National Center for Education Statistics, U.S. Department of Education, 1982.

Hadju, David. "Wave of Future in Computer Software May Come Over the Radio," *St. Louis Post-Dispatch*, September 20, 1983, p.

Houle, Cyril O., *Patterns of Learning*, San Francisco, California, Jossey-Bass, 1984.

Naisbitt, John, *Megatrends: Ten New Directions Transforming Our Lives*. New York: Warner Books, 1982.

A Nation at Risk: The Imperative for Educational Reform, Washington, D.C., National Commission on Excellence in Education, U.S. Department of Education, April 1983.

New York Times Education Supplement, October 16, 1981. Tele Learning Network Systems, (Press kit), September 1983.

Smith, Wendell, *Collaboration in Lifelong Learning*. Washington, D.C.: The American Association for Adult and Continuing Education, 1983.

Tough, Allen, *The Adults' Learning Projects*, Toronto Ontario: Institute of Studies in Education, 1971.

Yankelovich, Daniel, *New Rules: Search for Fulfillment In a World Turned Upside Down*, New York: Bantam, 1982.

ADULT VOCATIONAL EDUCATION

Robert M. Worthington

Vocational education is education's response to society's need for a skilled and productive workforce. As the education and training needs of our citizens have changed, there have been corresponding changes in the goals and focus of vocational education. Today, with few exceptions, workers can no longer expect to spend their entire working lives in the same occupations. The need for adult training and retraining is now a fact of life. Vocational education faces the challenge of preparing adults for employment directly related to their ability, interests, and capacity to work. Thus, adult vocational education plays an important role toward lessening the supply of persons for welfare-assisted programs and future poverty roles in society.

This chapter looks at the current context for adult vocational education, paying particular attention to the federal role in promoting vocational education and training. It describes the demand for learning among the adult population through the year 2000 and examines changes under way to help the adult worker adapt to rapid technological developments.

A Federal Role

Since the federal government became involved in vocational education in 1917 with the Smith-Hughes Act, it has included adults in its efforts. Prior to 1917, the National Society for the Promotion of Industrial Education and the Commission on National Aid to Vocational Education, an advisory body appointed by President Wilson in 1914, had identified the principles which were set out in the Smith-Hughes Act. In this early period, vocational education was intended for high school youth and for employed adults. During the 1930's, federal policy on vocational education for adults changed to also provide training for unemployed people so that they might obtain the necessary skills to seek and obtain jobs.

The vocational education system dominated workforce training during the 1940's. During World War II, vocational education provided more than eight million defense workers with the skills and knowledge necessary to sustain the nation's productive capacity.

In the late 1950's, it became apparent that additional changes were needed in the laws governing vocational education. In 1961, President Kennedy appointed a Panel of Consultants on Vocational Education to study vocational education and make recommendations for legislative changes, which were used in the framing of the Vocational Education Act of 1963. A number of these recommendations related to services and programs for post-high school youth and adults. As an outgrowth, the Congress stated in its declaration of purpose of the Vocational Education Act of 1963, "...so that persons of all ages in all communities of the State—those in high school, those who have completed or discontinued their formal education and are preparing to enter the larbor market, but need to upgrade their skills or learn new ones, those with special educational handicaps, and those in postsecondary schools, will have ready access to vocational training or retraining which is of high quality..." With this Act, Congress provided a broader basis for adult vocational education.

Pre-service and supplementary in-service training of adults became an important function of vocational education. The Congress, through the 1968 amendments, set minimum levels of expenditure of federal funds for postsecondary and adult vocational education. Efforts continue to serve equitably and adequately those adults in need of training or retraining.

Statistical Background

It is difficult—in many instances impossible—to separate clearly postsecondary from adult vocational education. Adult vocational education programs are either preparatory to employment or supplementary to employment. They enhance the productive capacity of the working adult in vocational education programs.

It is also difficult to know the level of participation in adult vocational education. The Vocational Education Data System (VEDS), established by Congress in the Education Amendments of 1976, is a prime source of statistics relating to all components of vocational education. Under the current system, however, no distinction is made between postsecondary and adult vocational education. For 1978-79, however, such distinction was made in the data presentation. Therefore, since these figures are relatively constant, by total enrollment and by program area, appropriate projections can be made for 1981-82.

The total national enrollment in vocational education programs approximates 17 million annually. Nearly five million (29 percent) are on the adult level. Those five million do not include postsecondary students enrolled in associate degree technical programs but are limited to adults in the two categories; short-term and long-term students. Short-term students include those enrolled in programs of under 500 contact hours' duration. Short-termers outnumber long-termers by about four to one. Trade and industrial education programs have the largest enrollment in both categories. Thirty percent of the short-term adult enrollments and 44.3 percent of the long-term enrollments are in these programs.

Other leading short-term and long-term program categories for adults are consumer and homemaking and office occupations. As is to be expected, a substantial majority (nearly 90 percent) of long-term adult programs train individuals for specific occupations. Slightly more than half of the short-termers are occupationally specific enrollees.

A Changing Workforce

The demographics of the adult population provides evidence of the need for adult vocational education. The organization and structure of vocational education has the potential to make positive gains toward solving many of the nation's acute social problems. Geographical shifts in the population, movement of business and industry, changes in the job market, increased immigration, an aging of the population, women's growth in the labor force—each of these is an indicator of change, and each presents a challenge to adult vocational education.

"Mobility of labor" was recognized as a national problem by the President's Commission on National Aid to Vocational Education in 1914. It is more acute today as the population migrates to the West and South. Some dramatic population forecasts have been presented:

The West, now the region with the smallest population, is projected to have a population growth of 22 percent during this decade and an 18 percent growth in the 1990's. By the year 2000, the West will have nearly one-fourth of the United States population.

The South will increase its number of inhabitants by 16 percent during the 1980's and by 13 percent during the following decade.

The Northeast will continue to lose population—from 49.1 million in 1980, to 48.4 million in 1990, and 46.4 million in 2000.

These population shifts affect the availability of and competition for jobs. Frequently, workers who migrate will need to upgrade their skills and knowledge to compete for available jobs. Or, people unprepared to work may change their location in the hope of finding employment. Many of this latter group may be suffering from frustration and disappointment; many lack the simple skills needed to command a job; and many lack basic functional literacy skills needed in everyday living.

Another changing demographic is the aging of the population. In 1970, the median age of our population was 27.9 years. By 1990, it is projected to be 32.8 years. But the largest sector of this population will be comprised of people aged 65 and older. For both financial and psychological security, growing numbers of older people are postponing retirement; many who have retired are interested in returning to work. Many of these retirees seek skills training for second careers, part-time employment, or for developing entrepreneurial techniques to establish and manage their own businesses. An increasing number of older persons are seeking instruction of an avocational nature such as home repair, automobile maintenance, and sewing. Rather than looking for gainful employment, this latter group may be seeking economic savings by peforming their own repair and maintenance work. In any event, vocational and avocational education is in demand.

The growing participation of women in the labor force is another example of the growing need for adult vocational education. State sex equity coordinators, along with the educational and employment communities, have worked to remove sex-biased barriers and stereotyping in vocational education programs. During recent years, female enrollments have not only been increasing but also changing. This is particularly reflected in nontraditional programs. Two forecasts underline this increase in women in the labor force:

> Women will provide about two-thirds of the total labor force growth between now and 1995, increasing from 45 percent of the labor force in 1985 to 47 percent 10 years later.

> By 1990, women will contribute 40 percent of all family income compared with 25 percent in 1980.

Yet another group with an exceptional need for adult and vocational education programs is the immigrant population. Legal and illegal immigration accounts for almost one-third of the total U.S. population growth each year. Some economists estimate that immigrants, particularly Hispanics and Asians, add as many as one million people to the population each year. Needs of this population, in addition to crossing the language barrier, may include obtaining new occupational skills or learning to transfer existing skills to the new work environment.

The challenge of these changing demographics to adult vocational education is tremendous. Adult vocational education must respond!

A Changing Job Market

Some labor market projections suggest that more technical and sophisticated skills will be required in this age of advancing technology. Other experts suggest that the need for less-skilled workers will exceed the need for highly technically skilled workers. A growing need is projected for service industry workers who lead all other occupations in job openings projected for 1980-1990. That need is followed closely by a need for clerical workers.

The Bureau of Labor Statistics projects that, for the 1980's, 23.2 million job openings will occur annually. Of these, 93 percent will be due to replacement needs, that is, persons transferring to other occupations and those leaving the labor force. Only about 1.7 million of the annual openings would result from growth.

The ten occupations with the highest projected openings in this decade are retail trade sales workers, waiters and waitresses, cashiers, secretaries, cooks and chefs, bookkeepers and accounting clerks, assemblers, typists, kindergarten and elementary school teachers, and carpenters. Nine of these occupations do not generally require a degree for entry; about half do not require specialized training or experience. High turnover rates are frequent in these occupations. Eight of these occupations are predominantly held by women. Conversely, the occupations with the fewest projected job openings require substantial training, are dominated by male workers, and support workers who tend to remain until retirement.

While very rapid growth is projected for computer-related jobs, few job openings will occur due to the limited size of the occupation and low separation rates. Computer service technicians are projected to have 11 percent as many openings as carpenters and 13 percent as many as automobile mechanics.

Adult Vocational Education's Response for Special Populations

A major activity in adult vocational education is to aid special adult populations to prepare for, find, and adjust to new employment. These workers must also have personal counseling, information and income assistance, job search and job placement training, skill assessment, job counseling, and relocation assistance services.

Retraining for Displaced Workers. Displaced workers are those who have become unemployed because their jobs have been eliminated by economic, technological, or structural changes in American business and industry. The exact number of these workers is difficult to determine, but it is estimated to be approximately 1.5 to 2 million. Many of these workers are unionized and have seniority in blue-collar jobs that provide adequate earnings. Many do not have the knowledge and skills needed for other occupations and are also reluctant to enter a new occupation. This is particularly true for older workers. Displaced workers may also have poor job search skills, and, may not wish to move or disturb their home environment. Therefore, their re-employment is delayed and difficult to secure.

There are many exemplary efforts to retrain displaced workers. For example, a General Motors retraining project operated from January 1982 to August 1983 at its Jefferson City, Missouri, plant. The Missouri State educational agency played a direct role in planning and implementing retraining programs for workers displaced by auto plant closings. The new plant GM established in the area was highly automated and required the workers to have new skills. General Motors had made a commitment to retrain displaced auto workers and employ them in a new, highly automated plant. The workers were trained in skills needed to operate the plant.

Retraining for Displaced Homemakers. Programs that provide displaced homemakers with education and training have proved to be viable routes from public assistance and dependency to self-sufficiency, economic independence, and citizen participation and contribution.

In 1979, the Department of Labor estimated that 11 million women were disadvantaged financially and in need of job skills. Of that 11 million, approximately 5 million were displaced homemakers - widowed, separated, or divorced. Vocational education programs annually serve an estimated 67,600 of these groups, such as single heads-of-households, homemakers, and part-time workers who wish to secure full-time jobs. The Vocational Education Act of 1963, as amended, requires that each state assess and meet the needs of these special groups.

Occupational instruction for displaced homemakers is offered in a wide variety of settings. Those special services that are critical to gaining self-confidence and ultimate employability are often delivered through special institutional mechanisms. According to a 1981 survey conducted by the National Displaced Homemakers Network, nearly 400 programs throughout the country provide counseling, workshops, skills training, and job placement assistance to displaced homemakers.

As an example of available services, one county public school system established a "displaced homemakers' resource center." This center offers specially designed guidance and counseling programs, arranges for training, and provides placement services in non-traditional jobs. In addition, the center provides inter-agency referrals, reference materials, support groups, specialized workshops, and self-directed computerized career search programs.

In another instance, a state has established a statewide information and referral service for both displaced homemakers and those that serve. This network not only serves as a clearinghouse for information on existing programs, but also provides technical assistance to all agencies with vocational education programs that serve displaced homemakers. Federal vocational education funds are a major source of support for this network and its activities.

Retraining for Those with Limited English Proficiency. Language difficulties are considered by far the most important barrier to job success. Recent census data indicate that over 18 million people in the United States, aged 18 and over, speak a language other than English in the home. Of this number, nearly four million do not speak English well or do not speak English at all. Those adults with limited proficiency in English do not comprise a homogeneous population. They range from those who are illiterate in their native language to those highly educated in their native language; from unskilled and inexperienced workers to highly skilled workers; from newly arrived immigrants and refugees to American-born or long-time residents. For adults with limited proficiency in English, bilingual vocational education may be the most efficient method of instruction. In addition to linguistic skills and occupational, these adults may need instruction that focuses on pre-employment and an understanding of the cultural values that apply in the workplace. They need to know general life and survival skills, how Americans value work, reasons for taking entry-level jobs (when necessary), and how to assess their experience and skills in relation to job opportunities. Once employed, they will also have to deal with work conditions and responsibilities as well as relations between employees and with employers.

An exemplary bilingual vocational education program for limited English-speaking adults operates in the Community Learning Center at Metropolitan State College in Denver, Colorado. Trainees become employed in a short period of time. This program has provided training in specific occupations in the hotel and restaurant, health service, banking, and clerical fields. Program emphasis is on moving into new and emerging occupations. The program works closely with small corporations in urban settings to develop specific training programs that ensure employment opportunities for trainees.

The trainees are permanent residents, mostly Laotian, Vietnamese, and Hispanic. Most are in their late twenties and have some knowledge of English. They are taught the basics needed for an entry-level job. Participation in role-playing workshops and job-simulated interviews is a part of the training. Training is usually completed in 18 weeks, after which trainees are placed in jobs, and teachers and interpreters then provide follow-up services, such as job-specific instruction.

Retraining for Offenders. In the past ten years, the incarceration rate has increased 70 percent. Nearly 2.5 million of the national population are under the jurisdiction of the criminal justice system; 600,000 of these are imprisoned in federal, state, and local correctional facilities; the others come under some other program, such as probation, and are not discussed here. Approximately 85 percent have not completed high school, and a large percentage function at the fifth or sixth grade level. About 40 percent of those incarcerated were unemployed at the time of arrest.

This population needs education and training. Lack of functional literacy and marketable skills aggravate a released offender's difficulties in securing employment and returning as a contributor to society. However, less than 12 percent of the total incarcerated population has access to academic and vocational programs.

In 1983, the Secretary of Education announced that the Department, through its Office of Vocational and Adult Education, will "assist state and local jurisdictions to develop, expand, and improve their delivery systems for academic, vocational, technical, social, and other educational programs for juvenile and adult offenders in order to enhance their opportunities to become law-abiding, economically self-sufficient, and productive members of society."

Contractual arrangements are underway for the development of a handbook/guide for use by correctional educators and administrators. This handbook/guide will address planning and implementation of successful vocational and related adult basic education programs in correctional settings.

Building the Productive Capacity of the Working Adult

Basic Literacy Skills. In 1983, President Reagan launched a new initiative to recognize the plight of the functionally illiterate adult and promote functional literacy. He announced the Adult Literacy Initiative saying, "In this decade, America faces serious challenges on many fronts: to our national security, our economic prosperity, and our ability to compete in the international marketplace. If we're to renew our economy, protect our freedom, we must sharpen the skills of every American mind and enlarge the potential of every individual American life. Unfortunately, the hidden problem of adult illiteracy holds back too many of our citizens, and as a Nation, we, too, pay a price."

In close correlation are the economic future of our Nation and the literacy of its workforce. Today, basic literacy can no longer be defined only on the basis of a fixed inventory of skills—reading and writing. Rather, basic literacy includes the ability to cope with the needs and demands placed on individuals in the society. Literacy must be defined by stressing its functional aspects—possession of the essential knowledge and skills that enable an individual to function effectively in his or her environment—the home, the community, the workplace.

In 1979, the Bureau of the Census reported that only six-tenths of one percent of the adult population could not read. But when functionality is also considered, the picture is not as bright. The Department of Education estimates that 26 million people are functionally illiterate today and an additional 46 million do not function proficiently. That makes a total of 72 million adults in this nation who function at a marginal level or below.

Basic or literacy skills are important tools for obtaining and holding employment. Adults lacking these skills are at a particular disadvantage when competing in the labor market. The economic and social costs of adult functional illiteracy are high: approximately 40 percent of all minority youth may be functionally illiterate; 15 percent of the workforce may be functionally illiterate; a disproportionate number of those who are functionally illiterate are found on the public assistance rolls. The nation pays a high price—an estimated $225 billion annually resulting from lost worker productivity, public assistance, crime, prisons, unrealized tax revenues, and remedial training programs.

A 1982 national survey by the Center for Public Resources found that, in the workplace, competencies in basic skills are lacking and there are deficiencies in speaking, listening, reasoning, and problem solving. These deficiencies prevent many youth and adults from getting and keeping employment. Upgrading or retraining for new or expanded occupations is seriously compromised when individuals lack basic literacy skills.

Providing the Basic Skills

There are a number of providers of basic literacy skills: vocational education, state-funded programs, and business and industry, adult vocational education, adult basic and secondary education. Vocational education programs promote the mainstreaming of all students in regular classes, but job-related literacy skills may also be offered to disadvantaged students. Several states provide learning labs for the purpose of offering remedial assistance in basic skills such as reading and mathematics. Postsecondary education institutions and other learning environments for adults may offer tutorial assistance to help students keep pace with their peers in technical subjects.

Business and industry, either independently or in collaboration with the public sector, are assisting in basic literacy instruction. Both employee and employer benefit. Benefits include higher productivity, job satisfaction, reduced absenteeism and turnover, and improved communications. There are many examples of effective approaches to basic literacy by business and industry. The Polaroid Corporation in Cambridge, Massachusetts, for example, offers fundamental skills education classes. Attendance is voluntary. The classes are available to employees during working hours and/or after work. The classes provide job-related skill development to improve job performance or to enhance job growth. Employees—from non-readers to those who need help with postsecondary courses— may receive assistance with reading, writing, mathematics, or other basic skills. Tutors are arranged for employees who cannot perform their current jobs effectively because of problems with reading and writing.

General Motors and the United Auto Workers, through an agreement with the California Department of Education, provide remedial instruction and job training for eligible GM and UAW workers displaced by plant shutdowns at Freemont and South Gate, California. On completion of the remedial instruction, all students are assigned to classes for further academic study in conjunction with skills training.

Promoting basic literacy is also a component of many adult vocational programs such as the telephone service/repair program at the Wisconsin Indianhead Technical Institute in Rice Lake, Wisconsin. This program won the Secretary of Education's Award for the Outstanding Vocational Education Programs in 1982. The program has a placement rate of over 90 percent. Employers throughout the nation have visited the Technical Institute to recruit the program's graduates.

Adult vocational education as well as adult education, must coordinate and cooperate in the effort to help eliminate illiteracy. These two educational communities should seize the initiative in dealing with this problem.

Career Guidance. Guidance and counseling are integral ingredients of successful adult vocational education programs, and they are mandated services in federally-assisted vocational education programs. A review of recent empirical studies on the effects of career guidance, published by the National Center for Reserach in Vocational Education, found that career guidance has positive effects on the career development and adjustment of individuals. These services are provided directly to students to help them realistically choose an occupation, and to determine if their individual characteristics, such as aptitude, interest, values, energy level, and temperament, are appropriate to the occupational and educational skills required for that occupation. A good match between individual characteristics and a particular job benefits the employer and employee.

Federal vocational education discretionary research funds are being used to facilitate a comprehensive range of improvements in guidance programs. An example is the federally funded project, "Linking Community-Collaborative Initiatives." This project will assist twenty communities in implementing collaborative programs of career guidance so that these programs are accessible to and meet the career development, vocational education, and employment needs of persons of all ages in the communities.

The Office of Vocational and Adult Education has initiated activities to achieve better cooperation among the education, business, and industrial communities. In a 1983 conference on "Making Partnerships Work: Career Guidance and Work Related Education and Training," recommendations were made on how to build and improve national, state, and community partnerships to enhance and expand the quality and impact of career guidance. The Department of Education also supports projects to update counselors' skills developed by other federal agencies such as the "Improve Career Decision Making Project." This project trains counselors in the use of labor market and occupational information to better meet the needs of their students and clients.

Quick-Start Economic Development Programs. The Nation's economy no longer enjoys the overall dominant position it did during the three decades following World War II. The manufacturing sector, especially, has gone through a period of stagnation. U.S. goods have lost parts of the international and domestic markets; our competitive edge has dulled. This calls for economic revitalization.

One of the most dramatic economic revitalization services provided by vocational education is the customized quick-start economic development program. Such programs are notable for their adult training/retraining requirements. The primary purpose of quick-start programs is to meet employer-specific needs as a means of economic development. These training programs, generally coordinated with other economic development authorities, are relatively short-term and can be made operational within 15 to 30 days.

At least twenty states have special programs established through formalized arrangements for the sole purpose of performing quick-start economic development functions. Many other states are involved extensively in quick-start activities, but those activities are integrated into the regular adult and vocational education programs. Financing may come from federal, state, local, or private sector sources. In Michigan and Ohio, for example, some funding for quick-start programs is derived from businesses and industries. In-kind contributions, such as facilities, equipment, and materials from local educational agencies and the private sector are available in a number of states. New York and Ohio each used more than $1 million of federal funds in 1981-82 for their respective quick-start programs.

Ohio is an example of a highly industrialized state where significant funds (nearly $8 million) are allocated to a quick-start program effort to serve nearly 60,000 persons. The Ohio program is designed to assist both new and existing industries, with the main thrust made on behalf of expanding existing companies. For example, the state vocational education agency, in concert with the Ohio Department of Economic and Community Development, persuaded a company to remain in a community of approximately 15,000 people by providing training to 1,000 people within a four-month period. In another instance, an international corporation located in Ohio and employing some 12,000 workers, threatened to move 6,000 jobs out of the country unless the workers became more productive. Management training was provided. The result: the 6,000 jobs were secured.

In some states, quick-start programs serve to entice new or established companies to settle in their areas. This is the case in Georgia, where an outside company established a $90 million plant in the state, employing 900 people, all trained through the cooperative efforts of the Georgia Industry and Trade Department and the state vocational educational agency. Georgia is also negotiating with several international companies in an attempt to bring new business and industry into Georgia. South Carolina also has an impressive record of attracting new employers; many overseas firms have opened branch offices and plants there.

Quick-start programs strengthen industrial and economic development, employ more workers, slow the migration of workers to other states, improve wages, and provide overall economic gains for particular communities. Customized, quick-start programs have helped achieve a net gain in jobs nationally, rather than merely causing a migration of workers to other communities or to other states.

Adult Vocational Education's Response to Technological Innovations

Career Change/Advancement. Rapid advances in various technologies and the emergence of completely new technologies are changing the nature of work. A careful scrutiny of education and skill requirements and their relationship to training and retraining programs is essential. Economic revitalization cannot be a success without a renewed commitment by both the vocational education community and the private sector.

Our businesses and industries are currently in a major technological transition period not unlike the Industrial Revolution in scope and impact. As new technologies are put in place, there will be a considerable impact on the work force as we now know it. For example, information processing will have a principal effect on the banking industry. In the area of manufacturing, the rapid automation in the machine, sheet metal, and assembly areas is changing the workplace. Computer-aided design (CAD) coupled with computer-aided manufacturing (CAM) can allow an impress design to be fabricated by computer. Adding automatic material transfer and robot assembly techniques will greatly affect the number or traditional-type manufacturing jobs.

To illustrate, the Chrysler Corporation has doubled production over the past decade with 30 percent fewer workers. Within that same period of time the United Auto Workers of North America has experienced a 25 percent reduction in membership. This occured in a period when automation and robotics were just being introduced. The new manufacturing technology requies fewer workers, but they must be more technically proficient. The implication for retraining for career change and for career advancement are evident.

In general, a robotics maintenance set-up job will require two years of post-secondary training. This has enormous implications for the older work force—many of whom have less than a high school education. The many technical skills required dictate a secondary education, particularly in mathematics, the physical sciences, and communications skills. The outlook for retraining many adult workers lacking these skills is rather bleak.

Many basic industries, such as mining and steel, are going abroad; those that remain in the States will be using the newer technologies. Employment in the new technologies is predicated on training and retraining of workers. Productive members of society will increasingly be expected to modify, upgrade, and update their knowledge and skills in response to the pace of technological change. The problem of designing training and retraining programs to meet the changing skill requirements is that there is no consensus on what the skill requirements will be. Given this uncertainty, it appears that the ability to adapt to the changing requirements of the labor market must be a top priority.

More than conventional wisdom and traditional approaches will be required to formulate educational policies and to plan training and retraining programs that ensure technological leadership, improved productivity, and an adequate labor force to meet the demand both in terms of numbers and in terms of adaptability to changing skill requirements.

Electronic Telecommunications Network (ADVOC-NET). Under sponsorship of the Office of Vocational and Adult Education, the National Center for Research in Vocational Education has pilot-tested a national electronic telecommunications system for use by Federal, State, and local vocational and adult education personnel. Known as ADVOC-NET and placed into operation in May 1984, the system provides communication channels across State, regional, and geographical boundaries and is not bound by time zones or by local office hours and operations.

Defense-preparedness Efforts. Under President Reagan's leadership, the national defense is being strengthened, creating new opportunities for vocational education. Studies have identified skilled worker shortages for engineers, precision machinists, skilled assemblers, tool and die makers, shipfitters, and others. Coping with skill shortages is essential to the military services and to defense industries. Here again adult vocational education will be challenged to respond to the need.

Sponsored by the Office of Vocational and Adult Education, a 1984–85 project of national significance in vocational education will increase collaboration between vocational education and the defense establishment. The National Association for Industry-Education Cooperation (NAIEC) in conducting the project will identify exemplary education or training programs involving vocational education with the defense industries or military services. An analysis of factors contributing to successful linkages will be performed. Project results will enhance defense preparedness, improve the quality of vocational education/industrial training programs, and increase the availability of skilled workers.

The Departments of Defense and Education have established a Joint Committee on Training and Education for National Security. This working group, co-chaired by Lawrence Korb, Assistant Secretary for Manpower, Reserve Affairs and Logistics (DOD), and the author seeks collaborative means to further strengthen our national defense through identifying criteria for skills shortages and finding innovative ways to train for them.

Projects by the Department of Defense indicate that in the period 1982 to 1987 there will be a need for 10 million new workers in 41 occupational fields that span both defense and non-defense industries and require vocational training. In the projections there was an attempt to isolate that part of the need directly related to defense production. For example, total employment for electrical and electronic technicians is projected to rise from 204,440 in 1982 to 241,190 in 1987, an annual increase of 3 percent without counting replacement needs. At the same time, as part of this total increase, the job openings for these technicians in defense-related industries are expected to rise from 50,770 in 1982 to 60,710 in 1987, an annual increase of almost 4 percent, again without counting replacements. In many key occupations (e.g., machinists), the annual growth rate in defense-related industries is expected to be twice that in all industries.

Typical responses to defense needs by State vocational education agencies are illustrated by programs in Mississippi and North Carolina.

Through diversified training efforts, the Mississippi Department of Education has made significant contributions to the defense effort. Over the past 20 years it has been involved in training skilled craftworkers, welders, and shipfitters for the Ingalls Shipbuilding Corporation. Recently the State educational agency concluded a short-term program in electronics providing 120 trainees for Lockheed in its work for the Air Force. The State educational agency is completing a third year of work with Mason-Chamberlin, Inc., under contract with the Department of the Army. This project involves the construction and operation of an ammunitions plant, the first one started in the U.S. since World War II.

The North Carolina community college system is involved in long- and short-term education and training programs for soldiers stationed at Fort Bragg. Programs are often designed to provide basic skills, including reading, mathematics, and English as a second language, as well as operational skills, such as communications, vehical maintenance, and operation of military equipment.

Epilogue—Participation in Organized Programs of Adult Education

A 1981 study, by the National Center for Education Statistics (NCES), on participation in adult education found that more than 21 million persons 17 years old and over participated in organized adult education activities. This figure represents 13 percent of the total adult population. Approximately 56 percent of all participants were women. Among women participants, over 70 percent were employed, 20 percent were full-time homemakers, and the remainder were either looking for work, going to school, or retired. Almost 96 percent of male participants were working. The dominant group of participants in adult education was professional and technical workers, who comprised over 30 percent of those taking courses. Clerical workers (18 percent) were the second most likely group of participants.

More than 37 million courses were taken by adults. Of these, 22.5 million (60 percent) were taken for job-related reasons. Of the job-related courses, 74 percent were taken to help the adult improve or advance in a current job. In the non-job-related reasons, personal or social benefits led with over 10 million courses.

The NCES study also reported courses taken for trade or professional objectives. Approximately 2.6 million courses were taken by adults to obtain a license or certificate. Just in excess of that number were taken to renew a license or certificate.

Census tabulations show that 156,000 adults were enrolled in courses to obtain or renew a license. Only participants working toward a license or license renewal in vocational/trade, technical, business, or commercial school are included. Licensing for a professiona, such as medicine or optometry, is excluded. Over half of these participants are employed full time; over 70 percent are ages 16-34 years.

An American Tradition

The role of vocational education in furthering the learning of adults reflects our tradition of American know-how. In a speech to the 19th Annual National Vocational Industrial Clubs of America Conference, President Reagan summarized this role and our tradition:

America's tradesmen and women are the pistons that drive the engine of our economy. This country was built with the sweat and determination of hardworking men and women who, like many of you, love to work with their hands as well as their minds. Your forerunners were America's link between our dreams and reality. They were the people who transformed this continent into one of the wonders of the modern world. We are a nation of people who believe it's not enough to be good. You've got to be good at something.

References

Current Population Survey. Washington, D.C.: Bureau of the Census, U.S. Department of Commerce, October 1982.

Duvall, Marcel R. *A Report on Quick-start Economic Development Programs.* Washington, D.C.: Division of Vocational Education Services, U.S. Department of Education, April 1983.

Golladay, Mary A. and Wulfsberg, Rolf M. *The Condition of Vocational Education.* Washington, D.C.: U.S. Department of Education, July 1981.

Hecker, Daniel E. "A Fresh Look at Job Openings," *Occupational Outlook Quarterly.* (Spring 1983):27-29.

Kay, Evelyn R. *Participation in Adult Education, May 1981.* Washington, D.C.: National Center for Education Statistics, U.S. Department of Education, July 1982.

Moore, Kris and Hull, Daniel M. "Laser Technicians: Will Demand Outrun Supply?" *Lasers and Applications.* (February 1984):91-93.

Seaberry, Jane. "Unprecedented Changes Forecast for Population," *The Washington Post*, January 22, 1984, p. G1.

Vocational Education, Report by the Secretary of Education to the Congress. Washington, D.C.: U.S. Department of Education, 1981.

THE CAUSES AND TIMING OF ADULT LEARNING

*Carol B. Aslanian**

During the past decade, there has been a significant growth in adult learning—both formal and informal. Today, more than one out of three college students is 25 years of age or older, and 40 percent of all college students study part-time. Most of these part-time students are adults who hold jobs and have families. Further, it is expected that these trends in the characteristics of college students will continue for the rest of the century. By the year 2000, there will be more students over 25 years of age on college campuses than under 25 years of age, and at least half of these adult students will be studying part-time. Millions more adults are learning at their places of employment, through private lessons, in local school districts, in their churches, through their professional associations, and in voluntary community organizations. Even more are learning on their own through television, libraries, museums, correspondence courses, and other sources.

This growth has not been well understood. Why has the rate of participation in learning exceeded the rate of population growth? If there were a better understanding of the dynamics underlying adult learning—the interplay of psychological, social, and economic forces that drive adult learning—perhaps there could be an explanation for the current rate of growth.

The Office of Adult Learning Services (OALS) of the College Board believed these questions were important enough to warrant a nationwide study to identify the causes of adult learning and to understand its timing. This article reports the major approaches to and outcomes of that study.

Why Do Adults Study?

Sixty million Americans learn each year. Educators know who they are. They know when they study. They know how they study. And they know what they study.

But they don't know why they study.

Learning was already finished for these adults—so many thought. Why did

---

This article is based on Carol B. Aslanian, *Americans in Transition: Life Changes as Reasons for Adult Learning.* New York: The College Board, 1980. Portions of that study are included in this chapter.

they come back? And why did they come back last year? Why not 1980? Why not 1990?

Adult educators can describe adult learning. Why can't they explain adult learning? Why can't they answer this question:

Why sixty million? There are 125 million American adults. What caused one out of two to learn last year?

Or this question:

Why more last year than ever before? One out of three college students was over 25 in 1980. Will there be two out of three over 25 in 1990?

Or this question:

Why do adults choose to learn some topics, not others? Most of them study job skills. They already have jobs. Why don't they study something they don't already have—philosophy, let's say.

Or this question:

What makes adults learn at certain times, not others? Some have been waiting years to study. What have they been waiting for?

Or this question:

What do adults expect to get out of their study? What knowledge, what skills, what feelings?

Or this question:

Why do the advantaged learn and the disadvantaged not? Because learning is what makes them advantaged? Because being advantaged is what makes them learn? Which is the cause, which the effect?

If adult educators could answer research questions like these, they could plan for years ahead, not weeks or months, because they could better predict which adults would study what topics in what numbers. They could better anticipate what kinds of institutions adults would choose, and what credentials adults would want. Adult educators could better predict the times, places, and teaching methods adults would prefer and the prices they would pay.

If educators could answer research questions like these, they could also make practical decisions like what mailing lists to buy, where and when to advertise, whether to cooperate or compete with other institutions, when to begin a course on small business administration for local doctors and end one on keypunching for data entry operators.

Such predictions would help five groups interested in adult learning: (1) those who provide adult learning; (2) those who supply information and counseling to adults; (3) those who make public policy for adult learning; (4) adults who are learning or who should be learning; and, (5) scholars who study adult learning.

Beneficiaries of Predictability

Providers. Two types of providers could benefit from reliable predictions about adult learning. They are those institutions and agencies whose primary function is education and those whose primary function falls in other areas— business, art, religion—but that also offer learning opportunities. Hence, providers include colleges and universities, professional and graduate schools, employers, museums, libraries, churches, civic organizations, the media, the military, publishers, and others.

Information and Counseling Center Staffs. There are roughly 25,000 centers in the United States that offer information and/or counseling to adults. These include special centers in colleges and universities, brokering centers, libraries, YMCA's and YWCA's, and private agencies, among others. As adults turn to learning in ever-increasing numbers, information and counseling centers that can assist them with educational planning will be in greater demand.

Public Policymakers. As lifelong learning becomes more prevalent, federal and state governments will become increasingly concerned about the supporting role they can play. Their support could include financial as well as technical assistance with institutional programming, provision of information services, coordination of public resources, etc.

Adults. About one-half of adults are current learners; all are potential learners. If educators could understand what makes some adults learn, they could offer advice to other adults about what, when, how, and where they might also want or need to learn. Educators could help them recognize opportunities or obligations to learn when they occur and help them anticipate the benefits of learning and the costs of not learning—or perhaps the reverse. In short, if educators assume that learning is a constructive adult activity and if they can understand why some adults undertake it, they should be able to help other adults know whether they should do the same. Moreover, by displaying the entire range of adult learning, educators might even be able to help the current learners see whole new possibilities for learning still more.

Scholars. A small number of scholars have made adult learning their speciality. A larger number of investigators—some in college and university institutional research organizations—have examined adult learning. The number of studies has grown as adult education has expanded. What previous research has been able to do is to describe adult education and offer some explanations of it. Further insights into the causes of adult learning would stimulate further research in this area.

But better predictions must wait for better answers to the question, "What causes adults to learn?" Educators need an explanation that identifies at least the main streams in the adult learning movement and that helps them anticipate which way those streams will flow in coming years.

Current Explanations

Descriptions of adult learning are fairly complete; explanations of why adults choose to learn are incomplete.

Descriptions
Adult educators know how many adults choose formal study in institutions rather than learning on their own. They know what kinds of institutions—two-year or four-year, public or private, educational or otherwise—adults attend. They know how many enroll full-time and how many enroll part-time, and whether they go to school days, nights, or weekends. They know what they study, and whether they are studying for academic credit or not; whether they are seeking degrees or certificates. Adult educators know how many adults take examinations to demonstrate what they have learned rather than taking courses to learn it.

In addition, educators know a great deal about the characteristics of adult learners and how they differ from nonlearners according to age, sex, marital status, race, education, occupation, income, and other demographic indicators.

Explanations
A fully satisfactory set of explanations would have to encompass at least three phenomena: the widespread participation of adults in learning; the unequal participation of adults, the rising rate of adult learning; and the fact that adults often do not learn what they say they will.

The lack of an adequate explanation of adult learning has been substantiated in different ways. Bernice Neugarten sees the problems broadly. She says educators don't have an overarching theory of human behavior, and that they paid too much attention to the first two-sevenths of life, at the expense of the five-sevenths that follow.

Michael O'Keefe agrees that there is no theory about adult learning. When he made estimates in 1977 about how many adults were going to learn in the future, his predictions were based on current trends, not theory.

K. Patricia Cross thinks it is hard to predict learning rates because there are only weak explanations of why adults decide to learn. She says that this is a big problem when you want to make "demand curves"—just what O'Keefe was trying to do.

Twenty years ago, using 22 case studies, Cyril O. Houle said that adults learn for one or more of the following reasons: they have concrete goals to meet—like learning to deal with teenage problems, using a word processor, decorating a new home; they want to socialize—find a new husband or wife, make new friends; they love learning—they learn for its own sake.

Cross explains why adults who learn keep on doing it:
- Learning is addictive. The more you do it, the more you want it;
- Learning has been successful. You want to return to scenes of earlier success; and
- Learning is natural. Human beings are basically curious, and they enjoy learning for its own rewards.

Cross also explains why other adults do not learn. She identifies three barriers:
- *Dispositional*. Feeling too old, lacking confidence, being bored with school. Attitudes you have about yourself and about education;
- *Situational*. No time, no transportation, no child care. Things which stop you from learning because of your own circumstances;
- *Institutional*. Inconvenient schedules, high cost, wrong courses. Features of institutions that discourage learning.

Despite the substantial contributions of Houle, Cross, and others, current explanations fall short in several ways. First, they classify adult learners into types, without explaining what produces each type. Second, they do not explain the timing of adult learning. Third, they do not explain the uneven distribution of adults across different curriculum areas. And, fourth, they lean more heavily on circumstances that keep adults out of school rather than on circumstances that lead them into school.

A Better Explanation

The College Board's Office of Adult Learning Services began its search for a better explanation by turning away from those who study adult learning toward those who study adult life. If it could understand adult living, maybe it could understand adult learning. Two areas of investigation are highlighted here.

The Adult Life Cycle
Those who have looked at adult development generally agree on one thing: adult life is divided into stages which adults move through in a certain order and at

certain times. But, they disagree on whether it is internal events (like a fortieth birthday) or external events (like a recent divorce) that signal the beginning or end of a life stage. Most authors see the events as setting the time for new stage rather than causing it. They also add that passing from one stage to another constitutes a significant transition—a transition which can bring about a challenge, create stress, or offer an opportunity for growth.

For example, Daniel Levinson, in *The Seasons of a Man's Life*, saw four periods in the life cycle, each lasting about 25 years, separated by five short transitions. We go from one to another, he says, in a given order and at a fixed age. In *Four Stages of Life* Marjorie Lowenthal, like Levinson, sees adult years broken down into stages, and says that moving from one to another requires stressful transitions, often causing personal reassessment. Roger Gould, in *Transformations: Growth and Change in Adult Life* says, "Adulthood is not a plateau; rather it is a dynamic and changing time for all of us." Gould stresses the significance of specific life events as milestones along the adult life course: events like buying a first house, experiencing a first job, or having the first baby. He says growth is necessary to cope with change. In *Passages*, Gail Sheehy, like Gould, finds adult life to be a period of dramatic growth. She identifies a series of life stages separated by transitions which she refers to as passages.

What caught the Office of Adult Learning Services' attention most was that transitions challenge adults and require them to grow. Could this be the explanation of adult learning OALS was looking for?

Some support for this connection came from Alan Knox. He examined the life events discussed by these authors and made this connection: the events signal role changes; role changes require adaption; learning is one of several ways adults can adapt, along with others such as frantic activity, trial and error. To put it simply, when some major event occurs in adult lives—a divorce, loss of a job, a severe illness—some adults learn to meet the challenge of a new status in life. The learning can be related to the event. Take, for example, a recent divorcee who studies single parenthood. But there doesn't have to be a direct tie. A competitive Madison Avenue advertising executive, for instance, who suffers a stroke will study real estate law to get licensed as a broker in rural Vermont. Of all the authors reviewed for the OALS study, Knox went furthest in linking adult learning to adult life changes.

Societal Changes

But where do life changes come from? Social and economic changes? Most likely. OALS examined recent social trend data, and it came as no news that American life is in a virtually continuous state of rapid social change. Lives have become more turbulent, and can be expected to become even more so in the future. How would Alan Knox expect adults to cope?

OALS had one more clue that it was on the right track in looking at life changes. The College Board had done an earlier study which probed career changes in adults. It found a very large number of adults anticipating a job or career change. Most important, it found a high percentage—60 percent—who said they would have to learn something new in order to make a transition to a new job or career. The OALS considered, "If career transitions led many adults to learn, could other transitions do likewise?"

Life Transitions

This line of thinking—life changes requiring further learning—led OALS to two propositions.

First, moving from one status in life to another requires learning. Learning new information, new skills, new attitudes or values. Becoming a foreman or an executive or a lieutenant requires new relationships with people as well as new technical knowledge or skills. So does becoming a wife, or a mother, or a widow. So does joining a political party or a fraternal organization. It's the same with becoming a member of a church, or attending a concert series, or taking up tennis. All of these choices require learning. If the learning is not accomplished, the adult can't make the transition into the new status.

The transitions OALS had in mind sound less significant than those talked about by others. But the strength of the OALS proposition is that it does apply to all types of changes—small and large—giving it the power to explain and predict adult learning whether it takes one week or one year. The size of the change doesn't really matter to us as educators, does it? Depending on our institutions, we are as interested in teaching a secretary how to use a newly installed electronic typewriter for about one week as we are in preparing the ex-schoolteacher to train middle managers in a local industry for about one year. Don't both of them have to learn to be successful in carrying out an existing job or in taking on a new one?

Second, some identifiable event triggers an adult's decision to learn at a particular point in time. The need, the opportunity, even the desire, are necessary but not sufficient to seek out more learning. Something must happen to convert a latent learner into an active learner. The effect of the event is to cause the adult to begin learning at that point in time rather than at an earlier or later point. Getting hired or getting fired, getting married or getting divorced, getting sick, getting elected, or moving to a new city were the kinds of events that OALS' investigations told adults it was time to learn.

In short, transitions set the reasons for learning, triggers set the times for that learning.

Finally, OALS thought that if life transitions were times of learning, and specific events triggered the decisions to learn at particular points in time, then both transitions and triggers would occur in several life areas. OALS used seven life areas to classify the transitions and triggers identified in the lives of 2,000 Americans—career, family, health, religion, citizenship, art, and leisure.

A Profile of Adult Learners

To test these propositions, OALS used a structured interview guide to speak to roughly 2,000 Americans, 25 years and older, in nine geographic regions across the country. The overall profile of the 2,000 adults interviewed is quite similar to what the census shows for the nation as a whole, particularly in geography, age, marital status and employment.

OALS asked over 40 questions about how, when and where the learning took place. Most important to testing the proposition regarding transitions and triggers were these questions:
- Are you studying or learning anything now, or have you in the last twelve months?
- What topics?
- When did you begin?
- Why then?

OALS found half of all Americans 25 years and older (over 60 million adults) had learned one or more topics in the past year. There are differences between the adults who said they had learned from those who said they had not. The learners are younger; better-educated; have higher incomes; are more likely to be employed, and employed in professional and technical work; are more white than black; and, more likely to live in urbanized areas and in the Pacific coast states.

Life Changes Require Learning

The findings showed that most adults—83 percent—said they had learned in order to cope with some change in their lives. They were learning to use new machines their companies had acquired; learning the histories of the churches they were joining; learning to take care of their aging parent in declining health; learning tennis now that they had moved to the suburbs; learning how to give up smoking when ordered by their doctors. In short, their lives had changed, were changing, or would change, and learning was the way to cope with these changes. The remaining 17 percent gave other reasons. They were more like Houle's socializers and lovers of learning. They found it to be a satisfying activity, keeping them mentally alert, giving them a chance to be with other adults, filling up their spare time.

To put it plainly, 83 percent wanted some reward from learning; 17 percent found the process of learning to be its own reward. For 83 percent learning was utilitarian, for 17 percent it justified itself. For 83 percent learning was the means, for 17 percent it was the end.

OALS classified the life change reasons given by the 83 percent according to the seven life areas and found that more adults learn in order to make career transitions (56 percent) than for all other reasons combined, with family and leisure transitions competing for a distant second place.

Life Events Set the Time for Learning

OALS also found that all adults who could name a transition in their lives as causing them to learn, could also point to specific events triggering their decision to learn. The triggering events they talked about were sometimes cataclysmic, such as a contested divorce, an illness, or the death of a loved one; but sometimes they were lesser yet significant events, such as the last child leaving for college, getting a promotion, or moving to a new town. Whatever the case, the adults who attributed their learning to transitions in their lives had little trouble in singling out the events that made them decide to learn when they did.

OALS also classified the trigger events according to the seven life areas. More than 90 percent of the events triggering adult learning occur in career or family lives. The career clock and the family clock obviously set the time for learning. This is not surprising, given the fact that the adults in the study also reported that they spent about 80 percent of their time with their career and families. This suggests a cause and effect relationship between how adults spend their lives and the life changes that cause them to learn.

Examples of Transitions and Triggering Events

Generally, adults' transitions and triggers for learning were clearly evident.

Career
Most career transitions had adults moving into a new job, adapting to a changing one, or advancing in their careers. The career triggers were very clear: getting

hired, arrival of new equipment, getting a promotion, stopping work. For example:

> First, I was a criminologist. I worked in the prison as a correctional officer and I evaluated prisoners' progress. That job was too hard for me; it was a terrible job and dangerous as well. People were getting killed in the prison and there were riots. I couldn't stay in that occupation, so I gave it up and looked for a very low stress area. Now, I'm working on my Master's degree in library science and working in a small library in Florida.

There are others who need to learn just to keep their current jobs:

> I graduated with a degree in teaching, decided against teaching, and got a job in business. When I was going through four years of college, learning how to teach students American history, I missed a lot of math courses and other subjects I now use daily on the job. I'm taking a U.S. Department of Commerce course in advanced export administration. I am in the export business and my job has grown by leaps and bounds—more commodities and more countries to deal with. I need to improve my administrative skills so I can keep up with the expansion in my job.

Running faster to stay in the same place requires continual learning, especially in fields with changing technologies, government regulations, intense competition. This is, for example, why adults who hold more professional and technical jobs are twice as likely to learn as those in mining and construction.

Family

Major events in family life can trigger learning.

One effect of the skyrocketing number of husbands and wives who cannot get along together has been to promote a special kind of learning, as one husband told OALS:

> You can't call it a course, really. But I'm learning or I'm trying to, and I by God hope she is. It's marriage counseling. Twice a week. Might as well be a course—and it'd cost a hell of a lot less if it were. Anyhow, I'm trying to learn that it's okay for her to work outside the house. That's really pretty easy. Hard part for me to learn is that it's supposed to be okay for me to do her work inside the house. It's learn it or Goodbye, Gladys, I suppose.

Divorce statistics doubled in the 1970s; unmarried couples tripled; their separations didn't even make the statistics.

Leisure

Americans spend 16 percent of their time in leisure activities. It is no wonder that close to 16 percent of all transitions are leisure ones. Further, less time in paid employment means more leisure. In leisure transitions, the triggering events always came from outside the leisure world.

One person reported:

I was widowed at 25. I began taking lots of classes involving dancing. I needed something to do, now that my husband was gone. I wanted to be a good dancer and meet lots of new people. For a single woman at my age in life, associating with other people was extremely important to me.

For this woman as well as for many others who have lost a spouse, making a successful transition to a new life often requires learning. Learning is obviously a reorienting experience that can help put the pieces of a life back together again.

Health

Some adults learn to regain their health, and some to maintain it. Here's the testimony of one person OALS talked to:

Since I was 17 I was a big beer drinker. But in 1973, I had a physical examination. My doctor said I had a high amount of triglycerides, so knock off the carbohydrates. The next day I got a book on what carbohydrates were—I couldn't even spell the word. I found out that each can of beer has 15 grams of carbohydrates and dry wine has comparatively little. So I started drinking wine and cut way down on beer consumption. After a while I began to appreciate the taste of good wine and said, "Too bad I can't get really good wine cheap." Then it dawned on me that you could get really good wine cheap if you had the time and patience to do it yourself. I've been making my own wine for five years now. I read a lot of books and talked to people that are also making wines to find out what they are doing so I don't make the same mistakes they made. Now I'm aging some Zinfandels. I always make dry wine.

Poor health habits that had little effect on one's energy and appearance at a younger age take their toll at an older age. But something has to happen to make the adult aware of the accumulating negative effects of these habits. In this case, the doctor's diagnosis did the trick. Seventy-five percent of all adults now reach age 65, as compared with only 40 percent in 1900, and the life expectancy of those who reach 65 today is 16 more years. As the nation's population ages, more adults will need to learn how to recover from personal injury or illness, or to maintain physical fitness.

Religion

Some adults have an intensely personal relationship with God. Some told OALS that intensifying that relationship caused them to start learning more about religion or more about God's plan for their lives. One adult said:

> My church had always held retreats every summer. We would bring in an outstanding preacher from some other church and he would lead the retreat while our own minister was on vacation. I had gone to these retreats for years but, two summers ago the preacher we brought in was so good. He prayed with me every day for God to take over my life. Nothing happened at first. But then, nearly at the end, God answered my prayers and came into my life. That's when I started adult Bible class at the church. Then I went on the retreat last summer and I have kept on.

This person underwent a major religious transition, and had to learn new values, new ways of relating to other human beings, and new ways of spending her time. The Bible was her textbook; the minister her teacher.

Citizenship

Other adults learned because of changes in their lives as citizens. Most of the reasons focused on becoming a citizen or becoming a volunteer. One man in the Southeast said:

> I moved here with my family from Caracas three years ago and decided to take out my U.S. citizenship—my wife and I—about a year and a half later. I had learned a little English in high school in Venezuela, but not much, and my wife had never studied it. The local high school ran classes and both of us went for almost a year. At the end we took our examinations and both passed. We are very proud.

More and more adult immigrants are arriving on American shores, and many of them are deciding to stay. All will need to learn their way into citizenship.

Study Conclusions

Several major conclusions about adults learning are obvious based on OALS' work:

- America has become a learning society. Half of the adults in the nation are learning each year—surgery and sales; sewing and sailing; Swahilii and swinebreeding. And, virtually all of America's children learn.
- America is a society in which adults learn everywhere. It is not just that

some adult learning takes place outside of formal education; most of it takes place in workplaces, churches, prisons, libraries, museums, the military.

- Many adults learn completely on their own. Close to 30 percent in the OALS sample did. If educators want to understand their competition, they should pay a lot of attention to the independent learners, those people who go on without regular teachers or formal instruction; who buy or borrow whatever books or materials they need. They can watch television or talk to a friend, or use just plain trial and error.
- Most adults do not learn for the sheer pleasure of learning. For most, learning is not its own reward. For four out of five Americans, it is not the process of learning that counts; it is using the results. OALS has found this conclusion to be quite disappointing to most educators, who like to think that learning— both getting it and possessing it— should be inherently rewarding. But this is not the case with adults. The value of the learning for them is in its utility.
- Most adults learn in order to cope with some change in their lives. It is being in transition from one role in life to another that makes adults learn. They learn what they need to know to be successful. They come to schools, colleges, bases, in one status, but expect to leave it in another. Most of them would be disappointed if they were to go out exactly as they came in. The test of learning is the success of the transition.

    The learning can come before, during, or after a life transition. Learning before a transition presumably is the best way, but it is the rarest. It is perhaps because most adults cannot plan their lives well enough to prepare ahead of time. Furthermore, some arrangements make it impossible. Military training, for example, is not available to most adults until they enter the armed forces. Company training is not available until an adult takes a job at the company.

    Other transitions occur more slowly, allowing adults time to accommodate to their changing circumstances by learning as their circumstances change. Their learning accompanies their transitions—a pregnant woman in child care classes, for example.

- Transitions, and the learning needed to accomplish them, are not evenly distributed across all life areas. More than half of them deal with careers, a smaller number with family or leisure lives. Very few are art, health, or religious transitions, and almost none concern citizenship. There are probably several explanations for this, but the best one is rather simple. The number of transitions in each life area corresponds exactly to the amount of time adults spend in each life area. The adults OALS talked to spent about 80 percent of their time with their careers and families, and attributed 80 percent of their learning to changes in their careers and their families. This means that the best way to predict what adults will learn is to find out how they spend their time.

- There is always a specific event in an adult's life that triggers the transition, and thus the learning. It is those events that set the time on the learning clock; to know an adult's life schedule is to know an adult's learning schedule.

The value of OALS' finding that life transitions cause most adult learning lies in its power to predict what they will learn. The value of its finding that specific life events trigger most adult learning lies in its power to predict when they will learn. These findings answer the questions the OALS study set out to address: (1) Why one out of two adults? Adult life cycle and social change. (2) Why more than ever? Faster rate of social change. (3) Why some topics, not others? The way adults spend time: 80 percent in their jobs and with their families. (4) Why some times, not others? The schedule of life events. (5) What do they expect to get out of it? Success in their new status. (6) Why the advantaged—not the disadvantaged? The advantaged control their life changes; for the disadvantaged, their life changes control them.

Implications for Providers

The OALS study drew five separate sets of implications from its findings. One set is aimed at those who provide learning. They suggest how to identify prospective clients; design programs; market services; and work with organizations. A second set is aimed at counselors who want to locate clients and want to be helpful at just the right point in people's lives. A third is for public policy makers, who should read the conclusions and legislate and administer accordingly. A fourth is for adults themselves, who can get clues as to when they may have to learn. And, a fifth set is for scholars. It provides good questions that could help advance educators understanding of adult learning even further. What follows are examples of the implications for providers, counselors, and scholars.

Providers would want to recruit people like these: parents who attend high school graduation might be seeing their last child off to college. This could free many mothers for full-time work and part-time school. Do you find parents through your local schools (where many of you are located) or through the colleges their children attend (where others of you are located)?

Mothers who had babies five years ago and who are over 25 now have these children in kindergarten. Some of these mothers are ready to go back to school. Hospitals can give you their names.

Military personnel who retire after 20 years of service have many years of active life ahead. They need training and occupational skills just before or just after they leave the military to enter another career or leisure life. This is not any less true for police departments, fire departments and other municipal agencies that offer retirement after 20 years.

People at 65 with a limited income need to learn how to manage their finances. You can find them in senior citizen groups or housing complexes, or at companies right before they leave.

You can also locate adults in transition by keeping in touch with others who see them often. For example: Do the counseling staffs in your institution or your community know you? Are the personnel directors of the companies familiar with your catalogues? Do lawyers and court officials know when you're available? Have medical staff visited your facilities? Are school superintendents and their staff up to date on your programs? If not, they cannot direct their clients, employees, patients, and parents to you.

You can also locate adults through organizations. The most important one would be employers, who have enormous requirements for training, and the resources to support it. Generally, they do not want to do it, but they choose to do it because it is the least expensive way to supply their own personnel with the skills they need. You can go to these organizations and offer to take over some of their training activities. If you can do it at less expense, you have got a good chance of getting the program transferred to you.

Finally, you must assess the learning demands of your community on a regular basis. Information should be collected from adults themselves, from employers, voluntary associations, and the government agencies, which require training for their employees as well as for their constituencies. Findings from such surveys can help you predict what types of adults in your service area will need what sorts of instruction for what purposes, now and in the future.

Counselors can locate adults much as providers do. You will find that many adults cannot predict when, and for what purpose, they will need to learn. You can help them forecast life events that will trigger the need to make a transition, and thus the need to learn. With that kind of help, adults will be able to better plan and schedule their future learning. Many adults who are most in need of learning—the disadvantaged and the minorities—are least engaged in it. You need to reach out actively if you want to serve these people, since they are as unlikely to seek information or counseling as they are to seek learning itself.

Scholars could address such unanswered questions as:
- Presumably all adults are in transition. Why do some adults seek learning as a means to succeed while others do not? Do other adults fail at their transitions, or do they have alternative ways of coping that make it necessary for them to learn?
- What is the anatomy of career entry, progression, and exit as it relates to learning? Does it work in the same way for women as for men? Will the growth of learning as a means of career re-entry for women be followed by a similar growth as a means for career advancement?

- Is there some optimum match between a given type of transition and a given provider of learning? Are employers the best providers for those in career transition, for example, or are churches best for those those in religious transition? Or are all providers equally suitable as long as the learning itself matches the transition?
- What are the limits to the growth of adult education, if any? Is there some maximum proportion of adults in the society who can be engaged in learning at the same time? Is there some maximum proportion of all adult time that can be constructively dedicated to learning, rather than to other activities needed to maintain the society?

OALS' findings, and the evidence of social and economic change demonstrate that American lives are changing. The lives of workers—young and old, women in and out of the home, senior citizens, military personnel, the recent immigrant. These adults will have to learn to cope with new life roles. If they are not your students or clients now, they will be.

WHAT WE KNOW ABOUT ADULT LEARNING STYLES

Patrick R. Penland

Each person has a learning style—characteristic ways of processing information, feeling, and behaving in learning situations. Successful adult education depends on an appropriate match between an adult's learning style and the form of instruction.

This chapter examines the interaction between learning styles and modes of instruction and how these relationships may be used to facilitate adult learning.

Forms of Instruction

There are three modes of instruction: informal, formal, and technical.

Informal learning encompasses two major modes—mentor and self-developed activities—and does not include any person in a teacher role. A peer model or authority figure could be used for initiation purposes, but that person may not be conscious of the influence being felt by the learner. The learner absorbs clusters of related activities, with little, if any, deliberate awareness of the embedded rules and patterns. For example, some persons watching television may accept variant lifestyle behavior as normal regardless of whether such behavior has much if any relevance to their own situation.

Informal learning may be self-directed and self-planned around a number of developmental steps that the learner deliberately considers. While such learning may be embedded in a "natural" cognitive style, the learner should make a considerable effort to "converse" with other persons using other styles and to retrieve information from resources of variant design and complementarity. An individual may use an interpersonal network and many resources, but must learn to remain responsible to the self and squarely in control of the self-instructional processes.

In *formal* learning, however, the teacher directs learning by means of prescriptions; the instructor sets the standard and plans, and directs and evaluates the results of the instructional processes. Usually, the teacher does not present a framework of right and wrong up front, but invariably reveals it only when correcting a mistake. With repetitions, the activities add up to a formal behavior system that nobody questions.

In *technical* learning, corrections for mistakes are administered explicitly, transmitted in a "packaged" instructional system from a teacher to student, orally or in writing. The "course" outline, syllabus, or programmed text presents content and competencies to be developed in a logical and coherent manner. The student tries, makes a mistake, is corrected and makes another effort. This linear instructional process, employing directed feedback, can be quite unemotional and detached. Under ideal conditions, the learner and instructor work closely together to ensure that learning does take place.

In order to accommodate greater variety in the modes of learning, enriched learning systems are needed that will allow greater flexibility for the learner. Some abilities may be best developed in a self-directed mode, others may be developed to better advantage in non-formal and informal modes, leaving some skill development to teacher directed instruction in formal modes. In any event, some advanced instructional methods and systems are needed in order to prepare individuals for achievement in employing the high technology of interactive and intelligent environments.

How do people naturally become self-instructors in informal, formal and technical education?

For adult educators, answers are available in the analyses of the patterns to be found in cognitive behavior and learning styles. Many cognitive styles have been identified and 19 types of learning patterns have been widely researched and generally accepted. These various dimensions can be integrated and be considered as aspects of the more widely recognized field sensitive and field independent learning styles associated with right and left brain information processing.

Adult Information Needs

Adults' learning needs are often related to employment. But, adults' personal circumstances make their other information needs different from those of younger students. That is:

- Because adults are more restricted with respect to times and places for learning activities and career moves, they require information which is highly detailed regarding local learning resources and employment opportunities.
- Adults' prior learning and work-experience histories mean that they require information on transferable skills and credentials and on the potential and procedures for occupational crossovers. Perhaps equally important, adults need to unlearn non-productive skills or job hunting approaches before they can develop new competencies.
- Adults, whether they are career-changers or new entrants to the labor market,

typically do not want the same kind of entry-level job information as youths. They need to know about such things as middle and upper level salary ranges, "transition trade-offs" (what they can gain or lose by changing job fields), and relationships between educational training and salaries or advancement.

- Since adults are no longer part of the formal schooling system, they require information on nonformal as well as traditional learning opportunities.
- Adults need information about support services for adults in transition such as, community resources, informal support networks, and organizations counseling, tutoring, financial help and "human touch" support.

Encouraging Performance and Achievement

Adults have demonstrated over and over again that they can learn almost anything they want, given sufficient time and assistance. Continuing self-directed education is a "fact of life" for eight out of ten American adults. Many individuals plan self-instruction projects, imposing their own structure and sense of timing on the knowledge or skill to be learned. Self-directed learners undertake two to three personally developed learning projects in a year, each of which averages 156 hours in length and ranges upward of 900 hours or more. Adults use various types of information resources as well as a considerable number of planning strategies and self-instructional aids within any particular cognitive and learning style.

To take advantage of adults' diverse and experientially rich backgrounds, effective teachers use informal conversation, and participant information forms as part of an initial session to obtain sufficient information about such participant characteristics as self-learning activity, recent relevant experience, and related proficiencies. They also assess interests and expectations in order to gain an accurate estimate of the fit between preliminary program objectives and participant abilities and background. Then, objectives are modified, if necessary, to take account of inadequate or variant study skills as well as the personal situations of the participants.

Participants can be helped to recognize specialized interests shared by subgroups, and assistance and materials can be provided to enable them to engage in productive small group discussions through demonstrations, participant presentations and panels, and focused discussion sessions. In some instances, teachers and program coordinators actively recruit participants with differing backgrounds in order to obtain contrasting viewpoints. Such a practice can be especially significant for programs in which the understanding of various viewpoints and values is important to the achievement of program objectives.

Topics of interest relevant to any group of participants easily extend beyond program limits. The participants use agenda-building procedures to gain agreement on topics that will be covered or excluded. Client-centered teachers are sufficiently flexible to give attention to relevant and important topics that emerge as the program progresses. Referral is made to other programs on related topics offered elsewhere by the same educational agency or by other providers in the community.

Effective teachers also realize that adults' use of self-directed learning projects benefits the formal instructional program and is a way to deal with variability among participants. Self-directed study can be encouraged by having participants discuss relevant learning projects in which they have engaged. Client-centered teachers provide guidelines and examples to assist participants in undertaking newly developed learning projects, such as a contractual study project involving preparation of a report. They also encourage relevant and challenging learning activities that avoid both boredom and threat, in part by encouraging participants to select learning tasks that fit their interests and backgrounds.

Some variations among participants, including lack of necessary experience, lack of transportation, child care responsibilities, or vision and hearing problems of older adults may result in barriers to learning for some participants. Effective teachers act to minimize these barriers by using concrete examples, suggesting where to obtain requisite experience, referring to sources of information about transportation or child care arrangements, and providing satisfactory acoustics and printed materials of sufficient size and clarity.

Vocational education teachers can recognize special backgrounds and interests of participants that would help achieve objectives if they were reflected in the educational program. For example, if participants want to apply what they learn to the jobs they hold, individualization may include modifying practices, based on education materials, participants' contributions, teachers, and other resource persons. Such contributions might include descriptions of standards, critiques or plans, identification of useful resources, discussion of alternative procedures, and consideration of issues and value questions that are part of a proposed course of action.

Participants' commitment to enhancing their own proficiency requires them to assume responsibility for their lives. In addition, they must make planning and implementation decisions regarding their needs, their learning environment, objectives, activities, and evaluation. Ways to help learners become more self-directed include:

- Providing self-assessment forms that enable participants to assess anonymously their own educational needs and evaluatate their own progress.
- Spending program time helping participants clarify and order their own educational objectives within the scope of the program.

- Encouraging alternative materials and activities that enable participants to select ways to enhance their proficiency that fit their purposes and learning style.

Adults who actively seek to enhance proficiencies tend to think of themselves as users of, instead of recipients of education. Successful teachers help adult learners understand how they can actively use education by respecting them as mature people, by helping them use education to clarify their purposes and standards of excellence as well as to master procedures, by helping them select educational activities likely to serve their purposes, and by giving attention to proficiences throughout the educational process.

Some teachers mistakenly equate attrition with vigorous instruction. However, effective teachers try to prevent dropouts and achieve participant satisfaction through processes that lead to persistence such as:

- Helping participants and others understand that they must increase their performance in order to produce proficiency.
- Designing educational activities that allow learners sufficient practice in becoming proficient.
- Giving attention to affective issues in achieving proficiency and its use in practice.
- Emphasizing the anticipated applications of proficiency in family or work and community.

Facilitating Transferable Skills

The most important learning of all is learning how to learn. Such learning includes the social survival skills and interpersonal behaviors which depend upon the ability to gather information (perception and interaction), and the ability to process information (thinking and learning). The most basic transfer skills are to:

- Observe consistencies in diverse information that is retrieved, organized and communicated.
- Understand the viewpoints surrounding a controversial issue and reorganize aspects of the issue into a new perspective.
- Learn from experience by integrating cognitive with effective decision-making, learning and communicating patterns.

Transfer skills can be acquired in any of the three modes of learning—informal, formal, and technical. But the rate of acquisition varies with the mode. Practical, transferable skills—such as being interviewed—may be learned to better advantage in formal learning and take longer to acquire in informal learning. Short-term performance improvement can be expected in the technical mode; but lock-step problem solving all too often degenerates into role learning behavior.

Efforts have been made to take advantage of the opportunities offered by each of the three models to develop systems of instructional activity and learning behavior. (On-the-job training capitalizes on the person's motivation to acquire practical subsets of the necessary competencies.) For some students, it appears that technical learning is best used in the beginning states of new skills acquisition. But such trainees have to be appraised at the start of course content to determine whether such skills are important or else optimal learning may not take place.

In any event, educational content and training skills should be developed together so that they reinforce each other, whether training is basic, remedial or enrichment. In such contexts, the gradual removal of structure allows individuals to assume increased responsibility. Greater self-discovery becomes possible as control over content and skill acquisition is turned over to the learner. Parallel with the move from pedagogy to andragogy, the student emerges from a "helped" position to one of self-initiative and achievement through self-directed learning.

It is essential to develop an awareness and understanding of the differences between transfer skills and content acquisition. For example, the teacher emphasizing content acquisition may on occasion return papers to students with corrections made for grammatical mistakes. Such feedback almost "guarantees" students' resentment unless they have been previously involved in considerable orientation to, and training in communication skills. (If, however, a combination of content and process is sought and consistently practiced, the teacher may end up learning more about cognitive style and learning skills than the students involved.)

Teachers can facilitate content learning by posing questions (low to higher order) that are developed from one of the instructional taxonomies widely used as tools for organizing levels of complexity.

In contrast, instructors can teach transferable skills by developing questions about how they process information and their learning styles. For example, in a learning contract approach to instruction, students are directly involved in setting up their own performance standards for the evaluation of learning skills. The skills of comprehension, analysis, appreciation, evaluation, creativity or synthesis, implementation and communication are embedded in and can be drawn out of any content area.

Naturally, the acquisition and retention of basic skills will be extremely valuable to future job seekers. Vocational education especially must concern itself with student's proficiencies in the basic skills by employing models such as the following:

- An integrated model combining basic skills instruction with vocational instruction in a vocational classroom.
- A nonintegrated system using subject matter specialists to deliver basic skills instruction in a conventional context.

- A combination model gains strength by using different learning styles that are appropriate for different learners' needs and interest.

Those who enter the job market today and want to overcome its vicissitudes must be more skilled than previous workers—especially in the basic competencies of reading, communications and mathematics. Turmoil in the job market, due partially to the influx of high technology, calls for workers to be flexible and adaptable in order to meet changes. Basic skills, more than specific vocational skills, are readily transferable between jobs.

Educators, employers and the general public are concerned that a decline has occurred in the basic skills proficiency of American youth. Dealing with that decline is a growing problem, especially for vocational educators. Vocational researchers, policymakers, and practitioners must have the background necessary to devise means to approach the problem.

Current literature on basic skills teaching in vocational education points to a need for attention, time, and materials to assist vocational students in obtaining the skills basic to survival in the workplace. Three conclusions can be drawn from this literature:

- Achievement in basic skills should be considered as a valued and valuable objective.
- Vocational teachers need preservice and inservice training in delivering the basic skills.
- Instructional materials in vocational classrooms must match the skill levels of the students who use them.

Vocational educators are concerned about the frequently made assumption that dropout students who have poor academic success will succeed in vocational education. Thus, potential dropouts land in vocational programs, where they must develop basic skills under the guidance of vocational educators. Dropouts and potential dropouts typically lag behind their peers in basic skills acquisition, the very skills necessary to function in society. Research data categorize three areas of concern in dealing with basic skills instruction for the potential dropout: content considerations, methodological considerations, and organizational considerations.

Sequence of Instruction

It is helpful to begin a learning sequence with questions about the learner's prior experience that are relevant to the essential features of the desired area of proficiency. Effective teachers use anecdotal information to emphasize important features of the desired outcomes. It is also helpful to proceed from simple to complex concepts and procedures, and to provide opportunities for adults to acquire useful explanations by using analogy whether inductively or deductively. Effective teachers involve participants in the preparation or modification of the instructional program so that learners can relate their own objectives, experiences, and learning style to the collective plan and make adjustments as needed.

Serious attention to content, objectives, learner preferences and teaching style will benefit the selection and organization of learning activities. When the methods selected are effective enough to achieve the objectives, familiar enough to overcome apprehension of the unknown, and varied enough to sustain interest, successful learning activities typically result. Towards the end of the sequence of learning activities, the learners can be involved in giving increased attention to consequences, applications and commitment to use the increased proficiency.

Learning generally consists of powerful and systematic activities designed to modify knowledge, skills, and attitudes. A distinguishing characteristic of continuing education is that adults seldom participate in educational activities just to increase knowledge, acquire skill, or modify attitudes. The adult's purpose is usually to modify capability, which entails changes in cognitive and learning styles in order to enhance proficiency.

Cognitive Styles and Learning Styles

Greater support is needed for the efforts being made by institutions and professionals to build upon learning best accomplished in a self-directed mode before involving adult students in the non-formal and informal modes and the further constrained efforts of formal and technical learning.

Two researchers in particular have been involved in applying the findings of cognitive and learning styles research to vocational education. Patricia Kirby has tracked the development of cognitive style and has examined the results obtained from the psychological literature for their applicability to transferable skills. William L. Knaak has taken similar prescriptions and has translated learning style theory into the mastery learning and competency-based models of vocational education.

Cognitive Styles

Cognitive styles are the ways in which individuals perceive, gather, and process information in order to learn, solve problems, work, relate to others, choose a career, raise children, act in groups, or participate in activities. Adults' personalities and behaviors are greatly influenced by their preferred cognitive style.

Given circumstances, one style appears to be as effective as another; no particular mode of thinking has been found to be related to intelligence. Research on styles identifies preferences about what adults are naturally motivated to learn and why. Cognitive strategies (decision-making processes) enable learners to select diverse processes to carry out learning activities. The cognitive and learning styles of *both* teacher and student have to be taken into account. Though different in their teaching approaches, field dependent and field independent teachers appear not to differ in competence. No appreciable differences in this regard have been found in students' scores for field independent as opposed to field dependent teachers.

However, it has been found that teacher and students who were matched in cognitive styles liked each other more than mismatched teachers and students. This relates to the concept of interpersonal attractiveness and suggests that self-matching as a general strategy is perhaps the best approach for compatibility. Informed student choice is presumed to be the most desirable route in education.

Research has demonstrated that field independent learners do not consider a friendly or caring attitude to be as important as knowledge proficiency. Field dependent teachers prepare lists and outlines; whereas field dependents, essentially right-brain learners, prefer to use pictorial or descriptive models of knowledge. It is possible that field independent teachers could be accused of not providing enough structure for learners who have field independent preferences.

Instructors who are relatively field sensitive have been found to favor class discussion and group interaction more than lecture or discovery approaches. The discussion approach allows students to influence content and classroom management. Field independent teachers, however, favor corrective feedback, a reinforcement technique which provides students with corrective information.

Learning Styles

Learning style describes individuals in terms of those educational conditions under which they are most likely to learn. Knowledge of one's own learning style can influence and enhance the development of particular conceptual levels. "Educational cognitive" style focuses on the amount of structure individuals require and on the unique ways in which an individual searches for meaning. Individuals approach their environments differently; they construct relationships differently; they process information differently. The brain's knowledge structure and learning style provide a "natural" basis where transfer skill acquisition can be especially functional. Learning how to learn is developing the ability to learn the language of various cognitive styles in order to function successfully with high technology. Within any ability or content to be learned, the individual oscillates between intransitivity (field sensitive) and transitivity (field independent) as some repertoire of behaviors are tested and applied.

The individual creates personal information out of the data of sense and perceptual experience which is gathered, processed and stored in long-term memory. On a primitive and essentially universal level, human beings create knowledge by assembling information to support a personal position in relation to various alternate points of view. In these processes, the field sensitive person prefers to gather and exchange informative data among peers. "New" students may be more field-dependent because of their need for approval and their sensitivity to others' opinions.

Learners'performance is affected by factors as sound, light, temperature; the need for either a formal or an informal design; motivation, persistence, responsibility; interpersonal relations; day or night energy levels.

Learning style is the product of the organization of a group of information-processing activities that individuals prefer to engage in when confronted with a learning task. Information obtained about learning styles can be used as a basis for a conference between the learning consultant and the client as adult student. The consultant can go over each of the important learning style areas profiled with the student and ask what that information means to the student. For example, why does the student prefer considerable structure, direct experience and close affiliation with the instructor? The conference provides a basis for a client-oriented relationship centering around learning and ways of presenting information that will be compatible with the student's preferences and the teacher's instructional alternatives.

Diagnosis of Learning Styles

Learning consultants have used learning style information to decide which students would do best in groups (as opposed to contractual learning by individuals). It is also possible to identify students who are not highly motivated and have difficulty persisting, and to determine how students prefer to have educational, personal, and career information presented to them. Research has demonstrated that students with learning disabilities have learning style preferences related to learning in a tactile and kinesthetic manner. They prefer that the instructor be present when they learn.

Educators can diagnose learning styles in order to make better decisions about program (curricular) development and instruction as well as in counseling individuals about problems, strengths and opportunities. Style diagnosis can be carried out by watching the student in action, by asking about preferred ways of learning and learning environments, and by administrating tests. When learning style preferences are taken into account, learner achievement and satisfaction have been shown to increase. Although much of this research has not involved adults, the usefulness of learning-style diagnosis for vocational and continuing education has been clearly demonstrated in practice.

Conclusion

The traditional philosophy of teaching has centered upon humanistic and personal concepts of human nature. However, since it has been concluded in the literature that cognitive styles affect teacher behavior, a question could be raised as to the impact of cognitive styles on the perceptions teachers have of their students. From current research findings, it appears that cognitive style, not one's model of human nature, establishes the perception of students about teachers and their roles.

The literature is full of processes, methods and techniques for the education of adults; but such profusion can be frustrating. On the other hand, cognitive style maps and learning skills offer the instructor a client-centered alternative to approaching individual development. Cognitive and learning styles are embedded in the ways human beings gather and process information in real life. Thus, advances can be taken which are not limited to the professional philosophies of human nature nor the sociologies of institutional enhancement.

Instructors conduct themselves and their classes from the perceptions they have about their roles, their students, and the nature of the learning situation. The philosophy generally advocated by client-centered consultants has included the premise that adults should be self-directed in both information gathering and processing. But, in so doing, it appears that educators are biasing learning approaches toward field independent students. Not so well recognized is the fact that field sensitive persons can exert as much or more self-initiative than do the field independents.

The methods being used for all students may not support the field dependent's preferred style of learning; but, if attention were directed toward alternative strategies, assistance could be provided to learners using different styles. At present, it seems that all too many educators cannot get over this dilemma. On the one hand, various lists of teacher characteristics favor field dependent styles such as personal warmth, caring supportive behavior, responsiveness, etc. On the other, the teaching profession expects instructors to help adults become self-directed. There appears to be a need for an instructor of adults to have, perhaps not a split personality, but an ability to operate in what may seem to be opposing styles.

Change in behavior involves considerable risk-taking and the achievement of a change does mean work. But are we going to persist in not using new knowledge and techniques that we know can assist the learner in learning? The answer seems to be in the ability of the instructor to become a helping consultant able to adjust like a chameleon to variant styles while the learner assesses opportunities and constraints, sets goals and moves towards self-realization.

Thus, the development of self-concept around functionally operating cognitive styles appears to be more appropriate than limiting personal growth to a philosophy of human nature or the sociology of institutional support systems. Only client-centered consultants can respond fully and adequately to the unique style configurations of actual human beings.

Most adult learning activities entail some blend of knowledge and attitude change, and often skill as well, applied to real life situations. It is this close correspondence between learning and action, beyond the educational program, that is one of the main distinguishing characteristics of the continuing education of adults.

References

Cross, K. Patricia. *Adults as Learners*. San Francisco: Jossey-Bass, 1982.

Gross, Ronald. *Independent Scholar's Handbook*. Reading, MA: Addison-Wesley, 1982.

Kidd, J. Roby. *How Adults Learn*. New York: Association Press, 1973.

Kirby, Patricia. *Cognitive Style, Learning Style and Transfer Skill Acquisition*. Columbus, Ohio: National Center for Research in Vocational Education, 1979.

Knaak, William C. *Learning Styles: Applications in Vocational Education*. Columbus, Ohio: National Center for Research in Vocational Education, 1983.

Knowles, Malcolm S. *Modern Practice of Adult Education: Andragogy Versus Pedagogy*. New York: Association Press, 1970.

Knox, Alan B. "Helping Teachers Help Adults Learn." *New Directions for Continuing Education*, 6, 6:73-100, 1980.

Penland, Patrick R. "Design of Alternative Learning Environments," in *Designing Learning Programs and Environments for Students with Special Learning Needs* (Phillip J. Sleeman, ed.). Springfield, IL: Charles C. Thomas, 1983, p. 48-61.

Thorndike, Edward L. *Adult Learning*. New York: Macmillan, 1928.

Tough, Allen. *The Adults' Learning Projects*. Toronto: Ontario Institute for Studies in Education, 1971.

NEW RESOURCES FOR ADULT EDUCATION AND TRAINING

Paul E. Barton

The purpose of this chapter is to identify new prospects and opportunities for funding adult education and training. It also suggests new financing possibilities that may not have been given much thought, may not be well known, or may still even be on the drawing boards. In doing so, it does not discuss traditional sources such as direct government appropriations to students, nor does it review the new Job Training Partnership Act, since that legislation is the latest in a long history of federal aid to retraining begun under the Manpower Development and Training Act of 1962.

New sources of funding may be of considerable significance in the future. It will require extra effort and attention to take advantage of them, and it may also require educators to exercise imagination and leadership in order to turn possibility into reality.

Employment Based Tuition Assistance

Over the years, more and more employers have begun to pay all or part of the tuition of workers who go back to school on their own time. While such plans began by supporting education and training that was fairly narrowly related to the worker's current job assignment, there has been considerable liberalization. The standard frequently applied is that the course of study be helpful to any job in the company. Increasingly, the course does not have to be related at all to the firm's employment opportunities.

As might be expected, larger companies are more likely than smaller ones to have tuition aid plans. While just over 80 percent of companies with from 500 to 1,000 employees have tuition aid plans, this figure rises to 92 percent for companies with 1,000 to 10,000 employees and to 95 percent for companies with over 10,000 employees.

These plans are not well known among educators, except for a few who have consciously tapped into this market, but there is potentially a very considerable sum of money available for financing education. Ivan Charner, who has done the principal research on tuition-aid plans, estimates that "about $6 billion is committed annually for tuition assistance through unilaterally offered company

79

plans. Another $100 million to $1 billion is committed annually through plans that are collectively bargained through union and management."However, only a small proportion of these funds are actually spent for tuition assistance. Charner estimates that about $275 million is spent each year from company plans and from $20 to $40 million from collectively bargained plans. It is this discrepancy between what is theoretically available and what is actually spent that constitutes both the opportunity and the challenge for the education community.

The rates of utilization of these tuition assistance plans are quite low, only four or five percent for all employees, and as low as one or two percent for blue collar workers. Although it is hard to know what the outside limits are, there are some very practical steps by which these participation rates can be increased. Just doubling the participation rates would make an additional $300 million available for adult education and training. For example, about 10 percent of the employees of Polaroid Corporation take advantage of these benefits. The highest participation rate known is 30 percent, at the Kimberly-Clark Corporation.

Methods of Raising Participation Rates

A few of the steps that could raise these participation rates are:
- Getting better information to workers about what their benefits actually are. Studies by the National Institute for Work and Learning found that only half of the eligible blue collar workers even knew of the existence of these plans in their companies.
- Providing employees with more access to counselors or advisers who can help them take advantage of these benefits and help them understand what educational opportunities are available in their community. It may be possible to make arrangements with employers and unions to provide counseling services through a consortium of the community's education institutions.
- Having education institutions do a better job of finding what kinds of courses employees eligible for this assistance want, and making adjustments in when and where the courses are offered to fit employees' schedules and needs.
- Lifting barriers. One barrier in most plans is that the employees get reimbursed for expenses—only after completion of the course. Participation rates would rise if employers could be convinced to advance the money up front. Alternatively, the school could delay collection until the course was completed, or work out some kind of interest-bearing loan.

Of course, many postsecondary institutions already have part-time students as a result of these plans. But the potential availability of funds from this source is not widely appreciated. Tapping them will require some initiative on the part of schools, perhaps on a community-wide basis.

The Training Role in Economic Development

Substantial experience with economic development and planning is emerging at the state and local level, aided and abetted by various government programs.

The state level efforts vary considerably in their form and scope. Looking at programs developed prior to 1980, David Bushnell, Director of the Center for Productivity identified three basic models. In the first, the development programs are concentrated in one state agency which coordinates the whole effort, with vocational education looked to, among others, for the training component. He cites Alabama, Georgia, Louisiana, and North Carolina.

In the second model, the economic development functions are shared, but vocational education provides training services and plays a central role in the state effort, as in Iowa, Mississippi, Minnesota, Oklahoma, New Jersey, South Carolina, and Tennessee. In the third model, cities or counties have plans that are usually less ambitious than the state plans. These plans tend to emphasize help to firms that are expanding rather than attempting to lure new firms. Training is one element of such local plans.

Case studies of 17 plans, prepared by the American Vocational Association, and published in 1982, provide greater familiarity with the different types of approaches available. The provision of training has become a standard feature of these development plans, although there are a variety of ways to deliver training services. Services may be offered in traditional classroom settings, in new facilities established for serving a new industry, or provided in the employer's establishment under joint arrangements and shared responsibilities among the employer, school, and community college. To take maximum advantage of these opportunities for funding adult training, educational agencies need to be flexible, adapting to the shape of the overall plan for the state, and to the methods employers prefer.

In a sense, of course, this is not an absolutely new source of funding for adult occupational education. However, it is a development that has gathered force within the last decade, and has considerable possibilities for continued growth, both in states that have economic development plans and in states that are now forming them. The situation is far from static; new developments are taking place right now in many places. Where education institutions involve themselves, even take the initiative, there is potential opportunity.

Examples of cooperative efforts are numerous. Massachusetts recently established the Bay State Skills Corporation, in which the state puts up 50 percent of the funding for projects proposed jointly by employers and schools. Massachusetts Senator Paul Tsongas introduced a bill in 1984 that would use the Bay State Skills Corporation as a model for a national program which would encourage other states to adopt similar approaches. According to the *Employment and*

Training Reporter, Washington State and Minnesota have just established similar programs.

As part of a comprehensive approach to development, Iowa created the Industrial Jobs Training Program in July 1983. It made $1.5 million available to defray the costs of training for new businesses, and 15 community colleges in Iowa are participating. In Mississippi, a new program, Strategies Toward Economic Progress (STEP), has a component to establish a link between economic development and training for companies that might relocate within the state.

There is no tally of how much new money is becoming available through these economic development programs, or what would be available if all states adopted them. While the future is not clear, there seems to be a rush to catch up, as more states realize that some other states are well ahead of them. While it is not clear how much of a "zero sum game" is involved in attempts to attract firms that might otherwise locate in other places, the use of training as lure does increase the quantity of training paid for by the public.

Working for Industry

Those involved in training and education have recently become aware of the vast amount of training and education carried on by industry. While there are no exact figures, the commonly used estimates are that every year industry spends from $30 to $40 billion on education and training.

The reasons for this growth are complex. But a lot of this training is highly specialized, narrow, and so integrated with the production process that separating it out would not make sense, nor would it be the kind of training that an institution serving the public in general should undertake. Therefore, industry does much itself, rather than turning to the community colleges, technical schools, and secondary vocational education.

Nevertheless, education casts an envious eye on the large outlay involved, particularly as school budgets come under increasing pressure from declining enrollments and less generous taxpayers. And there are opportunities for schools and colleges, for it is often the case that a firm starts its own system without being aware that there is a real alternative. It remains open to the possibility of being convinced that there is.

Contracts with corporations to train their employees, either by bringing the school into the firm, or taking the employees to the school, will not simply fall into laps of educational institutions. To secure such contracts, schools and colleges will have to first find out what these firms need. Then, they will have to secure the organizations' confidence that they can do the job, and perhaps do it better. A school bent on securing such business will have to invest money in development in order to secure it.

It is hard to know how much of this training could be transferred to educational institutions. Such programs are likely to start fairly small and grow as schools become more responsive to businesses' needs. Very often, some perceptions on both sides will have to be changed. Employers may feel that the schools have already let them down, given the number of graduates they find are ill-prepared. Schools may feel defensive, simply because they have long been under attack from several quarters. But much of the gap that sometimes separates corporations and schools is the result of a virus almost as common as the cold: the virus of lack of communication. Lack of understanding can infect relationships that could otherwise be quite healthy.

There have been breakthrough efforts to have corporations contract out training to educational institutions, and there has been enough success in this somewhat limited base of experience to encourage others to go to the trouble of trying. A few examples will illustrate.

Not long ago, the American Association of Community and Junior Colleges (AACJC) surveyed its membership to find out which colleges were pursuing such contracts on an organized and systematic basis. As a result, 15 colleges became the subject of case studies. These fifteen had established separate offices and programs. AACJC found that four of the programs were in the continuing education or community service departments, three in the president's office, one the provost's office, and the remainder elsewhere. Initial funding came from general funds, with the expectation that these funds would be repaid from additional revenues, and that they would come to "make money" for the colleges.

The College of DuPage (Glen Ellyn, Illinois) established the Business and Professional Institute in 1979, with a first year budget of over $200,000. By the third year, revenue had risen to $430,000. In three years, 17,508 students were involved.

Portland Community College (Portland, Oregon) created the Institute for Community Assistance in 1969. About 35,000 students have been served since it opened, and revenues were just under $180,000 in the 1982-1983 school year. In addition to 40 businesses, 11 associations and unions and 20 public agencies have been served.

The Williamsport Area Community College (Williamsport, Pennsylvania) established the Center for Lifelong Education in 1979. Enrollments climbed to about 1,000 in just a couple of years.

The specific payoff in these cases has been new sources of funding for the college offerings in adult occupational education, but there are indirect benefits as well as schools become more closely associated with the business community.

A Better Fit Between Unemployment Insurance and Retraining

Since the Great Depression, unemployment insurance (UI) has been the principal means used to alleviate the hardships of unemployment. To be sure, other efforts are made from time-to-time, such as federally-funded public employment and retraining, but not with the consistency of UI, nor with a legal entitlement.

It had long seemed to me that UI was formed so as to discourage unnecessarily a separated worker from retooling in order to keep pace with a changing economy. As a member of the Secretary of Labor's Policy Planning Staff, I helped shape the 1970 amendments to the Federal Unemployment Insurance Law. Until then, an unemployed person who enrolled in a community college or technical school as a means of getting a new job would be denied UI benefits because he or she was "unavailable for work." The 1970 amendments prohibited such disqualification from benefits for any person enrolled in state-approved training.

The reasoning behind this change was that if a person needs additional training or education in order to become re-employed, a very good time to do it is while UI benefits are available to live on; it is a more likely sequence that this need is recognized after benefits are exhausted. Of course, a number of safeguards are needed. But this new provision of law had practically no effect.

The states conformed, of course, to the federal law, and persons denied benefits had the right to appeal. But no positive steps were taken to inform workers of this new right, or to facilitate their taking advantage of the education and training available in the community. Only about one-fourth of one percent of UI recipients were enrolled in training courses in 1982.

States can make an effort to help. The State of Delaware has recently taken positive steps to identify those persons commencing their UI benefits who are not likely to be re-employed with their current skills. They are so advised and referred to a community college. This program was instituted by the secretary of labor at the direction of the governor.

It has been my experience that vocational education administrators are unaware of this right that claimants have under UI law or of the potential it could have for expanding training opportunities. It might be brought to life if state vocational education authorities worked with the state department of labor to facilitate taking advantage of this "retraining right" under unemployment insurance law.

Even if fully implemented, the UI does not itself pay the tuition of a community college or a technical institute. But many workers still have savings and assets when they lose their jobs. Many can afford the tuition at these relatively low cost schools, if they have income to buy the groceries while they are attending. Of course, many would not do so, so this provision does not work for everyone.

There is, however, continuing interest in some states to use such funds in ways that would more directly contribute to re-employment. For examples, California recently transferred $55 million from its unemployment insurance system to retrain unemployed workers and to prevent unemployment through retraining. The Employment Training Panel administers the funds. And, Delaware's governor recently proposed that .1 percent of the UI tax be used for retraining. Delaware's employers have been paying an increased tax to repay a federal UI loan. This is almost repaid and the proposal is to continue a .1 percent tax to be used for retraining; it has received considerable support among Delaware's employers.

From time to time, rather ambitious schemes have been proposed to link training to unemployment insurance and thereby use tax revenues for training purposes. This is what West Germany did over a decade ago to provide workers with training sabbaticals. At that time, the country had had many years of low unemployment, and the UI fund had a considerable surplus. Such is not the case in the United States. And, if the present trend of deep recessions followed by ever higher unemployment rates continues, the U.S. is not likely to have surplus UI funds in the foreseeable future. However, the possibility described above, of training while drawing UI, is a real one. And individual states may find it possible and desirable to follow California and Delaware's proposals.

Tapping the Market

It is well known that the enrollment of adults in postsecondary education has been expanding over the last two decades, due to the increased willingness of schools to go after the adult market and to adults seeking to go back to school. While this growth is spread across the educational enterprise, it has been concentrated in job-related programs.

What is not clear is whether the potential in this market has been fully explored. The pattern of adult participation is positively related to the amount of previous education adults have. This pattern has two implications for educating adults. First, each new cohort of those entering adulthood has had more formal education than the preceding cohort (the World War II baby boom is now a more highly educated bulge entering the middle years of life, and a group more interested in further education). Second, more information has been developed about the barriers perceived by those with more limited education, and how these barriers can be lowered.

There is now a base of experience which suggests that the adult learning market lacks the kinds of information and services that would enable it to function more effectively. On one hand, there are adults with only a vague notion that they want to, or ought to, renew a relationship with education and training. On the other hand, there is a growing complex of educational institutions in larger metropolitan areas that are eager to serve adults. But making the match between this two segments of the market is still often a matter of chance. The adult just may not know to pick and choose, what these offerings are, or how to relate a half-formed occupational objective to an educational goal by which it can be more precisely defined and pursued.

This is not unexplored ground. More than ten years ago, the Syracuse Regional Learning Service developed the concept of "educational brokering". Seven centers supported by the Kellogg Foundation, were established in New York State, serving the communities, that "brokered" between the adult and the educational community, helping adults to work out their educational plans and sort out the opportunities available to them. Later, Francis Macy established the National Center for Educational Brokering, which publishes a directory of the growing number of similar efforts around the country. At the end of the pilot period, these brokering centers were picked up in the educational budget of New York State. The National Institute for Work and Learning (NIWL) developed related approaches in its experiments and pilot programs that brought "educational advisement" services or "learning organizers" directly to employed workers at their place of work, or through their unions.

Another effort to bring adults and educational institutions together is a four-year old project to help local collaborative councils (composed of employers, educators, and unions) get into the business of aiding the adult learning enterprise. The project is under the direction of Richard Ungers of NIWL and with funding from the Kellogg Foundation. Ten out of 150 existing local councils were selected by NIWL to take part in broadening their activities (focused mainly on youth) to include adults.

A single institution acting alone is unlikely to develop adult learning to its maximum potential. Instead, several involved sectors must act in concert. If the level of awareness and participation is raised in the community, all educational institutions with offerings for adults are likely to benefit. There is an analogy to the job market; persons seeking jobs and employers seeking workers are aided through public and private employment services. While there are many other routes to jobs, these services are important in making the market work. The need is similar in the adult learning market.

Retraining Workers

There are other developments that may have a future impact on the availability of resources for adult education and training.

Collective bargaining and employer-union relationships have long played a role in adult training, in apprenticeship, in negotiated tuition-aid, and in training funds. There is, however, a new type of training arrangement that results from increasing recognition of the wrenching effect of dislocation due to imports and technological change.

There have been two path breaking agreements. One agreement has occurred in an industry that has been shrinking, automobile manufacturing. The United Automobile Workers has negotiated a comprehensive agreement to protect workers affected by production cut-backs and plant closings. It includes a provision to fund the retraining of separated workers. Much of this training will be done by community colleges and technical institutes; millions of dollars are already committed; and, training is underway in some places. The other agreement is in an industry characterized by growth, but with a rapidly changing technology. Realizing that technological changes could affect the jobs of the existing workforce, the Communications Workers of America has negotiated a retraining agreement with the Bell system to retrain existing workers for the new jobs developing in the industry. Local plants and unions will decide who will provide retraining. Whether there is a growing practice along these lines in other industries remains to be seen.

While there have been a number of general proposals over the last decade for a national system to provide workers with retraining opportunities on a large scale, and with assured financing, as is done in West Germany, the possibility has assumed a more concrete form in the proposal advocated by Pat Choate of TRW for Individual Training Accounts (ITAs). The parallel drawn is with Individual Retirement Accounts. In 1984, 17 members of the House of Representatives introduced the National Individual Training Accounts Act. The program would be voluntary, with the employer and the employee both making contributions to the account, until a maximum of $4,000 was reached in the account.

A new approach is being tried in Ohio. The Ohio Bureau of Employment Services will administer a loan fund of $2 million to go to unemployed people with low credit ratings. Borrowings for retraining, available in September 1984, will be provided up to $2,000 per year, for up to two years. Eligible individuals will be interviewed by vocational education counselors.

An Exciting Opportunity

For well over a decade, the enterprise of adult education and training has been undergoing rapid change. The growth of community colleges, the availability of guaranteed loans and Pell Grants, and new efforts by four-year educational institutions to reach "non-traditional learners" have greatly expanded adult enrollments. This state of flux continues, and a host of emerging developments promise to expand opportunity for adult education and training further.

To realize these opportunities, educational systems must keep up with these developments and become active agents in fulfilling their potential. In the United States, the school room has been reserved largely for the young. Educators today have the exciting opportunity to be part of a mega-change: the creation of a comparable system that allows learning to continue throughout life.

References

American Vocational Association. *Vocational Education and Economic Development. Case Studies*, Arlington, Va.: AVA, January 1982.

Barton, Paul E. et al. *Worklife Transitions: The Learning Connection*. New York: McGraw Hill, 1982.

Bureau of National Affairs. *Employment and Training Reporter*. February 29, 1984.

Bushnell, David. "The Role of Vocational Education in Economic Development." Background Paper Prepared for the American Vocational Association, 1980.

Charner, Ivan. Testimony before the National Commission on Student Financial Assistance, Washington, D.C.: April 25, 1983. Available from the National Institute on Work and Learning, Washington, D.C.

Mahoney, James R. *Community College Centers for Contracted Programs*. Washington, D.C.: American Association of Community and Junior Colleges, 1982.

PREPARING FOR A SOUND ADULT EDUCATION PROGRAM

Beverly Copeland and Meredyth A. Leahy

Adult education is unlike most other professions for a variety of reasons. First, it is a profession which has built in an ability to remain aware of and responsive to societal changes and consequent national, local, community and individual learning needs. As a result, there is an ever present need for flexibility in organizational structures, staffing patterns, program content, design and delivery systems.

Second, adult education is found in a variety of settings under the sponsorship of numerous agents. Profit and non-profit corporations, foundations, institutions and large and small agencies are involved in providing a vast array of education and training programs for adults. These agents are further differentiated by the specific needs of the clientele they serve.

Third, adult education activities generally take place as a subsidiary or secondary function of the sponsoring agent. As a result, the funding base is often tentative. Funding depends upon the program's ability to impact directly upon the sponsor's primary goals and objectives; to be self-supporting, and, in many cases, show a profit; and to generate funds from outside sources to support its efforts.

Finally, adult educators bring to their profession wide-ranging backgrounds with regard to orientation, preparation, experience and levels of proficiency. While at first glance the profession may appear to be complex and fragmented, there exists a strong common denominator to which the profession as a whole is committed: helping adults learn.

The Need for Teacher Training and Staff Development

In light of the nation's growing economic crunch, the technologically changing world, and the increasing older population, adult educators must facilitate learning that goes beyond factual information. Today, a person can expect to have six or seven careers in a lifetime; there is tremendous diversity in lifestyles and cultural patterns that influence people throughout their lives; there is a greater emphasis placed on improving the quality of on-the-job performance. Therefore, in order for instruction to be relevant to adult learners and for teachers to be able to help adults, teachers need to be prepared to deal with instruction that helps adults change their quality of life in varying situations.

When teachers develop course objectives and course content and conduct their classes, they do so from the perception that they have of their own roles, their students, and the learning environment. Teachers gain understanding and develop generalizations about adult learning from their practical experience of working with adult learners. However, those teachers who know research-based theory can more effectively create a setting for learning that helps adults to realize their full potential.

Teacher preparation is designed to broaden teachers' perspectives and to help them perform at a higher level than those without such preparation. Teachers can become increasingly helpful to their clientele by acquiring knowledge of adult development, by understanding the philosophical approaches to adult learning and thereby sharpening their own philosophy, and by using research and evaluation methodologies to develop effective learning activities. In short, teacher preparation enhances the teacher's practical experience by offering competencies and proficiencies for teachers to become more effective, to achieve goals, to involve learners, to offer relevant courses, and to achieve greater personal satisfaction. The adult learner is the ultimate beneficiary of teacher preparation.

The Diversity of Teacher Training and Staff Development
Because of the nature of adult education, teachers of adults typically have a strong technical base for the topic being taught, whether they are teaching on a part-time or full-time basis. At the same time, teachers often move into adult education positions with little or no formal or structured preparation for understanding adults as learners and without a clear perspective of the field. Although the need for teachers to have preparation beyond their technical expertise has been demonstrated, there is no widely accepted model used in the preparation of teachers of adults. In the past, the trend has been for teachers to enter the field of study, and then to engage in some form of training or professional development program.

The number of teacher preparation and training programs has grown in recent years, however, with the increasing number of those involved in the teaching or training of adults. The programs vary considerably, yet each offers opportunities for teachers to acquire proficiencies in teaching effectively and in understanding adults as learners. Because of the diversity of both the field of adult education and the careers of teachers of adults, a single model for teacher preparation has not been and probably will not be developed.

Part-time and Full-time Teachers

Some adult education theorists differentiate the training of part-time teachers and the training of full-time teachers. They contend that part-time teachers are primarily prepared in some disciplinary area and are responsible only for the course(s) they are teaching. Full-time teachers, on the other hand, often are involved in the total educational and planning process—curriculum development and evaluation, long-range planning, recruitment and retention—which requires specialized competencies. Therefore, training for part-time and full-time teachers should be differentiated since each has different responsibilities and requires different proficiencies. In reality, due to inadequate funding, agencies and institutions seldom offer training programs that differentiate such instruction.

Part-time teachers often engage in in-service training programs which are geared to classroom techniques, interaction between the teacher and adult learner, and individualized instruction to meet the learners' needs. Saturday workshops and seminars commonly occur since most part-time teachers are employed full-time in their subject matter field and are teaching part-time to supplement their income. Generally, part-time teachers are not interested in teaching full-time in adult education. However, in-service training offers them methodologies and techniques which can improve their ability to offer quality learning experience to adult learners.

Full-time teachers who engage in in-service training programs are typically served by training and staff development activities provided by the agency employing the teacher. Workshops, seminars, institutes, conferences, and university courses designed to respond to training needs also serve as in-service training. In most states, the state departments of education provide in-service training opportunities or information on the availability of training for adult educators and teachers.

Full-time teachers often choose in-service training activities dealing with curriculum development, philosophy and history of adult education, and adult development. Full-time teachers are more inclined to enroll in university courses and graduate programs in adult education that are offered by over seventy-five universities in the United States. Many institutions offer off-campus programs that are convenient and accessible to teachers.

Graduate courses in adult education offer various program concentrations but all have one mission in common—to prepare persons to help adults learn effectively. Graduate programs offer courses structured to impart the body of knowledge about the vast field of adult education. Standard courses include opportunities for graduate students to learn about a broad range of topics; adults as learners, adult development, learning patterns and theories, philosophical approaches to adult education, teaching methodologies, program planning, course and curriculum development, societal issues, assessment of adults' needs, utilizing research and evaluation, self-directed learning, teacher and administrative proficiencies, goal-setting, staffing, group dynamics, and funding of adult education programs. All graduate programs are designed to offer the knowledge persons need to become competent professionals in adult education.

Training

Training has been tagged by numerous adult educators as a sub-field of adult education. Training generally occurs within an organizational setting and deals with the performance and productivity of a teacher or employee. Training sessions vary from organization to organization, but their common goal is to assist people in fulfilling effectively the requirements and responsibilities of their work and in developing their full potential within the organization. Training programs in organizations, particularly in business and industry, have grown tremendously. Increasingly, participation in training programs is a requirement in the workplace and professionals in the field of adult education are called upon to conduct, organize and supervise training programs.

The training of volunteers is an area that is growing with the recent national emphasis on volunteerism. Organizations employ a full range of training techniques; however, the underlying intent is to balance the organization's needs and goals with those of the volunteer. In the area of adult education, the training of volunteers is currently most evident in the literacy movement in which thousands are trained each year to teach illiterate adults to read.

Apprenticeship relationships with knowledgeable and experienced practitioners and teachers provide another form of teacher training and staff development. Observing a master teacher or professional can provide invaluable insights to inexperienced teachers. Likewise, inexperienced teachers who are willing to be observed by a master teacher and evaluated in a supportive, productive atmosphere gain meaningful learning experiences. This informal training method has proven beneficial in many agencies, although it is not a widespread practice.

Professional Development

Membership in professional associations offers teachers of adults limitless opportunities for professional development. Associations vary in their mission, scope and services. Whether local, state, regional or national, adult education associations offer a broad range of services and benefits to their members: research journals, newsletters, magazines, conferences, seminars, resource publications, networking, information on federal and state legislation, monographs, audio-visual materials, press release, institutes, job referrals and announcements, talent banks, insurance packages. The primary reason people join professional associations is to have contact with other colleagues in the field; the secondary reason is to stay abreast of current developments, issues and trends in adult education. Active involvement in associations can enable teachers to discover innovative practices that can be adapted to their own classrooms, provides avenues for teachers to make comparisons of their own practices and programs with those of colleagues, and serves to broaden teacher awareness of available resources.

Professional development for teachers is not and should not be limited to participation in formalized programs. Self-directed learning is an important facet of teacher preparation. Teachers learn from reading books, journals and newsletters about issues and programs related to their teaching. Visits to other teaching sites and agencies, participation in professional associations and activities, and sharing innovative practices and ideas with colleagues also constitute self-directed learning. Self-directed learning activities contribute immeasurably to teacher effectiveness and professional development and should be an ongoing process for all involved in the teaching of adults.

Recruitment of Adult Education Instructors

Whether the mission of the adult education program is to have a long-term or a short-term relationship with its clients, the employment of effective teachers is one of the most critical factors in achieving program success. The teacher "makes the class" and, in effect, becomes the program. Prior to initiating the search for instructional staff, and assuming that the administrator is knowledgeable about all legal and contractual regulations which govern employment practices, the program administrator needs to decide what kinds of persons will best serve the program. While organizational mission statements and overall goals and objectives provide general guidance, several other factors impact upon the selection process.

Staffing patterns are often influenced by factors which may not be written, but are crucial in setting the tone of the program, and should not be taken lightly. These include: the administrator's own philosophy of adult education, management, style, observations of what characteristics seem to make a teacher effective in a particular program, and his or her perceptions of the nature of the adult learner.

Expectations of the teaching staff should be clearly defined. Job descriptions for part-time teachers, however, particularly if their role is of a short-term nature, are often considered to be impractical. And, the supervision of part-time staff often presents the greatest challenge. The teaching staff's essential role has an important impact upon the quality of the total program and upon the ability of the program to retain its clientele and to attract new participants. Ideally, adult education programs should provide job descriptions for part-time staff. However, letters of agreement for part-time personnel may suffice. Such documents should always include clearly stated job expectations, pre- and post-activity requirements, and evaluation procedures.

Many programs which rely upon part-time personnel develop handbooks or manuals designed to give short-term teachers a greater sense of involvement and to acknowledge their important role in the program. Administrative details such as employment forms, payroll procedures, and student data-gathering forms should be included in the teacher handbooks. Information such as the location and availability of instructional resources and supplies, duplicating facilities, audio-visual equipment, snack bars, and vending machines should also be included in handbooks. This general information saves time, eliminates confusion, and frees the teacher to concentrate on the task at hand—of helping adults learn.

Job descriptions should be available for full-time teachers and should delineate responsibilities and qualifications. Full-time teachers are generally involved in program development, curriculum design, evaluation, in-service training, recruitment and retention of students. Job expectations such as these which are outside the immediate realm of classroom instruction should be clearly stated and included in the job descriptions.

Other factors to consider when recruiting teachers or training personnel are course content and primary instructional approaches. Questions to be answered when recruiting teachers include: how skilled or knowledgeable should an instructor be to meet the learning needs of the students? is the hands-on approach so vital that experience in the practical application of the skill or knowledge is a must? to what extent are group processes and interactive teaching/learning techniques vital to student success and to a sense of accomplishment to the student?

Locating and Identifying Potential Instructors

While classified ads are useful, adult education instructors may be identified through various other means as well. As a result of student recruitment efforts, news releases or other media announcements, individuals interested in teaching often contact the program administrator directly. Administrators should read the newspapers, which are an excellent source of information about what is happening locally, nationally and internationally; individuals or organizations who are outstanding in their field or have special interests are often cited in feature articles. New product or service demonstrations, exhibits and trade shows, antique, hobby or craft fairs, and the like are a good source of skilled people who are accustomed to dealing with the public. Many program administrators find it useful to maintain communications or to become actively involved with various professional, technical, trade, service and/or volunteer community organizations. Members of such groups, if not willing or qualified to teach, are often in a position to recommend others.

Local, state and federal government agencies often have specialists in particular fields who are quite willing to have their staff members involved in local education programs. Regional and local headquarters for such agencies as the Small Business Administration, health and welfare, Internal Revenue Service, recreation, safety, and transportation, quite often have education programs already developed and staff who are trained and prepared to present short courses, workshops or seminars on their specialized areas of interest.

Not to be overlooked are the local chambers of commerce, museums, historical societies, local colleges and universities, and tourist and convention bureaus, all of which are excellent resources. Many have extensive networks, speakers, bureaus, or directories of those who are willing to assist others in a variety of ways.

Finally, many programs, particularly those related to public schools, community colleges and colleges and universities, rely heavily upon their own staff for referrals and recommendations. College and university alumni are another source to explore, as are graduate students who are quite often anxious to gain additional teaching experience in their area of specialization.

Sources for new teachers are limited only by imagination and energy. Good adult education program administrators are always on the lookout for teachers, particularly administrators who operate very broad-based programs. By watching others in action and in various leadership roles within the community and in special interest groups, administrators will quite often find teachers who are not only well versed in their field, but who are respected by their colleagues because they possess good communication and human relations skills, organizational competencies, and expertise in teaching.

Selecting Instructors

An adult education program administrator can identify individuals who are experts in their fields and interested in teaching through a variety of sources. While these potential teachers appear to be well-versed in their area of specialization and able to document both academic preparation and experience, how is the administrator to know whether or not they will be effective in a particular adult education setting?

Good interviewing skills help to answer this question and are a prerequisite for hiring. There are useful tips that can be incorporated in the interviewing process. Do ask indirect questions to give the candidate an opportunity to share his or her insights and observations; avoid answering questions for the interviewee; do not spend a lot of time selling one's self, the program, or the agency. While the candidate will certainly be evaluating the administrator, the administrator's first order of business is to examine and evaluate the candidate's potential for enhancing the program. Avoid the tendency to react positively to candidates who are just like you. On the other hand, one should take care not to dismiss a candidate because he or she is significantly different. Both reactions can be misleading and obscure objectivity. Finally, the job description must be kept foremost in mind. There may be a tendency to assume that when one quality is outstanding, all others will follow suit. While it is good to be aware of a candidate's obvious strengths, it is just as important to be alert to weaknesses which he or she may or may not be able to overcome.

Screening potential instructors can be time consuming, but administrators who prepare for the task will find it can be done effectively and efficiently. In addition to being clear about his or her own philosophy and having well-defined job descriptions or job expectations at hand, the administrator should consider the following brief list of proficiencies to look for while interviewing prospective teachers.

Proficiency 1. The candidate is aware of and takes into consideration the motivational and participation patterns of adult learners.

Due to the prolific growth and expansion of adult education in the last decades, a program administrator can expect to find applicants who have experience, direct or indirect, with adults as learners. They may have taught adults, participated as learners, or most certainly have friends or colleagues who have returned to the classroom. Answers to open-ended questions such as the following will provide clues as to the candidate's sensitivity and receptivity to adults as learners and to the motivational patterns of adults:

- What have you observed about adult learners that make them different from children and youth?
- Why did they (or you) participate in the learning experience?
- What was the background of the learner(s)?
- How did that background impact upon the learning environment and the teaching/learning process?

Proficiency 2. The candidate knows how to use various instructional methods and techniques.

The candidate should be able to select instructional strategies which are most appropriate to the goals and objectives of the instructional program, whether those are to disseminate knowledge, develop skills, change attitudes or any combination thereof. The candidate should also be able to implement those strategies. In addition, the candidate should have the ability and the willingness to adopt or modify his or her teaching style to meet the needs of the learner.

In the course of the interview, the administrator might select a specific learning objective relevant to the content area and ask the candidate to describe two or three ways in which the material can be presented. The candidate's response will alert the administrator to the candidate's range of techniques, as well as flexibility in approach to the subject matter. Similarly, the administrator should determine if the candidate is aware of the appropriate uses of large group, small group, and individualized instruction.

Proficiency 3. The candidate knows how to develop and/or locate and use educational materials.

While many programs supply instructional materials, it is not uncommon to find gaps, particularly in the areas of practice, reinforcement, or application of learning. As a result, it is often necessary for teachers to develop or seek out supplemental materials. Candidates can be asked to provide sample instructional materials which they have prepared that are related to the content area. If necessary, the candidate can be presented with previously developed materials and questioned on how he or she might go about adapting them in order to make them more relevant to a particular type of learner.

Proficiency 4. The candidate knows the community and its needs and demonstrates an awareness of and sensitivity to the community of the learners.

Few, if any, adult education programs exist without a clear statement of purpose which serves as their link to the community and the clientele they serve. Many programs are designed to meet the specific learning needs of a specific segment of the population. Others, as a result of their content and image, attract a particular type of student. Finding a good instructor is often a case of finding a person who seems, for a variety of reasons, to fit the program's goals or student body.

During the course of the interview, it may be important to discern whether or not the candidate is aware that the program is a response to a real or perceived community need and what that need is. Is the candidate aware of who the participants are? Is he or she sensitive to any apparent cultural differences which may exist between the learners and his or her own predominant culture? And, finally, is the candidate willing and able to accept the diversity of values, attitudes, lifestyles and priorities which can often be found in a class-room of adults?

Teacher Supervision

Supervision is generally defined as an activity which involves coordination and assistance for the purpose of helping employees (in this case, teachers) do their job better. A good supervisor not only has to be knowledgeable about the programs, philosophy, goals and objectives, but must also have an understanding of the teaching/learning process and why teachers and learners behave as they do in the classroom.

A supervisor should understand and acquire proficiency in human relations, communications, group process, participatory decision-making, and the delegation and sharing of responsibility and authority. Because supervision and evaluation go hand-in-hand, supervisory skills must be supplemented by a working knowledge of various theories and methods of evaluation and the advantages and disadvantages of each. Too often, supervision and evaluation of teachers is a sensitive issue for both parties involved. The supervisor, whether the image is true or not, is seen as one who is "out to get" those who are being supervised. Evaluation is often dreaded for fear that it will expose only weaknesses and yield only criticism. However, it is possible to approach supervision and evaluation in such a manner as to yield positive and productive results.

Supervision and evaluation of teachers, in order to be effective, should include all elements of the instructional program. Both should be based, first, upon the desired learning outcome; second, on the curriculum which has been designed to achieve the desired outcome; third, on the teachers' competencies or proficiencies deemed necessary to implement the on-going professional development of the teacher effectively. Supervision and evaluation of teachers should be planned and carried out in a way that clearly communicates that its purpose is to assist and support. Ideally, those who are to be evaluated should be involved in designing the process, procedures, and the criteria to be used. While this may be difficult in the case of part-time, short-term instructors, full-time staff can and should be consulted.

Various strategies are used for teacher evaluation, including student rating, supervisor rating, self-evaluation by teacher and student, peer evaluation, and learning outcome. Each method has advantages and disadvantages that should be carefully weighed. In addition, problems can arise when only one strategy is used, thereby placing too much importance on the observations, perceptions, and feedback of a limited number. Strategies selected should be a part of the total system, and should be practical. They should yield valid and useful information which can be used by both supervisors and teachers in decision-making.

Helping Adults Learn

Because of the tremendous diversity and complexity of adult and continuing education programs, there is not one comprehensive model for teacher preparation and training, staff selection, supervision, or evaluation. In order to be effective, the program administrator must keep in mind that the bottom line— helping adults learn—remains constant. It serves as a starting point for all aspects of program development and management. Identification of the learners, who they are, where they are and where they want or need to go, is the foundation upon which all other decisions should be based. Because the learner continues to change as the result of societal, philosophical, economical and developmental pressures, programs must adapt, change, and maintain flexibility in program content, design and delivery system, staffing patterns and organizational structure.

TODAY'S PROPRIETARY VOCATIONAL SCHOOLS

Lee R. Kerschner and Christopher Davis

Proprietary, postsecondary vocational schools account for almost two-thirds of the postsecondary institutions engaged in vocational training and nearly three-fourths—or more than two million students—of all postsecondary vocational school enrollments. But despite the significant training contributions being made by this industry, very few people really know why America's proprietary schools are in such demand.

The answer lies in what these schools accomplish. Private vocational schools are independent, job-oriented, practical, intensive, and student-centered. Since the colonial period, they have trained students for careers in business, trade and technical fields, and cosmetology. Unlike other forms of postsecondary education, meeting manpower needs has been the exclusive preoccupation of private vocational schools since their inception. And, they are finely attuned to knowing what manpower needs are and to training students for available jobs.

Delivering Services

Most of these schools are privately owned and operated and must be profitable to survive in the marketplace. With rapid advances in industrial and office technology changing many jobs, equally rapid training is essential to keep workers in touch with the newest developments. Private vocational schools help meet this need. They are market-oriented and sensitive to industry's demands for career-related training. They know how shifts in the labor force are affecting particular occupations. Consequently, these schools are constantly adjusting their courses and programs to reflect changing job needs. In making these changes, private vocational schools have historically depended on employers to help determine what constitutes "entry-level" skills or minimum qualifications needed to get the job, and therefore, they are better able to serve the needs of both the students and the employer.

Students attend these schools to learn necessary job skills. Students spend 41 percent of each day in realistic job settings, and the remainder of their time in classes. Their training is directly related to what they will be doing on the job. Concerned only with preparing students for successful employment, private vocational schools place a significant emphasis on specialized training with less attention to unessential or unrelated subjects. Students get "hands-on" training, usually in an environment that is compatible with working conditions that exist on the job. Almost from the very first day in the school, students begin training with the actual material and equipment they will use on the job.

Private postsecondary education is an intensive experience. For the convenience of their students, private postsecondary vocational schools operate year-round and offer day and evening programs, part-time and full-time. The average course is about 1,000 hours, or forty weeks. Classes generally meet five hours per day, five days a week. Programs range from four weeks to four years, and students can earn certificates, degrees, or diplomas. In most cases, students can enroll and start training within a few weeks. Most of the programs can be completed in two years or less. Many schools also provide vocational training for people who want special programs to help them advance in their job or change careers. For many students, the method of instruction, the ability to get "hands-on" experience, and the accelerated pace of training are the most appealing characteristics of a private postsecondary vocational school.

Students

Postsecondary, private vocational schools are achievement-oriented and place significant emphasis on producing employable graduates, so it is vital to recruit students who are likely to succeed and complete their training. Recruiters, therefore, look for potential students who are serious about learning a specialized skill, getting a good job after graduation, and earning a living as soon as possible.

Enrollment demographics for private vocational schools vary according to the occupational discipline in which the students are enrolled. In general, however, over sixty percent of the students are below the age of 25. However, because more people are now changing careers so rapidly, the number of older students is increasing significantly. Most of the students attending private and public vocational schools are men, but the National Association of Trade and Technical Schools, which represents accredited career schools, reports that 52 percent of its students are women. Changing attitudes and values, plus potential earnings, are apparently attracting more and more women to many of the traditional and nontraditional vocational occupations.

Although graduates directly from high school represent the largest percentage of recruits each year, today's private vocational schools are also enrolling college graduates, college dropouts, and displaced workers unable to find suitable employment. Many potential students discover private postsecondary vocational schools through high school counselors, but a significant number of enrollments are generated by referrals from former students.

Teachers

To maintain their relationship to the world of work, these schools hire teachers who come directly from industry with years of career experience. Teachers stress practical knowledge and believe the best way to learn is by doing. However, the role of the proprietary instructor is not just the transmission of skills. Instructors are hired, retained, and promoted on their ability to teach. Teachers must have the ability to motivate, instill confidence, and stress the importance of good working habits.

Since courses are revised often and new courses are introduced regularly to respond to frequently swift alterations in occupational requirements, instructors must keep abreast of changes and developments in their fields. Many instructors are active members of professional societies, attend meetings of technical associations, and subscribe to numerous trade journals. Schools hold special discussions and invite guest lecturers to present demonstrations to faculty and students.

Private vocational school instructors are not given tenure and are evaluated regularly, especially in terms of the satisfaction and employment success of the students. The absence of a tenure system encourages teachers to strive for excellence to ensure their own security and a solid future.

Job Placement

To serve employers needing trained manpower and to help graduates, most schools provide a formal placement service. For many schools, placement is considered a major responsibility for the entire staff. While many graduates are employment-oriented as a result of their training and do not always need the school's placement assistance to find a job, other graduates depend on the school's placement program.

The placement process involves much more than simply identifying possible job openings for graduating students. Usually, the placement process begins on the student's first day of training and requires continuous contact with employers: to tailor instructional programs closely to job opportunities and trends in the marketplace; to help find part-time jobs for students who need work; to match graduates with available jobs; and, to schedule placement interviews.

The school's placement program is also responsible for tracking graduates to help determine and evaluate the effectiveness of the school's training. Although no school can guarantee employment, private vocational schools work especially hard to place graduates because the school's ultimate success depends on finding good jobs for the students they train.

Accreditation

The primary function of accreditation is to help improve the quality of educational institutions and to serve as a significant indicator that an institution is meeting established standards as well as its own stated objectives. Although accreditation is voluntary, it is desired by many schools because it is a measure of quality. According to many experts, the quality of many schools may be due in part to four nationally recognized accrediting agencies: The Accrediting Commission of the National Association of Trade and Technical Schools; the Accrediting Commission of the Association of Independent Colleges and Schools; the Accrediting Commission of the National Home Study Council; and the National Accrediting Commission of Cosmetology Arts and Sciences.

- The Accrediting Commission of the National Association of Trade and Technical Schools accredits postsecondary trade and technical schools. NATTS was formed in 1965 and today consists of 660 member schools in 45 states, the District of Columbia, and Puerto Rico. As part of the accrediting process, a school is visited by an independent team of experts every five years who evaluate its educational objectives, management, faculty, admission and enrollment policies, course offerings, placement and completion rates, advertising, facilities, and equipment. Only those schools which have been in operation for two years are eligible to seek accreditation.
- The Accrediting Commssion of the Association of Independent Colleges and Schools (formerly the United Business Schools Association) accredits business schools and junior and senior colleges of business. AICS has been a recognized accrediting agency since 1956. AICS accredits 594 schools, of which over 125 are authorized to grant an associate degree.
- The National Home Study Council was organized in 1926 and became a formal accrediting body in 1955. Its standards focus on elements considered essential for successful correspondence instruction. Currently 90 institutions hold NHSC accreditation.
- The National Accrediting Commission of Cosmetology Arts and Sciences was created in 1968. NACCAS currently recognizes over 1,450 schools of cosmetology.

Accreditation is a prerequisite for institutional participation in many federal assistance programs, and for many schools, adherence to these standards often leads to higher completion rates and higher placement rates. In addition, by providing effective standards of accreditation, these four national organizations can build an increasingly positive image of proprietary education.

Today's Job Market

According to the Bureau of Labor Statistics, an estimated 25 million new jobs will be created by 1995, and only one-fourth of the occupations will generally require a college degree. Millions of Americans will have to be educated, trained, and continually retrained to fill both new and existing jobs.

Technical training at a private vocational school can be one road to success and can often serve as a stepping stone to many occupational opportunities.

Private vocational school enrollments continue to climb as the need for specialized job skills increases. Employers in today's job market prefer to hire people with training or previous experience.

Without proper job skills, the chances of finding suitable employment can be difficult. Thousands of people are unemployed in this country simply because they lack the skills and necessary training to qualify for many of the available jobs. Many of these unemployed citizens are unfortunately victims of change— change in the nature of work and change in the workforce, as the nation moves to a high tech, service-oriented society. But, for many people who have learned or are learning a specialized skill, these changes in the job market promise opportunity and prosperity.

INDUSTRY TRAINING EFFORTS IN ADULT EDUCATION

Robert Craig

As most vocational educators undoubtedly know, employers operate a massive education and training enterprise for adults. The American Society for Training and Development roughly estimates that employers in the United States spend some $30 billion annually for employee education and training. This is widely accepted as a reasonable figure, and it includes both direct and indirect costs, but not the trainees' wages, salaries, time off the job, etc. Most of this training is done "in-house" by employers using their own resouces. Some, of course, is procured from schools and colleges and some from the "training industry" that has evolved in the past decade or two in response to the growing need for employee training.

Employers invest in their employees to improve job and organizational performance. While traditional educators may enjoy educating for education's sake, employers clearly educate to produce a high quality product or service at a competitive price for their organization's success and survival. Employers provide employee education and training because they believe they must.

That belief has been the driving force behind the growth in employee education and training. Employees are the largest single force in retraining the American work force.

Business Educators

Most employee education and training goes on in large and medium sized organizations where there is an "in-house" training function. Often, where the training is not done in-house, the training department acts to procure training from outside providers.

Many, if not most, in-house training functions operate on a cost recovery basis, i.e., they must bill the costs of conducting the training to the "client" departments or divisions which use the training services.

In many instances, this means that the line operations have the option of going to sources or providers other than the in-house training function. More often, the in-house training function is a centralized activity that seeks quality training at the best price for in-house use, regardless of source. The in-house training department always faces the need to satisfy the line department client in terms of the end result—improving on-the-job performance. Where the course content is entirely specific to that company, this option is quite limited or non-existent. But for many generic programs, line departments can and do use outside sources.

The logic of who provides what kind of work force education and training seems pretty clear. The public, tax-supported education system is probably best suited to providing generic programs and employers are best suited to providing job specific training.

There are complications, of course. Many people enter the work force without the generic knowledge and skills they will need for their careers. Further, it is not likely that all employers, especially small employers, will be able to provide much job specific training except informal on-the-job training.

The logical pattern does not always occur. Some employers do a great deal of generic education, and some public institutions provide rather specific job training. However, when technology is changing rapidly, when team building is important, or when the content is proprietary, the employers usually do the training themselves.Few small businesses can engage in extensive employee training, usually because they do not have the necessary resources and economies of scale. Many employee training needs of small business often go unmet, although some small employers use external resources. Trade associations are a growing training resource for small businesses. In such group efforts, the training is tailored to the needs of the particular industry, and the development costs are shared over a broad base of many small employers.

Of course, some small employers use public education resources too. Overall, the need for employee training by small business is vast, but it can be a difficult market to serve because of the economics of the business organizations or the economics of delivering training services.

And who is trained? Recent data from the National Center for Education Statistics indicates that professional and technical workers receive about 32 percent of all the employer-provided education and training. Clerical workers got 18 percent of all training, sales 6 percent, managerial 18 percent, and blue collar and other about 26 percent.

Needs Assessment

A needs analysis approach is fundamental to much employer-provided training. Employers ask what these employees need to know and be able to do to meet the job and organizational performance objectives.

Needs analysis may show that not only do the employees need to know highly job specific skills, but they may also need basic skills which they do not have.

It is, unfortunately, all too common to find employees without the most basic skills that would enable them to advance beyond entry-level jobs. In some instances, employers find it necessary, for economic reasons, to redesign jobs and/or work stations rather than conduct extensive remedial education.

The needs assessment approach has the built-in benefit of setting criteria for measuring the effectiveness of the training. It is necessary to spell out clearly what employees should be able to do in order to set performance indicators that can be tested. Inadequacies that show up in testing can be corrected in subsequent training programs.

Needs assessment is also invariably an on-going process because of the constant change in the work place—changing technology, changing personnel, upward mobility, changing markets, etc.

With needs analysis, the training department often finds itself in the position of being asked to recommend solutions for performance problems that are not training solutions. This occurs when, all too often, line managers hastily conclude that some production problem can be resolved by employee training. Experienced training managers have reported that anywhere from 50 percent to 80 percent of the performance problems presented to them cannot best be solved by training. A better solution may be a redesigning of the system, the work station, etc.

Needs analysis, which encompasses an industry or a community as well as the individual company, should probably be widely adopted as a beneficial linkage between educators and employers. There are many fine examples of this kind of collaboration, and those now doing it would undoubtedly agree that there should be more.

Organizational Programs

When employees' jobs change and they move up or make other job adjustments, they need new job knowledge and skills. Most of what employees need to do in their jobs is learned informally ("on-the-job training"), but more and more employers believe it is worthwhile to make the learning of new knowledge and skills more efficient and relevant through organized training programs.

Supervisory training is perhaps the most popular activity in employee training. When a person on the shop floor or the office is promoted to foreperson or supervisor, he or she is often given supervisory training—how to get things done through people, a new kind of responsibility.

When an engineer has progressed to the point where he or she is offered a managerial responsibility, the company is likely to provide basic courses in management. In fact, employers now do a good deal more management development than do the business schools—training the first-line supervisor to the top-level executive.

Recent data from the Hope Reports, a market research organization, indicate that courses in management development, organizational development and supervisory training account for about one-third of all employer training purchases from the "training industry" in the U.S. The fastest growing topic, however, was data processing training.

The scope of those programs can be substantial. For example, one course catalogue of a corporate engineering and manufacturing technical education operation includes many broad gauge course titles—e.g. Introduction to Accounting Principles, The Employee Relations Function, Introduction to Computers, Basic Mathematics (sample topics in the math course: calculations, statistics and probability). It also lists courses in Design for Assembly and Customer Requirements. And this catalogue is only one of the many education and training activities of this large company.

A New Alliance

The quality and competence of the work force is a key factor in economic progress. The training and retraining of the work deserves more attention immediately. Employers cannot, and will not, be able to do all the work force training needed for the nation's well-being.

What the nation needs is a new, direct alliance between educators and employers, both committed to building the best work force possible. This means that employers and educators must work together, on needs assessment and other practical linkages for "win-win" results.

And this is best done at the local level, not through prescriptive national legislation. Those at the local level can best know what is needed. Accountability and ownership have been the common denominators of successful vocational education in the past. But vocational education, regardless of the source of the provider, must be driven by the discipline of the market place.

References

Carnevale, Anthony, and Goldstein, Harold. *Employee Training: Its Changing Role and an Analysis of New Data*. Washington, DC: American Society for Training and Development, 1983.

LABOR UNION EFFORTS IN THE TRAINING OF ADULTS

Edgar Czarnecki

Labor education deals primarily with the educational needs of workers as they arise out of their participation in the labor movement. Its objective, according to Joseph Mire, a noted labor educator, is to improve the worker's individual and group competence and to advance his or her social, economic and cultural interests, in order to become a "mature, wise and responsible citizen, able to play his [sic] part in the union and in a free society...." Labor education does not include within its scope any apprenticeship training, any on-the-job training, job skill training, or upgrading training—all of which are handled independently of those topics treated in this definition of labor education.

A Sizable Undertaking

Labor education is a sizeable undertaking. Herb Levine and Morris Freed, professors of labor studies, estimated in 1978 that "some 20,000 workers attend one week residential institutions generally conducted in the summer months by international unions in cooperation with universities around the country. Some 50,000 shop stewards, communication men and local union officers attend weekend seminars, or short courses, conducted by the national AFL-CIO Education Department, or the education departments of their international union".

The majority of education programs involving trade unions take place within education institutions that form the University and College Labor Education Association (UCLEA). Approximately 42 institutions are affiliated with this group; in addition, there are about 12 schools that engage in labor education but are not affiliated with this national group. UCLEA institutions average roughly 2,500 participants per year—100,000 overall.

Of the 96 unions affiliated with the AFL-CIO, approximately one-third have a full-time education director and offer a comprehensive program. These unions provide training programs for labor union officers and stewards, some rank and file members and, in some cases, national staff. They generally deal with traditional labor education topics and sometimes offer new course subjects.

Other programs may be conducted at a local level—special stewards education meetings, ad hoc attendance at union sponsored conferences, etc.,— that are not reflected in any union or university statistical compilation.

Basic Labor Education Programs

The primary purpose of labor education programs is to impart basic leadership skills to union officers and members so that they can improve their performance within the union structure.

Traditionally, the foundation course in most labor education programs is shop steward training. The traditional shop steward training program is a basic skill course to teach stewards how to identify and process a grievance. It may also include communications, human relations skills and labor law. It serves as a counterpart to corporations' efforts to train first level supervisors. An extension of this course is a course in arbitration, which is usually the last step in the grievance procedure.

In addition to these courses, the other major labor education courses are collective bargaining and labor law. These courses comprise the primary subjects of labor education. Indeed, a survey conducted by the AFL-CIO Education Department in 1979 confirmed that these were the courses most often offered in summer labor education programs sponsored by international unions.

A Variety of Courses

Secondary subjects include: union/administration/leadership, communication skills/public relations, organizing, politics, labor history and labor law (particularly as it relates to union elections, organizing and political activities). These courses have an immediate payback—information and skills obtained can be applied almost instantly to redress shop/office problems.

Auxiliary courses may include: time study, pensions, right wing politics, energy, pre-retirement, community services, plant closings etc., and specific legislative issues such as imports/exports, auto content law, etc. There is also a growing number of Quality Work Life programs, as well as new programs concerning the use of computers. None of these, however, could be considered in the same context as the other courses which form "core programs" because these courses are geared to special audiences—those facing particular collective bargaining situations, particular legislative action programs, or changing age composition of members.

The primary and secondary subjects offered share certain characteristics. They are offered almost universally by both union education departments and university labor education centers. Each topic has a wealth of excellent material, including ready-made role playing incidents, case studies and simulation exercises. There is a ready supply of instructors to handle these programs; in fact, individuals with any degree of union background have accumulated experiences that can assist them in teaching these programs.

New Additions to Core Subjects

Two relatively recent additions to labor education are now an inherent part of the basic curriculum: occupation safety and health training, and programs designed for women.

Ten years ago, safety and health training was a topic rarely included in labor education programs. With some grants from the Department of Labor to the University of California, Los Angeles, Ohio State University and the University of Wisconsin in the 1970's, labor education programs were developed in this area. During the Carter Administration, the New Direction Grants program allocated millions of dollars annually, up to $14 million in 1980, to unions and universities to train workers on potential safety and health hazards on the job, to understand the legal remedies available to them, and to promote programs within their local union to resolve safety and health problems. Most of these programs were established in unions and universities that already had educational programs; in a few instances, totally new programs were established at national unions, at community colleges, and with some local unions and central labor bodies and building trades councils, which previously did not have labor education experience.

A total of about $50 million has been spent since 1976 and has substantially altered the composition of labor education. In some cases, these programs became an integral part of an existing labor education program, in other situations, a separate Occupational Safety and Health Administration (OSHA) Department, completely independent of existing labor education functions, was established.

As women have begun participating in increasing number in the labor force, more attention has been paid to their needs both in the labor force and in the labor movement. Special attention needed to be focused on women who lacked confidence, experience and support networks to engage fully in union activities. Some unions, particularly the Communication Workers of America, have had considerable experience in incorporating the subjects of sexism in their annual summer school programs. Many others, of course, now cover this topic. Ten years ago, the UCLEA and the AFL-CIO jointly began sponsoring summer schools for women workers, initially through a national conference for women, and now through a series of annual regional conferences. Each year, over 400 women trade unionists participate in these schools.

These courses have the traditional number of basic skill courses, but also include a number of sessions devoted to promoting understanding in the union organization and its rules, so women can more actively participate in local union operations. Courses in assertiveness, risk taking, issue development, and action programs are also available. The intent is not only to encourage participation, but also to support issues that have direct significance to women. Special concerns such as child care, sex discrimination problems, occupation stratification and comparable worth have been actively pursued as a result of these education programs. Somewhat like the OSHA training programs, the women's courses have been assisted by grant money. The regional schools receive funding and in-kind contributions from both the AFL-CIO and the UCLEA. Substantial grants have been awarded to develop women's programs at Cornell University and the University of Michigan. In addition, the Coalition of Labor Union Women has received funds for an "empowerment of union women project". This project has published a handbook for union women, an anlysis of the role of women in American unions, and training models; produced a film on influential women unionists; and, compiled examples of unions' leadership training activities for women.

Overall, these courses provide the labor movement with a constant flow of educated officers and stewards who protect the interests of workers on the job. Nevertheless, a high turnover rate among these individuals makes education a never-ending task. The efforts of both unions and universities have accomplished a good deal in meeting the basic education needs of workers. However, more needs to be done to educate workers.

Other Labor Education Needs

"Let me suggest to you that the public educational system has failed the ordinary worker shamefully in preparing him for the work that he performs, the security of his family and his life as a responsible citizen.

If it is true, and it is, that many of our high schools are graduating students who are almost functional illiterates, then the students are not alone in their failure.

If it is true, and it is, that employers find many vocational school graduates have learned obsolete skills, are unable to be trained for the present low-level hiring jobs and even less trainable for the highly advanced positions of the future, then not only are many workers misguided.

If it is true, and it is, that the average employee can expect to change jobs six times during his work life and yet finds his present education doesn't equip him for more than a life on the assembly line, then more than the worker is redundant.

If it is true, and it is, that the major problems experienced by newly hired black workers are those caused by their fellow employees, then more than the workers' attitudes have been misformed."

This quotation is certainly applicable today. Ironically, however, it was written 15 years ago by George V. Boyle, the Director of the University of Missouri Labor Education Program.

Boyle argued that adult labor education: needs to remedy the failure of the public school experience for ordinary workers; needs to remedy the irrelevancy of their vocational training; and, must be directed to the broader needs of workers to know and understand the world in which they live.

These three needs still need to be addressed in whole or in part by the labor education network. There have been some recent important advances in these three areas.

Basic Education

The AFL-CIO Education Department has disseminated information on an innovative external high school diploma program developed in New York State. This program grants a high school degree to candidates who have successfully completed tasks that assess 54 basic academic skills. Models of these programs are now offered in 13 states, several with labor union participation.

Several unions such as the American Federation of State, County and Municipal Employees, Service Employees International Union, Amalgamated Clothing and Textile Workers Union, and International Ladies' Garment Workers Union have developed literacy and basic education programs primarily to help their members achieve the high school equivalency diploma (GED).

In addition, these national unions and others have actively begun to develop courses for their members who speak English as their second language. With the growing number of immigrants whose native tongue is other than English, these education programs are essential to learning on-the-job skills, career development, and participation in union activities. This is a program that could easily be duplicated by other unions, but is offered now by only a few.

Career Development

Similarly, labor education programs have developed a small number of excellent retraining and career upgrading programs but again, their sparseness only accentuates the problem. The AFL-CIO Education Department conducted a pilot program—Education and Life Planning Conference—from September 7-10, 1982, at the George Meany Labor Studies Center in Silver Spring, Maryland. The program was designed to have union education staff experience just what is involved in a career change or career reassessment program. Representatives from approximately 15 international unions participated. The program was conducted by representatives of CLEO (Compact for Lifelong Educational Opportunities), a consortium of 37 colleges and universities in and around Philadelphia.

The AFL-CIO Education Department has also participated in an education counseling program with the AFL-CIO Professional Employees Department. This program developed material and conducted training programs for local union volunteers who advise local union members on educational opportunities.

The Department participated in "Dual Enrollment" programs in which students are enrolled in degree credit community college courses and in union apprenticeship programs at the same time. At the conclusion of the program, workers received both their Journeyman card and their Associate of Science degree.

Adapting to Technological Change

Several international unions, such as the Communication Workers of America, Amalgamated Clothing and Textile Workers Union, and Service Employees International Union, have developed extensive programs to meet the needs of their members who are displaced by layoffs or technological changes. Most of these programs provide on-going services to unemployed members by providing counseling services and referrals to available community resources.

The United Auto Workers has established, with General Motors and the Ford Motor Company, programs to train and place dislocated auto workers laid off because of technological changes in the auto industry. The programs are supported with substantial funds. The UAW-General Motors fund receives about $40 million a year, the UAW-Ford fund about $10 million. These programs assess worker skills and aptitudes, provide education and training to prepare them for alternative occupations, and offer a placement component for jobs within and without the industry.

With the number of disclocated persons estimated at a minimum of 100,000 and a maximum of 3 million, primarily in union-organized industries, and with potentially millions more facing dislocation over the next decade or two, there is no question that their needs must be addressed.

Issue Education

Today, the social, economic, and cultural needs of workers are not included within the scope of most labor education programs at either the union or university level.

There are exceptions, however. The AFL-CIO Civil Rights Department, as well as the civil rights departments of individual national unions, constantly offer programs focusing on problems facing women and blacks, and civil rights. In addition, the A. Philip Randolph Institute, an organization of black trade unionists, and some universities, notably Cornell University and the University of Michigan , also offer such programs. Exemplary cultural programs include those offered by Local 1199 Hospital Workers (The Bread and Roses program), and the innovative cultural programs developed by the University of Michigan. The George Meany Labor Studies Center offers specialized cultural programs weekly throughout the year and has an ever changing exhibition of art and sculpture.

Two national education programs on political issues in the 1970's were also offered to the workers. One was an extensive program to educate union members on the so called "right-to-work" legislation proposed in Missouri. This program involved both printed educational material as well as radio and television commercials. The other program was the massive educational program undertaken in 1977 to instruct union members on the need to rewrite basic national labor law. While both were extensive educational accomplishments, the unions did not succeed in modifying national legislation, but did defeat the attempt to modify Missouri law.

These specially-directed political issue education programs help underscore the dearth of long-range and continuous programs to educate union members on major economic, social, political and international issues. One way to develop such programs would be to have unions take the resolutions adopted by the AFL-CIO Executive Council and the AFL-CIO convention, and include these in existing union and university education programs. Very little of such activity currently takes place. In fact, it is much more necessary today, given the Reagan Administration's massive demolition of social programs for which unions have long fought.·

What is really needed is for the unions to develop on-going legislative educational programs (not specifically oriented towards one or two issues). An example of a program that does accomplish this (unions are one of many sponsoring groups) is the Domestic Policy Association, started three years ago by David Matthews, former Secretary of Health, Education and Welfare. The Association is now supported by the Kettering Foundation. This organization's purpose is to develop on-going discussions on important domestic issues, similar to the national Foreign Policy Association, which conducts nationwide study discussions that focus on major international issues.

The Domestic Policy Association has focused on such important "trade union issues" as inflation, retirement and social security, jobs and productivity, the deficit and the federal budget, and priorities for the nation's schools. Next year's program will focus on the soaring cost of health care and on work in America—two other major concerns of unions.

There are two primary reasons why the Domestic Policy Association has been successful in educating union members. First, it has produced excellent educational booklets that offer both valuable statistical information but also present a list of alternative solutions. Second, it has developed a nationwide network of sponsoring groups which can use these materials to stimulate small group discussions in hundreds of cities.

Unions, because they represent a wide range of political viewpoints and because there is limited coordination both between individual unions and among the unions and universities, cannot easily launch a comprehensive and broadly based education program on issues.

This type of education, however, is offered through a growing number of university and community college sponsored labor studies programs, broadly defined as programs which "[encompass] the study of worldwide social, economic, political, psychological and ideological massive movement which affects every aspect of national life in both the civilized and developing areas of the world."

No statistics are available, but there may be only a maximum of a few thousand trade unionists enrolled in labor studies programs. These programs provide a structure to extend labor education beyond the typical skill oriented courses. Furthermore, because a semester course is much longer than a non-credit labor course of about 12 to 15 contact hours, much more extensive instructional material has to be developed.

A non-traditional education program called PACE (Program for Adult College Education) at Longview Community College in Missouri offers the type of program that meets unions' long run educational objectives. This program enrolls over 400 full-time trade unionists. PACE has a set number of core courses, some offered through television programs, others through traditional one night a week programs. A third component—week-end conferences—focuses on particular topics and themes. This component offers students an opportunity to explore, in depth, a wide variety of new subjects or new approaches to standard subjects. These conferences often include full length Hollywood movies as well as field trips and guest lectures. Among the topics offered over the past two years were: responsibilities of multinational corporations; myth of the American rugged individualist; federal reserve policies; conflict in society; analysis of advertising; domestic violence; sports and the sports hero; the burden of proof concept in law; and, political interest groups.

Limits on Labor Education

Why has labor developed an education program that is so narrow in scope? Why has it been so difficult to venture out into courses beyond the traditional skill courses? There are several possible reasons:

• Labor educators (and labor leaders) are comfortable with a narrow focus.

Everyone can see the relevance of these programs. The programs can be conducted in a relatively short time frame. They do not involve any policy matters. They can, if necessary, be supplemented by "special programs" that can bring together people for one day programs, without committing the union to continued programming beyond the "basic courses".

- The labor education role has been pre-empted or engulfed by others within the union and university network. Separate union departments covering civil rights, women, safety and health, staff training, industrial engineering, etc., offer courses independent of the education department. Individual university educators specialize (and sometimes consult) in areas of interest to them, such as computers, stress management, economics, etc.
- Rather than attempt to reach out and expand the content of trade union education, union leaders often turn to quick, simple messages in union publications or television to "educate" their members on issues. Of course, more and more "educations" will probably take place through the media. The prime illustration of this approach is the AFL-CIO's Labor Institute for Public Affairs. It has produced a number of excellent television shows on such important issues as plant closings, pay equity, voter registration, toxics in the workplace, and industrial policy.
- There is a lack of financial support to develop fully the resources needed to conduct an effective membership/staff education program. Union education departments, facing reductions in membership, and university labor centers, facing cost pressures, are in a down cycle. New print and video publications require considerable financial resources. Unlike the Canadian Labor Congress, which receives about $3 million per year from the government, the unions in America do not have any government allotment or private foundations to underwrite their programs.
- Finally, there needs to be a structure within which some of the neglected labor subjects can be addressed. In the case of literacy and retraining, a separate identifiable staff within an education department could be set up. Regarding issue education, there should be some program courses, like that of the Union Leadership Academy (ULA), which offers long-term certificate programs.

References

Boyle, George V., "Defining Labor Education Needs," *Adult Leadership. Reprint*. March, 1970.

"The Functions of University Labor Education Programs," *Labor Studies Journal*. 2 (Fall 1977): pp 139-144.

Levine, Herb, and Freed, Morris. "Labor's Role in Lifelong Learning." Unpublished: Rutgers University, 1978.

Mire, Joseph. *Labor Education, A Study Report on Needs, Programs and Approaches*. Washington, D.C.: Inter University Labor Education Committee, 1956.

COMMUNITY COLLEGES AND THE ADULT LEARNER

Michael Crawford

Community colleges are committed to "opportunity with excellence." And, for the adult learner, they offer accessibility and program diversity, two important factors in encouraging adults to participate in education. Overall, community colleges offer adults flexibility, allowing them to mesh family and job responsibilities with their schooling.

There is a community, technical, or junior college within reasonable commuting distance for more than 90 percent of all Americans. As of 1983, there were over 1,200 community colleges in the United States enrolling more than 11 million adult students.

These colleges prepare people for employment in over 1,400 different occupations. They offer programs in vocational-technical education, college transfer, developmental education, and a wide variety of courses, workshops and seminars in their division of adult and continuing education.

The community colleges also appeal to adults because they are an economical delivery system. These institutions charge an average tuition of $550 for the academic year. In addition, accessibility keeps travel expenses minimal. And, ninety percent of the part-time students, and fifty percent of the full-time students in the nation's community colleges are employed, causing less drain on the family budget.

Populations Served

Historically, community colleges have been especially aware of their responsibility to those people who have been on the periphery of educational opportunities because of their limited financial resources or their socio-economic status. Classes that focus on basic, vocational, or job-seeking and job-keeping skills are an integral part of community college programming, designed to benefit the adults in this segment of the community.

Today, however, the adult student population enrolled in community college classes also includes college graduates seeking additional training; business men and women newly promoted to managerial positions; and adults returning to the workplace after a period of planned or unplanned unemployment. The number

121

of college parallel courses, vocational-technical programs, short-term vocational seminars, and continuing education courses have expanded accordingly to meet the rising needs of this population.

In addition to serving the specific needs of various adult learner groups, community colleges are promoting, developing and strengthening partnerships with many different community entities. More and more, community colleges are developing cooperative arrangements with business and industry, other educational institutions, service agencies, local government, hospitals, and civic organizations. These arrangements occur in order to accomplish the community college mission more effectively.

As a result, the populations served by community colleges include all age groups, and all economic and social levels. Because of this commitment to the entire community, community colleges must continue to be comprehensive, open, accessible institutions.

Program Structure

The variety of needs of adults served by community colleges demands a complex program structure. Historically, these programs have been credit classes, both vocational-technical and college parallel, continuing education classes, developmental education, and special programs developed to meet specific and current unmet community needs. All of these are appropriately supported by a program of student services.

Credit Courses
Community college credit offerings are provided through a variety of two-year transfer college programs and through various vocational-technical programs. Most credit programs are of one or two years duration and culminate with the awarding of an associate degree, diploma, or certificate.

In addition, credit classes can be utilized to meet an individual's specific career needs. Often, an adult learner will enroll in a limited number of job-related courses to update skills and/or to obtain a promotion. In these cases, the individual seldom plans on completing a program or receiving a degree or diploma. Obviously, flexibility of program offerings is extremely important in order to meet the needs of this type of student.

Continuing Education
Non-credit offerings are structured in almost any way necessary to meet the needs of many adult learners effectively. They deliver selected non-traditional

educational experiences. Often calling these programs "community education," many community colleges offer a wide variety of continuing education programs, including short-term vocational, career supplemental, vocational preparatory, vocational special needs, and general interest courses. These programs are often developed in cooperation with, and to specifically serve, a local business or industry, organization or agency. Also, in some states community colleges administer and provide their continuing education programs through local school districts.

Continuing education courses usually require a smaller time commitment for the adult learner, and courses are often taught by professionals currently working in the field in which they are teaching.

Developmental Education

Adults who need remedial training in the basic skill areas, or whose current level of knowledge doesn't meet the minimal requirements to enroll in a college-level course, often take advantage of developmental education services offered by many community colleges.

Remedial training services include classes in reading, writing, general math, and job-seeking and job-keeping skills. Adults without a high school diploma are directed into the GED program, enabling them to earn their equivalency diploma. These services help adult students qualify as vital members of the workplace.

Those adults who lack minimal enrollment requirements for a specific course or program also find help through developmental education. For example, these services might include classes in basic computer use, beginning typing or short-hand, or any number of entry-level courses. Once a student has completed these classes, they are better equipped to enroll in a vocational or college transfer program.

Special Programs.

Community colleges are entering into new partnerships with local businesses and industries, forming new programs to benefit the community. Examples of such partnerships are community colleges' establishment of business and industry centers and Job Training Partnership Act (JTPA) programs.

Business and Industry Centers. These centers provide a high level of visibility for community college education within the community. They are created to give local business and industry a central resource for expert advice, education programs tailored to their needs, and planning, development, research and survey services. In effect, the business and industry centers act as a liaison between education and industry. Further, they are an important economic development resource and encourage new or expanding businesses to locate within their service areas. One of their primary responsibilities is to develop creative employee training packages for new or expanding industry.

Business and industry centers use various community college programs and services, particularly adult/continuing education, to carry out their responsibilities. A sampling of the services offered by these centers to business includes: assisting in the recruitment and screening of employees; providing employees with specific job-related training; and, in some states, coordinating a program of financial reimbursement to the company while employees are receiving job training.

Job Training Partnership Act (JTPA) and Private Industry Council (PIC). JTPA's goal is to create a partnership among businesses, local elected officials, and state government to administer a federally funded employment and training program.

The governing body for JTPA is the Private Industry Council. The PIC is composed of local representatives from business, labor, education, rehabilitation agencies, economic development agencies, community based organizations, and public employment services. In coordination with elected officials, PIC develops local employment and training programs, using businesses as on-the-job training sites.

Since JTPA is a federal program administered through the states, it is the state which determines the delivery area. The delivery system may differ in the areas JTPA serves, but many community colleges act as the administrator. In this way, community colleges are providing another community service—one that is sensitive to local needs and is administered and governed by local people.

JTPA matches area employers who need qualified workers to fill existing jobs with people who need work and are eager and able to learn. It also provides funds to enroll adults in vocational and technical classes offered at a community college, and this capability allows potential employees to receive customized training from the college. And, JTPA encourages community participation by providing up to 50 percent of a new employee's wages during the required training period.

Funding

Community colleges are funded through a variety of sources. Funds come primarily from a combination of tuition and fees, state aid, local taxes, and federal vocational education money.

However, because of today's economy, three of these sources have become static or are declining. On the state level, revenues are down because of increased unemployment and decreased consumer spending. On the federal level, the Reagan Administration has reduced the federal role in education with subsequent reductions in financial support for education. And, locally, taxes are down since there are fewer expanding businesses and fewer new homes being built and sold.

Therefore, community colleges are becoming more involved in the acquisition of "new" sources of support. For example, more and more community colleges are contracting with local business and industry to provide a given number of educational services. Rather than going through the traditional program structures offered by community colleges, the business contracts for the specific services it needs and pays accordingly.

Grants are another important source of funding for community colleges. Specifically, community colleges are soliciting money from state and federal sources, as well as from private and corporate foundations, and corporations.

More and more, community colleges are actively pursuing non-traditional sources of education funding—state development commissions, the United States Department of Commerce, and the United States Information Agency. Money from these types of grants is often used to encourage partnerships between business and industry and community college, to develop manpower programs to meet local employment needs, and to develop and improve educational delivery systems.

Community colleges are also more aggressively soliciting donations from businesses, organizations, associations, alumni, and private individuals, including the use of deferred giving plans.

Community colleges have recognized within the last decade that public funding is generally adequate to operate "good" public institutions. However, to continue the development of excellence in institutional programming an additional margin is required. That "margin of excellence" can only be realized in many cases by the acquisition of private funds. For this reason, more and more community colleges are establishing aggressive resource development offices and foundations, and are turning to private dollars to support their public educational efforts.

Restraints

Ironically, many of the limits facing community collges to meet demands are due to the recent increase in high technology jobs. The need for new and updated training has caused an increase in enrollment at these institutions.

Community colleges recognize the need to provide quality programs in the new technology areas, but the cost of establishing these classes is often prohibitive. Instructional equipment is expensive, and it is hard to offer sufficient guidance to qualified instructors, who are leaving the educational field and taking jobs in the more lucrative business sector.

Fifteen years ago, a vocational program in office education might have included a teacher, a stack of steno pads, and a few typewriters. Today, that same program involves sophisticated word processing and dictation equipment, in addition to the need for a highly qualified staff member to instruct adults in recent innovations. Because of these changes, increased expenses, and limited funding, some community colleges are looking at instituting entrance level criteria to limit enrollment. Obviously, this contradicts the open door policy traditionally associated with community colleges.

In partnerships between community colleges and business and industry, there is sometimes a problem because large corporations have traditionally been responsible for their own employee training programs. As a result, there are occasional misunderstandings to overcome and an "education of the industry" before anything else can be done. Once this is accomplished, it quickly becomes clear that it is mutually advantageous—both economically and qualitatively—for community colleges and businesses to join together in the training process. Businesses are slowly and steadily responding to this relatively "new" and direct approach to educating their workforce.

Marketing

Community, technical, and junior colleges have experienced many changes in the last decade. The changing economic climate, demographics, inflation and budgetary and staffing concerns have forced them to take a critical look at themselves.

The examination has brought a relatively new dimension to community colleges—marketing. As a non-profit organization, the community college's marketing plan operates in a very complex arena. Since it has multiple constituencies, the clients to whom it provides services and the many sources from which it receives financial resources, the marketing plan must be flexible. The approach used to influence potential clients need not be the same as the one used to influence its funding sources. This flexibility makes the marketing task more complex.

Many factors encourage educational managers to develop and implement marketing plans. These factors include, but are not necessarily limited to: fear of declining enrollments; increased competition from other educational institutions; educational programs offered by business and industry; taxpayer's resistance to further support; and, declining revenues and inflationary pressures.

Planned and effective marketing can make the institution more effective in meeting its objectives. Through more effective measurement of needs and desires of specific adult learner target groups, community colleges will be in a better position to provide programs that best serve the consumer and the community.

Serving the Community

When evaluating the community college's delivery system for the education and training of adults, the most important word to keep in mind is "community." The community college must be a reflection of the community. The cooperation generated between the community college and the community it serves is an extremely important contributor to a sound and comprehensive program of community and economic development.

MILITARY TRAINING

*Clinton L. Anderson**

The Armed Forces have the constant mission of maintaining this country's ability to use land, air and sea force components of the United States military power throughout the world in consonance with national goals and interests. In order to accomplish this mission, military training encompasses the Active Component (i.e., deployed and continental U.S.-based (CONUS) active forces), the Reserve Component (i.e., the National Guard, the Selective Reserve Units, the Mobilization Designes (MOBDES), and the Individual Ready Reserve (IRR)), and the Civilian Component (e.g., civilians employed by Department of Defense and the military services, defense contractors, etc.).

Trainees are voluntary service members of the Armed Forces. Recruits are usually 17 years of age or older and are on the threshold of adulthood. Most have completed at least 12 years of civilian education and now enter the Armed Forces with a variety of expectations and goals.

Each military service has a training strategy which provides the conceptual framework for planning, programming, budgeting, and conducting and/or overseeing all training and education necessary to accomplish its particular military mission. This military training strategy includes education and training for deployed, contingency, and reenforcing forces; the peacetime and mobilization training bases; and training and education support programs to sustain individual and collective job performance. Implementation of this training strategy and long-range military plans provide a coherent process that helps insure a smooth and timely integration of manpower, material, doctrine, technology, and other resources to produce a well-trained, modern, mission-capable fighting force.

Goals

The military services have set series of goals for themselves and their service members. The training goal is usually stated somewhat like this: "To develop and sustain a combat-ready force prepared to mobilize, deploy on short notice, fight, and defeat enemies of the United States in support of worldwide national

---

*The views expressed in this paper are those of the author and do not necessarily reflect the position or policy of the Department of Defense.

commitments according to the Joint Strategic Capabilities Plan (JSCP) as directed by the National Command Authority."

The Army, in conjunction with Air Force, has developed a new fighting doctrine called "Airland Battle 2000." This "how to fight" instruction calls for a quantum increase in required individual skills and knowledge. It envisions an extended and integrated battlefield that may require the individual service member to fight anywhere, at any time, against conventional, unconventional, chemical, biological, nuclear and electronic threats, in all types of terrain, in all kinds of weather and visibility for extended periods of time. Resources will be widely scattered and service members must be capable of operating as effective team members with various mixes of United States forces and Allied forces. Emerging new systems require the individual service member to operate on the battlefield in automated, semi-automated and manual modes as the situation demands. As a result, service men and women need many new system-related skills and knowledge.

Meanwhile, the military services must consider the "human goal." Military leaders would like to see their forces composed of military and civilian professionals who loyally serve their nation in rewarding careers. In order to achieve this end, each service attempts to provide all service members with meaningful and satisfying duty, adequate living and working facilities, equitable compensation, professional development, and advancement opportunities. The military training strategy must incorporate both personal development and military training goals in order to have able and willing personnel who can use and maintain high tech equipment and can fight in modern warfare.

Categories of Training

For the purposes of this discussion, military training is an all-encompassing term. It includes what is generally considered military training, military education and adult and continuing education provided in and/or for the Army. Therefore, military training includes a minimum of five categories (Figure 1). First, there is preparation for potential entry into and/or employment in the Armed Forces. Examples of this type of training are academic and vocational education and training. Physical, mental, and moral fitness, and willingness to serve are emphasized in this category. Pre-enlistment activities extend into the secondary school system, post-secondary educational institutions, civilian adult education centers, and job training programs sponsored through the Department of Labor and state, local and private organizations. Perhaps the best known formal training programs in this category are the

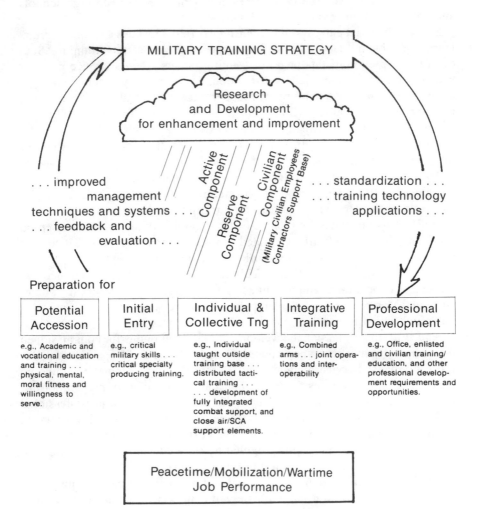

Figure 1

Junior and Senior Reserve Officer Training Corps (ROTC) in high schools and college and universities throughout the United States.

Second, is initial entry training. During the first 13 weeks or more, recruits learn common military skills and undergo critical specialty training. Successful completion of this phase of training occurs when a service member is awarded particular specialty certifications (e.g., military occupational specialty, rating), and sent to his or her first permanent duty station. For example, the Army Basic Training (BT), Advanced Individual Training (AIT) or a combination of the two called One-Station Unit Training (OSUT) are specific programs in this category. Incoming officers generally undergo a basic course in a particular branch or specialty before going to a first permanent assignment.

Third, is individual and collective training in units. This category includes individual skills training outside the formal training base (i.e., formal schools and training centers where initial entry training or basic courses are conducted). It also includes distributive tactical training or unit training essential for the development of fully integrated combat, combat support (CS), combat service support (CSS) and close air/land/sea support elements.

Fourth, is integration training. This includes intra-service combined exercises, joint operations among United States military units (Army, Air Force, Navy and Marine Corps), and interoperability exercises between United States units and Allied forces.

And fifth, the professional development. This training is for commissioned officers, warrant officers, non-commissioned officers and Department of Defense civilians. Service members and Defense civilian employees undergo these programs at various stages of their careers, usually in preparation for advancement. In addition, a large number of specialty courses and professional and personal development programs can be loosely included in this category: human relations training programs, personal effectiveness training. Adult and continuing education programs provided by base education centers and sub-centers worldwide generally fall into this category.

All five categories promote individual and unit performance during peace-time, during mobilization and, ultimately, during wartime. The military training strategy of each service provides criteria for standardization and for technology applications to the training and education programs.

In addition, evaluations and lessons learned from training and field performance feed back to the strategy planners and programmers to improve management techniques and systems development. The training research and development activities within the Department of Defense, such as those conducted by the Army Research Institute for the Behavioral and Social Sciences and its field stations, the Navy Personnel Research and Development Center, and Air Force Human Resources Laboratory, work toward the enhancement of education and training through model program development, application of engineering technologies, and solving research questions.

Critical Elements of Military Training

Perhaps another way to view military training is to look at its interlocking critical elements (Figure 2). One critical element is the caliber of personnel employed by the Armed Services. The military services, often *in conjunction* and always in *close coordination* with the Department of Defense and the Office of Personnel Management, establish qualification and classification standards for employment or enlistment. These standards are set for prerequisite skills and knowledge deemed essential for initial employment and likelihood of successful performance within the military organization. For the enlisted personnel in all military services, the Armed Services Vocational Aptitude Battery is used as the screening instrument. A variety of other evaluation tools are used to screen officer candidates and civilian applicants prior to formal employment and service.

The conduct of the training and education programs serves as another critical element. These programs may be individual skills training within the training base, individual and collective skills training in units throughout the world, distributive tactical and integrative training, mobilization training, unit endurance and performance training to include professional development.

Evaluation of the quality, effectiveness and relevancy of the programs is a critical element. This entails both performance measurement and evaluation of overall training effectiveness.

Another critical element is management training. Management is responsible for needs assessment, education and training, program development, methods and techniques. Management is responsible for making the process work, including *incorporating* evaluation findings into improved instructional programs. Management must maintain the prerequisite skills and knowledge base that helps set the standards for initial employment.

Individual Training Systems

While other categories of training are often fully integrated into general mission funding and become indistinguishable from normal military operations, each military service has a highly visible and well-defined individual training system with a budgetary line item. In fiscal year 1983 (October 1, 1982-September 30,

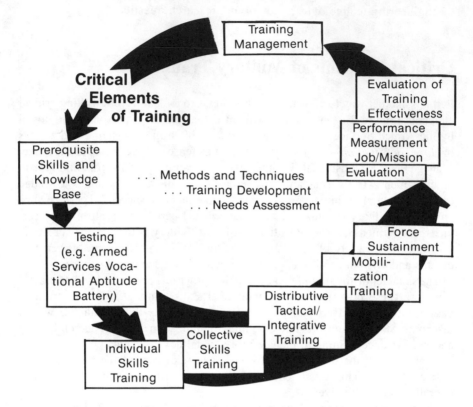

Figure 2

1983), for example, the Department of Defense had approximately $10.5 billion to spend on individual training. This amount covered:

- Recruit training (indoctrination and basic training) for approximately 338,000 students at a cost of $882 million.
- Specialized skills training for approximately 709,000 students at a cost of $2.4 billion.
- One-Station Unit Training (combined recruit and specialized skills training in the Army) for approximately 104,000 students at a cost of $322 million.

Other costs included flight training, some officer acquisition costs, some professional development education, medical training and overhead (support, management, travel and pay).

Military Training Evaluation

The overall purpose of military training evaluation is to determine if service members and civilian employees are capable of performing their required tasks and if military organizations can accomplish their missions. The military services attempt to formulate fair and realistic evaluation plans, validate evaluation instruments based on clearly established standards, develop a feedback system, hold prinicipal agencies accountable for carrying out evaluation, allocate personnel and train them in the process involved, communicate evaluation findings to the appropriate corporate management empowered to make the necessary changes in the system, and take action based on these findings.

Within the context of Instructional Systems Development (ISD), to which each military service ascribes, evaluation is not considered simply a process that follows implementation of the training program. The term "evaluate" is used to mean the continuous monitoring of a program or of the training function as a whole,and it involves both verification and validation. The process, as envisioned in ISD, consists of internally evaluating the training program during each phase of its preparation (at least to the degree that fiscal and manpower resources and time permit), while concurrently externally evaluating the overall training function. Thus, following implementation, feedback is used to evaluate the program, assess the quality of job performance and check the organization's overall responsiveness to training need (Figure 3). Without a dynamic systems approach, negative situations often occur because: (1) programs reflect tradition and inertia, particularly "core" program offerings that are outdated and not responsive to job requirements; (2) the purposes, goals and standards of training or education programs are fuzzy at best; (3) newer programs are plagued by fads, so that they include inappropriate use of new technologies, techniques, or gimmicks; (4) there is inefficient or non-existent liaison between training staff professionals and line managers to identify "real" needs in the organization; and (5) performance problems are only sometimes recognized as related to knowledge or skill deficiencies. Even if a systems approach is used, management at times does not push for necessary research and development to measure the results of training.

Even when objective evaluations are produced, the research data are usually sensitive information. Training managers often fear negative results with good reason. They could be relieved, or at a minimum, their efficiency reports could reflect poor performance. In addition, they could lose resources such as staff and money. Nevertheless, for an effective training system, honest objective evaluation is absolutely essential particularly in the area of field feedback.

A Model for a Systems Approach to Training

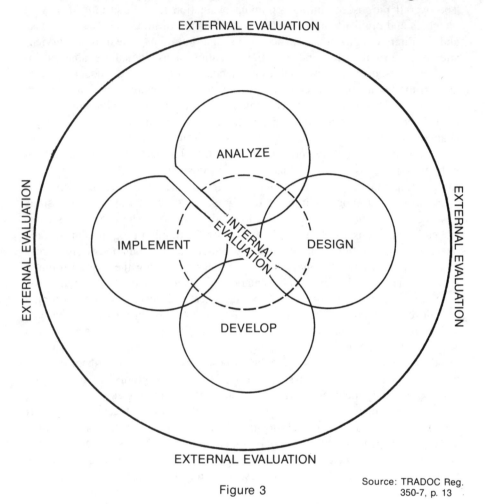

Figure 3

Source: TRADOC Reg.
350-7, p. 13

The Challenge

The "landmark" education reports of 1983—*A Nation at Risk, Action for Excellence, Adult Illiteracy in the United States, Report of the Twentieth Century Fund Task Force on Federal Elementary and Secondary Educational Policy*, and *Condition of Teaching*—call for education and training to raise standards, particularly to meet the needs of the disadvantaged and minorities within the United States. An article in the *Washington Post*—"Hard Times Close Army's

Ranks to the Inner City's Would-Be Recruits''—points out that the restricting of recruitment to high school graduates in the "higher mental categories" screens out most of the inner city youth. It goes on to say that closing military recruitment in this manner adversely affects the disadvantaged minorities. The chances for getting out of the ghetto are lost to them. Anger and frustration boil.

The message is clear. Military management, in conjunction with business and industry need to identify more precisely the prerequisite skills and knowledge needed for employment and career development. These needs should be conveyed to the civilian education and training community which, in turn, sets appropriate standards, reorders priorities, and uses available resources to produce qualified personnel for employment and development.

References

Department of the Army. *The Human Goal*. Shortened version of the "Human Goal" briefing given to the Army Policy Council on 20 May 1982. (Cover letter signed by Thurman, M.R. and Walters, Harry N.) Washington, D.C.: Office of the Deputy Chief of Staff, Army, for Personnel, 26 July 1982.

Department of the Army. *TRADOC Regulation No. 350-7: A Systems Approach to Training*. Fort Monroe, VA: Headquarters, U.S. Army Training and Doctrine Command, 5 November 1982.

Department of the Army. *Army Training 1990 (Final Draft)*. Fort Monroe, VA: U.S. Army Training and Doctrine Command, 8 April 1983.

Department of Defense. *Military Manpower Training Report for FY 1982*. Washington, D.C.: Office of the Assistant Secretary of Defense (Manpower, Reserve Affairs, and Logistics), March 1981.

"Excerpts from the Report of the Twentieth Century Fund's Task Force," *The Chronicle of Higher Education*. May 11, 1983, pp.5-7.

Feistritzer, C. Emily. *The Condition of Teaching*. Carnegie Foundation for Advancement of Teaching, August 1983.

"Hard Times Close Army's Ranks to the Inner City's Would-Be Recruits," *The Washington Post*. Sunday, 27 February 1982, pp. A1, A14.

Hunter, Carman St. John and Harman, David. *Adult Illiteracy in the United States*. New York: McGraw-Hill Book Company, 1979.

National Commission on Excellence in Education. *A Nation at Risk: The Imperative for Educational Reform*. Stock No. 065-000-00177- 2. Washington, D.C.: U.S. Government Printing Office, April 1983.

Schultz, James B. "Airland Battle 2000: The Force Multiplier," *Defense Electronics*, Vol. 15, No. 12, December, 1983, pp. 48-54, 59-67.

Task Force on Education for Economic Growth. *Action for Excellence: A Comprehensive Plan to Improve Our Nation's Schools*. Denver, CO: The Education Commission of the States, June 1983.

CONTINUING EDUCATION

Lee Transier

Continuing education programs in four-year institutions are diverse and multi-faceted. Their variety in objectives, programs, and organizational structure reflects both institutional differences and the changes that are taking place within higher education.

The term "continuing education" has a multiplicity of meanings. In some institutions, it includes credit courses, summer school, evening school, non-credit offerings and conference programs. There are a number of continuing education programs that also offer undergraduate and graduate degrees through a college or school of continuing education. In other schools, continuing education only handles non-credit offerings, although such programs may range from powder-puff auto mechanics to quantum mechanics.

It is difficult to categorize programs in relation to type of institution, public or private, or by size of the sponsoring organization. The current changes now affecting many programs further complicate any analysis of programs. What may be factual at the time this is written, may be nothing more than past history in the next month.

Continuing Education Program Objectives

Although some writers suggest that continuing education has been practiced since the first settlers arrived in the new world, the modern practice of adult education is of rather recent origin. Its current philosphy grows out of its past experiences in two distinct branches of education, the public school system and higher education.

With the diverse cultures coming together in the United States, the social need for programs in literacy and aculturation has always been acute. In the nineteenth century, the public schools responded with large evening school programs for adults wanting to become a part of the American dream. They provided English and civics courses and vocational programs. At the same time, there was movement among the nation's higher education institutions to spread culture to the masses. An organization was formed at the University of Pennsylvania for the purpose of expanding university extension work. Faculty members from a number of respected institutions fanned out across the nation, delivering lectures on science, literature and other disciplines.

In urban areas, a number of colleges were founded for the express purpose of providing college education for the working class. Many offered programs in the evening to allow students to support their families by working during the day.

The land grant institutions not only taught traditional undergraduates, but saw as their broader mission the spreading of knowledge to adults across their state. They used a variety of outreach programs, with an emphasis on acquiring practical knowledge.

Today, the philosophic objectives of colleges' continuing education programs are:

- To provide knowledge that enables adults to keep pace with the rapid changes taking place in society;
- To offer programs for retraining adults where job displacement occurs due to changes in technology or the economy;
- To provide information to adults that will assist them in understanding and coping with the meaning of life, through the study of the humanities;
- To assist the community or state in providing individuals with job-related skills that will enhance the pool of workers, thus attracting new industry to the areas;
- To provide opportunities for adults to learn for the joy of learning;
- To provide adults, who either did or could not attend college after high school, with the opportunity to earn a degree;
- To assist adults in acquiring the skills necessary to become self-directed learners; in taking responsibility for determining a learning need; in developing a plan to acquire the knowledge; and, in placing the plan into action;
- To provide current knowledge for doctors, dentists, engineers and other professionals.

From the institutional perspective, objectives may include increased revenue; fulfilling social responsibilities; carrying out the committment to the land-grant concept; stemming a tide of decreasing enrollments among traditional age cohorts, and conducting public relations.

Populations Served

The populations served by continuing education programs are as varied as the number of programs that exist, although some groups tend to predominate. Since most continuing education programs are not funded by state appropriations, they derive their revenue from student fees. This approach often requires them to have fees that are significantly higher than regular tuition. These fees limit participation to those with a higher level of disposable income. The policies of the federal government and many state governments further restrict participation because they limit financial aid to credit course work, and they often place adults at a significant disadvantage in financial aid evaluations. As a result, professional and managerial level individuals outnumber trade and clerical workers, except where programs are funded from grants or special appropriations.

There are also two other factors that affect participation of these higher income groups. Studies have shown that the more education a person has, the greater the probability that he or she will continue to learn. In addition, professionals must acquire the new knowledge necessary for effective practice and, in many cases, professional societies and organizations mandate continuing education.

Labor organizations have also recognized the importance of continuing education, and some have included funding in their contracts. The trend toward improved educational benefits, however, has been limited by the economic difficulties of the 1980's.

In the late 1960's and early 1970's, continuing education programs for women grew rapidly. With the women's movement and attitudes changing toward women in the workplace, there was a strong demand for programs that would provide services for women returning to the workforce and for displaced homemakers. This trend for special services has diminished in the past few years as the pent-up demand has abated.

Some institutions provide special programs for older adults. Among the most common are the Elderhostel program and legislatively mandated programs in some states that allow retired adults to sit in on credit courses for no fee or for a token payment. As the number of older Americans increases, there appears to be an increasing demand for programs to meet their needs.

Minorities pose a somewhat enigmatic issue for continuing education. Continuing education provides opportunity for advancement through education, but financial factors often prohibit participation. In credit offerings, where tuition and fees are moderate and limited financial assistance is available, participation by minorities tends to be higher than in non-credit offerings, in which minorities are under represented.

Funding Sources

By totaling expenditures in various governmental agencies, companies, and educational institutions, a case could be made that substantial funding of continuing education programs exists. In reality, there is little direct funding. On the federal level, Title 1 of the Higher Education Act was to be the springboard for substantial funding of continuing higher education. The level of funding for this program, however, has only been adequate for few demonstration projects, and there is little likelihood that funding of continuing education programs will become a national priority in the next several years. The perceived crisis in American education at the primary and secondary school level is bringing about demands for reforms and more spending for public schools, thus reducing the amount of funds that might have been available to provide funding of continuing higher education.

Where appropriations for funding of higher education are driven by formulas, credit courses for adults generate revenues that benefit the institution. In a limited number of cases, this money is returned to the continuing education program; in others, it is distributed to departments or kept by the central administration. In some states, programs designed to meet the needs of adults may actually penalize the sponsoring institution. In one state for example, institutions offering off-campus credit courses are financially penalized if the courses represent more than two percent of the total number of course offerings.

Most legislators and some university administrators contend that adults should pay for their own education and only youth should benefit from tax-supported education. The outlook for any substantial change in funding patterns is at best, bleak.

Program Characteristics

Program structure varies considerably from institution to institution. Most credit course offerings taught through continuing education divisions are scheduled in the traditional semester or quarter pattern, although a number of schools have established successful weekend credit programs.

Rather than being driven by the traditional semester system, most non-credit programs are structured in direct relationship to client need or to the amount of information being taught. It is not uncommon to see one week programs, six week courses, weekend programs and semester long non-credit programs in an institution. Work and family and community responsibilities make short courses attractive to adults.

Program locations range from on-campus, to off-campus centers, department stores, to malls. Many schools have been quite successful in offering courses in the client's workplace.

Continuing education programs often provide a greater degree of flexibility than that found in traditional academic units. As a result, there is often more innovation, experimentation and opportunity for interdisciplinary programs.

One such non-credit interdisciplinary program in underwater technology grew into a new degree-granting program. It involves the colleges of engineering technology, and health, physical education and recreation, and the departments of biology and physics.

The opportunity for experimentation has resulted in a new approach to teaching languages to adults. By blending together several accelerated learning techniques, one continuing education program has found that it is possible to teach an adult to speak a foreign language after 84 hours of instruction.

Not all continuing education programs are designed to teach traditional academic disciplines. At the University of Massachusetts-Amherst, for example, the Adult Career Transitions Program is designed to respond to the needs of adults who are choosing, or being forced to change, careers. A series of counseling sessions help adults participating in the program to: identify transferable skills, values and interests; assess potential career options; and, learn skills necessary for achieving these options.

Recruitment and Selection of Instructors

Like many things about continuing education, the most appropriate term to describe selection and recruitment of instructors would be "varied". At some institutions, administration policies require that all instructors teaching in continuing education programs be selected from the regular full-time faculty. Other continuing education units select faculty from the community, and, in still other cases, instructors come from both faculty and community.

Continuing educators find selecting faculty difficult. Unlike traditional students, adult learners will not tolerate poor instruction. Many faculty members have never taught adults and approach the instruction of adults in the same manner as they would a traditional undergraduate class, which often leads to unsatisfactory results. Therefore, evaluation of teaching is a primary concern of most continuing education professionals. Each course is usually evaluated by students and, in many cases, by the continuing education staff. Furthermore, many continuing education programs utilize advisory panels, with one of their functions being the recommendation of individuals as prospective course instructors.

Recruitment from the community is not considered to be a problem because a professional from the community is usually honored by the opportunity to teach at the university. Policies vary from institution to institution, but it is not unusual for an academic department to employ the external instructor as a means of maintaining quality.

Where flexibility allows continuing education programs to utilize both regular faculty and community experts, there are a number of benefits: the capability to provide both theoretical and practical knowledge; a closer relationship between the institution and the community professional; university faculty's improved understanding of what is happening in the "real world".

Marketing Strategies

Marketing strategies play an important role in continuing education programs. In most cases, credit is not attached to programs, thus the perceived benefit is difficult to market. This requires a marketing strategy that conveys the "value" of the program to the potential student. Since most programs are required to be self-supporting, marketing is necessary to insure survival.

Marketing strategies for continuing education programs depend on the type of program the institution offers and on institutional philosophy. In some cases, there are aggressive marketing units attached to continuing education programs, and marketing research plays a major role in the development of marketing plans. Each component of the marketing program is analyzed to determine the most cost-effective avenue for attracting clients. In other instances, the marketing strategy may be nothing more than publishing a bulletin each semester. Again, diversity is the best descriptor, from an institution that wants all promotional materials to feature a photo of "Old Main" on the cover, to some of the more sophisticated units that use telephone marketing to cultivate former students for future enrollment.

The primary method of marketing is direct mail, either through a periodic bulletin or brochures for individual programs. After direct mail, newspaper promotion, both paid advertising and public service announcements, are most utilized for marketing purposes. Electronic media are sometimes used, although the consensus among continuing educators is that television is effective, but its cost is prohibitive. Paid radio advertising, in general, appears not to be cost-effective.

Future Directions

Forces that are at work reshaping American society are also shaping the future of continuing higher education. The considerable diversity which now exists is desirable given the nature of the client population. There appears, however, to be a trend to integrate continuing education programs into the main institutional programs. This development can either be beneficial or detrimental, depending upon how the change takes place. If, by integration, the continuing education programs become less flexible and more like traditional programs, the responsiveness to community need may be lost.

If, on the contrary, continuing education programs integrated into the mainstream strengthen and bring about change in traditional programs, then there is a strong probability that institutions, traditional programs, continuing education, and clients will all derive benefits from the change. A new environment will be created that will enable this nation to grow and adapt to a changing world.

DELIVERY SYSTEM FOR ADULT EDUCATION: COOPERATIVE EXTENSION SERVICE

Mary Nell Greenwood

The objectives of the Extension Service of the United States Department of Agriculture (USDA), and the cooperative extension services at the state and county levels are spelled out in the Smith-Lever Act, of 1914, as amended: "An ACT to provide for cooperative agricultural extension work between the agricultural colleges in the several States receiving benefits of an Act of Congress approved July 2, 1862, and Acts supplementary thereto, and the United States Department of Agriculture."

Key purposes of the Act relate to adult education and the unique delivery system which has become a model all over the world: "In order to aid in diffusing among the people of the United States useful and practical information on subjects relating to agriculture and home economics and to encourage the application of same;" and, "Cooperative agricultural extension work shall consist of the giving of instruction and practical demonstrations in agriculture and home economics and subjects relating thereto *to persons not attending or resident* in said colleges in the several communities, and imparting information on said subjects through demonstrations, and printing and distribution of publications."

Although the cooperative extension system has been called the "educational agency of the Department of Agriculture," it is actually part of a three-way partnership—federal, state and county. Funding is approximately 39 percent federal, 43 percent state and 18 percent county, with considerable variation from state to state and county to county. In 1984, approximately $900 million in support came from federal, state and county governments, plus an additional $29 million in private funds.

Organization

Extension is the largest off-campus informal education system of its kind in the world. It has local offices in 50 States, the District of Columbia, Puerto Rico, Virgin Islands, Guam, American Samoa, and Micronesia. And, it has local offices in most of the 3,150 counties in the nation.

Extension Service is "where the action is", which assures that programs meet the needs of the public. Nearly 16,000 professionals, 5,000 paraprofessionals, and 1.6 million volunteers conduct adult educational programs in both rural and urban areas throughout the country. An estimated 66 percent of U.S. agricultural producers had direct contact with Extension programs in 1978, according to a 1980 national evaluation study. Cooperative Extension Services currently devote about 38 percent of their staffs' time and other resources to agriculture-related programs.

County extension agents are as close to the clientele as their computer, telephone, radio, TV, and mailbox; and many users of extension information are on a first name basis with the county extension staff. County agents provide educational information, materials, fact sheets, publications, and advice in the major areas of agricultural production and marketing, protecting natural resources, family living, food and nutrition, 4-H & youth, and community and rural development. They also use non-credit workshops, group meetings, demonstrations, tours, newsletters, and mass media.

Extension's educational programs for agri-business include both those persons engaged in processing and marketing farm products and those selling supplies to producers. Educational work is also done with producer and marketing or consumer cooperatives.

Extension's move into electronic technology demonstrates its concern about meeting its clients' needs. It is estimated that by 1990, all large farms and 75 percent of all middle-sized farms will be using computers or programmable calculators in making management decisions.

Computer technology hardware for farmers and ranchers is expanding more rapidly than the software. Therefore, the Extension system, in concert with agricultural researchers, is translating research results into software packages for family farms, particularly for farm and home financial management. For example, the Department of Agriculture recently published "Computers on the Farm" to guide farmers and ranchers in selecting and using computers. Extension Service staff contributed to and reviewed the text. And, programs conducted by State Extension specialists and county agents include workshops in farm and ranch financial management and computers.

Special Populations

A large cadre of paraprofessionals works with Extension in special programs for families with limited resources. One of these programs is the Expanded Food and Nutrition Education Program (EFNEP), which seeks to better participants' nutritional status and good management practices. Since 1968, 2.4 million low income homemakers have been enrolled in EFNEP, which currently operates in

861 independent sites, including cities and Indian Reservations. Approximately 60 percent of EFNEP participants are minorities.

The Extension 4-H program is conducted by over 600,000 volunteer adult leaders who are trained by the Extension Service professional staff at the county level. This program currently involves nearly 5 million boys and girls in over 9 million educational 4-H projects. 4-H has the largest staff development program for national, regional and statewide training of volunteers. In 1983, over 500 4-H professionals were trained in national workshops; over 4,000 volunteers were trained in week-long national and regional forums; and, some 10,000 volunteers were trained in state forums.

Extension home economics programs focus on household and individual decision-making on food, finances, housing, families, and leadership. Programs designed by local staff provide current research findings and established knowledge to solve problems faced by men and women of all ages and resources.

More and more farm and ranch women, who help their spouses or operate farms on their own, are participating in Extension production and marketing workships. Extension specialists in Missouri holding "swine farrowing schools for women only" have so many applications they have to restrict the number who can attend. These women are caring for the farm operation while their spouses work off the farm.

Linkages and Other Resources

Extension Service expands educational information and technology transfer to adults on a nationwide scale through its linkages with other agencies of USDA, other departments of government and two-way communication with national organizations. For example:

- *The Residue Avoidance Program* (RAP) is a shared agency program. The Food Safety and Inspection Service (FSIS) provides $2.39 million "pass through funds" to the Extension Service for state educational projects in 33 states. RAP is a cooperative effort between FSIS, ES and industry, and is aimed at helping farmers and others involved in animal and poultry production reduce the potential for drug and chemical residues in their products. Eventually, the program will involve more than 1,000 state extension administrators, and specialists and county agents will play a major role in reaching clientele at the local level.
- *The Extension Urban Gardening Program* teaches adults gardening skills and food use and preservation for better diets and improved nutrition. The 1984 program was funded for $3 million, was used in 16 designated cities for approximately 200,000 participants.

This money is used only for educational programs in gardening and produce, but the program has also generated another $500,000 in private contributions for the purchase of equipment and materials. Extension staff and 3,000 trained volunteers make up the delivery system. The retail value of the vegetables produced is conservatively estimated at $8 million. Other gardening help includes Extension's on-going gardening programs in all states and work with the "Master Gardening" program.

* *The Integrated Pest Management (IPM) Program* operated by the Extension Service system trains adults in the private sector to function as advisors and scouts to reduce the presence of chemicals in the environment, and their application on crops. Scouts are people trained to inspect the fields for the presence of insects to justify spraying. A report published in 1978 predicted the need for about 5,000 professional advisors and 70,000 parttime scouts to staff private consulting firms and cooperatives by 1985.
* *The Pesticide Applicator Training Program (PAT)* is an ongoing educational activity by the state cooperative extension services. Each year, 100,000 new pesticide applicators receive initial training from county agents and/or pesticide specialists in the states. Additionally, re-certification training activities reach over 300,000 of the more than 1 million certified pesticide applicators each year.
* *Farm Management Associations.* The Extension Service cooperates with Farm Management Associations in 10 states to provide highly intensive one-on-one assistance for farmers with their farm management problems. These associations reach many adult farmers—over 8,000 in Illinois last year.
* *Food and Fitness.* The USDA Food and Fitness Campaign, launched in 1983, is a nationwide effort with the Extension Service as the lead agency for conducting the program at the state and county levels. This program will work with school teachers and others to sponsor an essay contest with state and national awards. The year-long awareness program ended with a Food Fair on the Mall in Washington, D.C. in August 1984.

Marketing Extension Service

Extension Service programs are marketed in many ways. Clients often seek out the County Extension agent by going to the local office or by calling. Word-of-mouth referral is often important.

Or, clients may be made aware of Extension Service through the local media. Specific examples and methods used to make people aware of the Extension Service, or to provide educational materials and advice include:

* *Radio* is an excellent medium for making people "aware" of Extension

Service programs. Contact by radio leads to a followup because the recommendations on the radio are usually very short and not specific enough to be used if, for example, the recommendation deals with application of a chemical. Fact sheets or other educational materials in more depth are available at the county extension office and mentioned at the end of the radio spot announcement. Or, the radio spot may announce an upcoming workshop or short course, tour or demonstration, the farmer or consumer can attend, with more details available from the Extension office.

- *Local newspapers* are used daily and weekly by Extension agents to "market" Extension programs. Newspapers will usually give enough space to an extension item for an "educational message." Also, local newspapers will use photos from the agents, or often cover events and write stories and provide their own photographs. These stories attract the adults Extension wants to reach and teach.

- *Dial access*, which is also called "teletips," is a telephone service that stores subject matter information on tapes which the user calls for by number. This approach is promoted by direct mail, flyers in grocery stores, local media, even brochures in Braille for the blind. North Carolina has a statewide teletips system with about 1,000 tapes using eight 800-watt lines, and it averages over 2,000 calls per week. The Colorado Extension Service has 600 taped messages, with the most popular one being the "weight control" tape. California Extension reports that out of 1,000 calls about gardening/home horticulture, only about 150 have to be handled by an operator or other staffer to answer questions not covered to the satisfaction of the caller by the tape.

Use of Mass Media to Reach Adults

Extension Service makes the maximum use of state and county mass media outlets to reach the adult audience with educational messages and general information. For example:

Illinois. The county extension staff conducted a six-month mass media survey of how print and electronic releases were used in the local media. Totals were:
- Radio programs—66,210 on-air minutes
- Television programs—5,460 on-air minutes
- News releases—6,494
- Regular news columns—4,365
- Feature photographs—3,596

Nebraska. A telephone survey of 371 farmer/ranchers regarding their use of Nebraska Educational Television Network's full-screen text service, AGRI-VIS

22 years old and over who completed high school had incomes below the poverty level. For adults who completed nine to 11 years of school, 18.6 percent had incomes below the poverty level.

The percent of those with incomes below the poverty level increases as the number of years of school decreases. This phenomenon exists independently of differences in age, sex, and race. Thus, census data show that persons who completed five years or less of school were four times more likely to have incomes below the poverty level than were those who completed high school. Bureau of Census data also demonstrate the increasing importance of high school education in avoiding economic hardships. In 1970, 16 percent of adults aged 22 to 34 who completed 9 to 11 years of school had incomes below the poverty level; by 1981, the rate had increased to nearly 28 percent.

Corroborative data on labor force status and years of school completed are available from the Bureau of Labor Statistics (BLS). In 1983, BLS reported that adults without high school credentials had the highest unemployment rate, approximately 16 percent. During that same period, the national unemployment rate was 9 percent.

To understand non-economic reasons why adults need the skills and knowledge available through high school education, it is useful to turn to the national evaluations of programs supported under the Adult Education Act of 1966, as amended. This legislation supports adult basic education, English as a second language, and adult secondary education programs for adults who have not completed high school or its equivalent. Through formula grants to states, approximately 2.3 million adults pursue basic skills and high school equivalency.

Of the 2.3 million people seeking education under the Adult Education Act, approximately 45 percent are in Adult Basic Education (ABE), 26 percent in English as a Second Language Programs (ESL), and the remaining 29 percent are in Adult Secondary Education (ASE) Programs. Data show that the ASE program has emerged as an alternative for the recent high school drop-out. Forty-eight percent of those in ASE are between the ages of 16-21, and 81 percent are age 34 or younger.

A 1980 national evaluation of the Adult Education Act program sampled participating adults in the program. Approximately 75 percent of those contacted had previously been in the program but had completed or terminated their studies. Approximately 80 percent said they had fully or partially attained their goals. The benefit most frequently cited (by 85 percent of the participants) was that they felt better about themselves. While a variety of factors may have contributed to these improved feelings, this finding does support the importance of adult education to self-development and adult fulfillment.

Among those interviewed, less than 15 percent indicated they were in the program to obtain a job or to increase earnings. However, 49 percent indicated their goal was to obtain a high school diploma or equivalency certificate. Given the high correlation between high school education and improved earnings, it is reasonable to assume that for many the high school diploma is seen as an attainable goal and as aiding their economic improvement in the future. Under this interpretation, a much higher percentage of those in the programs were in the program for job-related reasons or for their economic improvement. Clearly, however these data are interpreted, at least half of those in the program are primarily motivated to learn for other than directly job-related purposes.

How Adults Achieve a High School Education

Today, an adult can earn a high school diploma or its equivalent in three ways:
- a regular high school diploma issued by a local educational agency when the adult satisfactorily earns the required Carnegie units;
- an equivalency certificate upon passing the General Educational Development (GED) tests and other requirements of the state;
- an alternative diploma that is competency-based and gives credit for prior experience and previous learning.

Carnegie Units

Before World War II, the only way an adult could obtain a high school diploma was to go back to school and learn the subject matter required for high school graduation. "Adult night schools" offered these opportunities, which were usually distinguishable from regular high schools only by being offered in the evenings and being attended by adults. This avenue is still available and preferred by significant numbers of adults, although the programs now are usually available during the day as well. In this approach, the adult earns Carnegie units, a standard of measurement used to describe the secondary school subject matter pattern that constitutes the entrance requirements of college. Like the graduation requirements for in-school youth, Carnegie unit requirements for adults in high school may vary from state to state and from community to community. This method of credentialization presents little opportunity to receive credit for prior experience or learning. Performance is usually measured by results of tests that refer only to subject matter in individual courses.

GED

In contrast to the traditional high school diploma awarded through earning Carnegie units, adults may take an examination that measures their "general educational development." Millions of adults have earned secondary school equivalency diplomas or certificates based on their performance on General Educational Development (GED) tests.

Introduced by the examination staff of the United States Armed Forces Institute, the secondary school equivalency program began in 1942. Under the auspices of the American Council on Education, the program was later extended to civilians. Over the past four decades, the program has grown considerably both in acceptance and in number of credentials awarded. The GED program is conducted jointly by the GED Testing Service of the American Council on Education and 69 state, territory, and Canadian Province departments and ministries of education. Each of the American state educational agencies participates in the GED testing program.

The following excerpt from a 1983 review by the GED Testing Service, summarizes the major purposes of the program:

- The GED testing program exists primarily to provide an opportunity for persons who have not graduated from high school to earn a high school level educational credential. This primary mission suggests that the GED Tests be developed so as to include the major and lasting outcome of a high school program of study.
- Mindful of the importance that examinees attach to the attainment of this credential, especially as an aid in obtaining employment and/or job advancement, the GED Tests should also include those *general* educational skills most highly valued by employers.
- Because it is hoped that GED examinees will be able to function successfully as adults in our society, the tests should also include those *general* educational skills that contribute to this end.
- Because the tests should serve beyond the primary credentialing function to document the level of educational skills and to attest to the examinees' degree of general educational development, the tests should measure a broad range of relevant educational skills ranging from basic through advanced.

Competency-based Diplomas

The third way available to adults seeking high school level skills and knowledge is less than 10 years old. It came about principally through the convergence of two projects. In 1971, the United States Office of Education gave funds to the University of Texas to conduct the four year Adult Performance Level Project (APL). In 1973, while this research was underway, the Syracuse University Research Corporation, in concert with the New York State Department of Education, obtained support from the Ford Foundation to develop an alternative high school diploma. The project sought to establish an adult high school diploma based on the life competencies needed to function in society.

The APL project was not specifically aimed at creating an alternative adult high school diploma. Its purpose was to identify the generic skills and knowledge required for adults to function in modern society. Its results were intended to begin to specify the goals and aims of the Adult Education Act in operational terms. These results, in turn, were designed to be useful to adult educators in developing an adult education system related to real-life needs. Curriculum materials, staff development programs, tests, and administrative systems could be checked or designed against these empirically identified requirements.

The projects shared results. The APL project identified 65 competencies or objectives in five knowledge areas: occupational, consumer, health, community resources, and government and law. In the meantime, the New York project identified 63 competencies required for an adult alternative diploma. New York added the two competencies identified by the APL project, and both rejoiced at the high degree of convergence of two projects using significantly different methologies.

The New York effort also developed an alternative high school diploma designed to recognize adult life experience and learning and to emphasize individual assessment. The program also emphasized independent learning by adults who use community resources as well as available adult education offerings.

In 1974, the Texas Educational Agency, which had been instrumental in administering the APL project, funded a curriculum project based on the APL results. It too sought to develop an alternative high school diploma. In this case, however, a more traditional classroom approach was used in which curriculum was designed to teach the objectives identified in the APL project.

Subsequent research indicated that the New York approach appealed to older adults with more life and community experience while the Texas model appealed to younger adults. These two approaches were both validated through the Joint Dissemination Review Panel of the U.S. Office of Education and incorporated into the National Diffusion Network. As a result, most other states now have competency-based alternative high school diploma programs. Rather than identify with one approach or the other, these programs tend to synthesize both the New York and Texas models in order to better meet the needs of a wide range of adults.

Where Adults Achieve a High School Education

The delivery of adult high school opportunities varies among the states. A majority of states use vocational and technical schools in their adult education programs in some manner. In Wisconsin, for example, the State Board of Vocational, Technical, and Adult Education (VTAE) is the sole agency responsible for administering and supervising the adult education program. Each VTAE district provides instruction for its population. Classes are offered in technical institutes, storefronts, community buildings, and at business and industry sites.

In North Carolina, the adult education program is administered through the North Carolina Community College System. Programs are offered in community colleges, technical colleges and institutes, as well as non-profit agencies and organizations. In other states such as Iowa, Oregon, and Washington, community colleges are the primary source for providing adult education, and they supervise outreach programs designed to make programs available in all areas of the state.

In many other states, local school districts are the primary or exclusive grantor of adult high school diplomas and equivalency certificates. Other states, such as Florida, also offer a state high school adult diploma based primarily on the GED test and supplemented by other requirements.

In 1979, amendments to the Adult Education Act re-emphasized outreach programs and flexible scheduling. A 1980 evaluation disclosed that 62 percent of all instructional programs were offered outside of elementary and secondary schools. Learning centers, storefronts, churches, community buildings and homes made up most of the out-of-school locations.

In metropolitan areas with populations of 150,000 or more, adult education programs support adult learning centers. These centers are located to provide easy access and offer individualized instruction and flexible scheduling. Nationwide, 25 percent of all adults in the Adult Education Program attend these centers. These centers frequently utilize a variety of funds from combined federal and state sources.

Accomplishments

The National Council of State Directors of Adult Education found that in 1982, 102,261 adults obtained a high school diploma and an additional 181,229 adults served by state programs passed the GED test. In the same year, the GED Testing Service reported that a total of 535,503 adults passed the GED—approximately 70 percent of those who took the test. Participants in the GED program ranged in age from 16 to 90. The average age was 25.

The Department of Education's Division of Adult Education Services reports that, in the 1982-83 school year, an additional 14,316 adults obtained alternative high school diplomas. Thus, a total of 652,080 adults earned a high school diploma or equivalency through one of the three available routes.

Conclusion

The demand for comprehensive high school adult education has increased significantly during the past 15 years as states have expanded programs to meet that demand. Three types of programs—the adult diploma, the GED, and the alternative adult diploma—provide different learning options for adults, although the largest number of adults prefer the GED. As alternative adult diploma programs become more available and better known, the number receiving diplomas in this manner can be expected to increase. Furthermore, the number of adults seeking a high school education should continue to grow throughout this decade because more than 52 million out-of-school adults lack a high school diploma, and the diploma is generally necessary to improve earnings and for self-development.

References

Adult Education Program Statistics, State-Administered Program, Fiscal Year 1981. Washington, D.C.: Division of Adult Education Services, U.S. Department of Education, June 1983.

An Assessment of the State-Administered Program of the Adult Education Act. Arlington, Va.: Development Associates, 1980.

Bureau of the Census. *Consumer Income: Characteristics of the Population Below the Poverty Level:* 1981. *Current Population Reports, Series P-60, No. 138.* Washington, D.C.: Government Printing Office, March 1983.

_____ *Persons in Poverty.* Series P-60. Washington, D.C.: Government Printing Office, 1983.

Bureau of Labor Statistics. *Labor Force Status and Educational Attainment, 1982 to 1983.* Washington, D.C.: Government Printing Office, August 1983.

FEDERAL TRAINING PROGRAMS

Thomas N. Daymont

In 1983, the Job Training Partnership Act (JTPA) replaced the Comprehensive Employment and Training Act (CETA) as the primary federal training program for adults. This new program provides job training for economically disadvantaged adults and youths and for dislocated workers. It is similar to CETA in that it authorizes a wide range of training options including classroom skills training, on-the-job training, remedial education, and customized job training. It also continues, and indeed expands, the decentralization of federal employment and training programs so that local officials have considerable flexibility in deciding upon the mix of training and other services. At the same time, the JTPA represents some important changes from CETA, including an emphasis on training rather than public service employment, a greater concern for program performance (as measured by job placements), and an expanded role for the states and for the private business sector.

Antecedents to the JTPA

The passage of the Manpower Development and Training Act (MDTA) in 1962 marked the beginning of a major, sustained federal effort to provide occupational training for adults. For the most part, previous federal efforts were limited to providing money to states to support vocational education. The MDTA emerged during the Cold War era. The aftershocks of the Sputnik scare were still being felt, and many Americans believed that it was vitally important to stay ahead of the Soviet Union in terms of technological development and automation.

From a training perspective, two main concerns of the Cold War period were:
- to upgrade the skill level of the labor force to develop and utilize the technological advances that were felt to be necessary for economic development and national security.
- to provide retraining for skilled workers displaced by automation.

The first concern was addressed by such new programs as the National Defense Education Act (1959), which provided incentives and opportunities to bright people to develop technological and scientific skills.

The MDTA was designed to accomplish the second goal. Indeed, in the beginning, the MDTA was quite narrowly focused on this goal, as evidenced by the fact that admission to training programs was restricted to unemployed heads of households with at least three years of work experience. Soon afterwards, however, the focus of the program was broadened to also provide education and training for the unskilled unemployed.

By the mid-1960's, the overall unemployment rate was on the decline, but it was not going down for most of those who were disadvantaged due to discrimination, inexperience, or a lack of basic skills. More generally, the civil rights movement and the concern for those in poverty led to a redirection of manpower programs during the Johnson Administration. A new goal for the MDTA was to help the most disadvantaged develop skills so that they could obtain jobs and break the cycle of poverty. In addition, a variety of new programs to target training to the disadvantaged were initiated, including the Neighborhood Youth Corps and the Job Corps for youths, the Work Incentive Program for Aid to Families of Dependent Children recipients, Operation Mainstream for older individuals, and the Adult Basic Education program.

The rising unemployment of the early 1970's led to a rethinking of manpower programs. The result of this reevaluation was the Comprehensive Employment and Training Act (CETA), which was passed in 1973. By the end of the 1970's, public service employment (PSE) was the major component of CETA in terms of level of expenditures and especially in terms of its public image. However, in the beginning, PSE was a relatively minor component. Moreover, CETA did not imply a significant change from previous programs in the types of training provided nor a change in targeted groups. Instead, it combined several elements of existing employment and training programs. For example, it focused on both institutional and on-the-job training (OJT) as did the MDTA. It also targeted services toward the disadvantaged as did the programs under the Economic Opportunity Act of 1964. In addition, it included a dose of PSE, as previously provided for in the Emergency Employment Act of 1971.

A key feature of CETA was decentralization and decategorization of the delivery system to shift the primary decision-making function concerning the service mix and target populations from the federal to the local governments. Under MDTA, Congress had appropriated money for specific categories of services and the United States Department of Labor administered the programs. Under Title I of CETA, monies were allocated to about 500 prime sponsors (usually local government administrative units) who were responsible for choosing the mix of services.

Despite these changes, and despite huge increases in the amount of money allocated to public service employment during the 1970's, unemployment failed to decline. By the beginning of the 1980's, public service employment had been thoroughly discredited in the eyes of the public. More generally, the public and many policymakers had become pessimistic about the effectiveness of almost any type of public sector employment program.

Job Training Partnership Act

In 1982, the Job Training Partnership Act (JTPA) was passed and by October, 1983, it had replaced CETA as the comprehensive federal employment and training program. Since it has been in place for a very short time, it is too early to tell just how JTPA will work out. However, we can identify some important differences between it and previous federal employment and training efforts, and this chapter provides some initial views of how it is being implemented. Important features of the new law include:

- An emphasis on training (no authorization for public service employment)
- A new dislocated worker program
- An expanded role for the private business sector
- An emphasis on performance standards
- An expanded role for state governments

Under the JTPA, no money is allocated for public service employment. The emphasis is on training. While total annual expenditures under the JTPA are much lower than under CETA, most of the reduction is accounted for by the discontinuation of public service employment; little reduction has occurred in the amount of money available for training. The two main parts of the JTPA which authorize training for adults are:

- Title IIA, which provides training and other services for economically disadvantaged adults and youths; and,
- Title III, which authorizes a new set of programs for dislocated workers.

Programs for Disadvantaged People

Title IIA authorizes a wide range of training service for economically disadvantaged workers including institutional skill training, on-the-job training, retraining for displaced workers, training for upgrading, advanced career training, literacy and bilingual training, education programs leading to a high school equivalency certificate, remedial education, basic skills training, and customized training conducted with an employer's commitment to hire individuals upon successful completion of the training. In addition to training, other authorized services include job search assistance, job counseling, outreach and dissemination activities to make people and employers aware of the training programs, education-to-work transition activities, employment generating activities (that are not substitutes for activities funded by other federal programs), and needs-based payments for participants.

Basically, the adult and youth job training programs under Title IIA are targeted toward the economically disadvantaged with eligibility criteria fairly similar to those under CETA. Participants must either: (1) have family incomes below the official federal poverty level or 70 percent of the lower living standard; or (2) be receiving welfare payments, food stamps, or certain other types of support. A "10 percent window" is provided whereby up to 10 percent of the participants do not have to be economically disadvantaged if they have encountered other barriers to employment (e.g., those with limited English language proficiency, displaced homemakers, school dropouts, teenage parents, handicapped people, older workers, veterans, offenders, alcoholics, addicts). Forty percent of Title IIA funds are required to be spent on youths age 21 and under.

A major complaint about CETA was that too much money was going to administration and support payments to participants and not enough to training. Under JTPA, 70 percent of Title IIA money has to be spent on training, with only 15 percent allowed for administration, and 15 percent for needs-based payments and support services. The constraints implied by these restrictions are eased somewhat by a liberal definition of training costs (which includes, for example, job search assistance, employer outreach, costs of developing OJT and customized job training, and employability assessment). Nevertheless, most local administrative units, called Service Delivery Areas (SDA's) under JTPA, feel considerable pressure to minimize administrative and participant support costs.

Dislocated Worker Programs

Title III of the JTPA authorizes federal funds for state and/or local programs to provide training and employment services to workers who have permanently lost their jobs due to plant closings and technological changes. A wide range of services are authorized, including training in job skills which are in demand, job search assistance, support services, and relocation assistance. As a result, Title III programs vary greatly in the types of services provided. One survey of early Title III projects by Westat, Inc. found that OJT was the most preferred strategy. Classroom training and job search were also commonly used strategies. In addition, counseling, customized training, and various types of support services were sometimes provided. Many Title III projects emphasize retraining through either OJT or classroom training. This, of course, reflects the fact that Title III participants already have work experience and general work skills, albeit often in specialized occupations that are no longer in demand. The Westat report also observed that the prevalence of OJT and customized training contracts with several large or expanding firms seems to reflect an economic development emphasis in many states.

Title III of the JTPA contains several features designed to overcome some of the problems encountered in dislocated worker programs. Previous studies have shown that a small proportion of dislocated workers have participated in training and retraining programs. A variety of factors appear to have contributed to this disinterest by dislocated workers. In part, the low participation rates for CETA programs resulted from the targeting of many of these programs to the economically disadvantaged. Despite their economic problems, few displaced workers had incomes low enough to qualify as economically disadvantaged. And while retraining programs under Title II-C of CETA did not have income eligibility standards, they did have other requirements that reduced their effectiveness in helping dislocated workers. For example, applicants for retraining often had to have a bona-fide notice of layoff within the last 6 months, even though it would often take displaced workers longer than that to begin looking for a new job and learn that training was necessary.

Restrictive and inflexible CETA rules can only be a part of the explanation for the low interest in training, however, since this phenomenon predates CETA. A basic reason seems to be a perception on the part of many displaced workers that training will not be helpful in obtaining a new job. The lack of job opportunities due to depressed local economic conditions often reinforces this view. For some displaced workers, the time until retirement is too short to realize a significant economic return on the training even if it should lead to employment. Indeed, one survey reported that many CETA prime sponsors believed that many of the dislocated workers who entered training programs did so not for the training but for the additional 26 weeks of Trade Adjustment Assistance benefits that they would receive.

In order to increase the participation rates and effectiveness of displaced worker programs, Title III of the JTPA provides the states with a great deal of flexibility in terms of who will be served and what services will be provided. Participants are not required to be economically disadvantaged. To be eligible, individuals must: (1) have been terminated or have received notice of termination from employment, be eligible for (or have exhausted) unemployment compensation and be unlikely to return to their previous industry or occupation; (2) have been terminated due to a plant closing; (3) be long-term unemployed with little chance of employment in a similar occupation near where they live; or (4), be unemployed older individuals with barriers to employment due to age. In addition, the states are given considerable discretion in operationalizing these criteria.

The JTPA also attempts to improve the coordination between retraining programs and the Unemployment Insurance (UI) system. The UI system is intended to provide income support to individuals who are able and available for work but cannot find a job. Participation in a training program usually implies that an individual is not available for work and this unavailability often conflicted with UI work test. To resolve this conflict, the JTPA stipulates that participants in training programs that lead to state-identified job opportunities are automatically in compliance with the UI work test. Since the states have broad discretion in identifying job opportunities and in designing Title III programs, they now have the flexibility to structure retraining programs so that receipt of UI benefits by participants is not contingent on their actively looking for work or accepting jobs referred by the employment service.

Expanded Role for Private Sector

The Job Training Partnership Act attempts to provide a more equal partnership between the public and private sector in planning and managing the job training effort through an expanded role of the Private Industry Councils (PIC's). The PICs were originally established by the 1978 amendments to CETA to increase private sector involvement in employment and training efforts. Although the precise functions of PICs varied from locality to locality, they typically provided advice to prime sponsors on such factors as the skill needs of area employers, and solicited employment and on-the-job training (OJT) positions and training resources from employers. In general, however, the PICs played a role secondary to local public officials and had a relatively minor influence on employment and training programs. The influence of the private sector was even less, since despite the name, most PICs under CETA included only a minority of representatives from private business. The JTPA requires, however, that a majority of PIC members must be from the private sector and that they should be top level executives in their companies. In addition, the PIC chair must be a private business representative. To promote a balanced partnership between the private and public sector, the JTPA stipulates that the PIC and local public officials must jointly decide most major policy issues such as the selection of the SDA program administrator and the job training plan and budget. Furthermore, the PIC has the authority and responsibility along with the local government to review, monitor, and evaluate the program.

Performance Standards

The JTPA also differs from CETA in that it emphasizes program performance standards and de-emphasizes regulatory compliance. For adult programs, performance is defined primarily in terms of placement in unsubsidized employment and cost effectiveness. The United States Department of Labor issued the following standards for adult programs for the transition from CETA to JTPA between October, 1983 and June, 1984:

- Job Placement Rate   58%
- Cost per Entered Employment $5,900
- Average Wage at Placement $4.90 per hour
- Job Placement Rate for Welfare Recipients   41%

Incentives built into the law include a stipulation that the governor of the state is required to reorganize any SDA that fails to meet performance standards for two consecutive years. In addition, 6 percent of Title IIA funds are reserved as incentive funds for the governor to distribute to SDAs which exceed performance standards.

It was recognized, however, that performance may be low in the beginning until local agencies learn to adjust to the new law. Thus, for example, SDAs are not to be penalized for non-attainment of performance standards during the transition year. In addition, some states have not yet established formulas to distribute the incentive funds to the SDAs. It is not yet clear to what degree the states will use their reorganization authority and incentive money to bring pressure to bear on the SDAs to increase their performance.

The JTPA also encourages job placement by providing incentives for SDAs to make contracts with training program operators that are based on a fixed unit price and stipulate that full payment will be made only when the training is completed and the participant is placed in an unsubsidized job at no less than the wage specified in the agreement. Such performance-based contracts are attractive to the SDAs since all costs associated with these contracts can be charged to training, thus easing the constraint on the SDAs mentioned above that at least 70 percent of Title IIA funds must be spent on training and not more than 30 percent for administration and support services.

Even though the JTPA has been operating for only a short time, there is little doubt that most SDAs are responding to the philosophy and intent of the law (frequently expressed through private sector PIC representatives), the emerging and potential pressures from the states, and the financial incentives to write performance-based contracts by placing a greater emphasis on performance as measured by placement in unsubsidized employment and cost per placements. While meaningful figures are not available at this time, it can be confidently stated that as they become available, the numbers will indicate that the performance levels of JTPA training programs will be significantly higher than for previous CETA training programs. However, intense debate over the explanation for the increase in measured performance can also be anticipated.

Some will argue that improvements in measured performance are primarily due to improvements in the service delivery system and in the training programs themselves under JTPA. That is, the JTPA provides the program operators with greater incentives, as well as pressure, to be more effective in raising the skill level of participants to the point where they become employable and in locating job openings. In addition, the SDAs have also been stimulated to provide more relevant training, an effort that has been enhanced by the more prominent role of the business sector PIC members and their knowledge of the skills needed in the local economy.

Others will argue that the improved performance is more apparent than real since the JTPA puts pressure on program operators to find ways to improve measured performance that do not necessarily imply improved training. For example, it appears that cost per placement performance standards have led some SDAs and program operators to emphasize short-term training at the expense of long-term training that is more costly. These placement standards also encourage SDAs and program operators to arrange with employers to finance OJT for existing and future job openings. Of course, an important question is the degree to which this approach amounts to the subsidization of training that the employer would have undertaken anyway.

A shift toward more short-term training implies a shift toward serving those who are already fairly close to being job ready and thus can take advantage of short-term training. More generally, the emphasis on performance standards seems to have led many SDAs to focus training efforts, either explicitly or implicitly, on the most qualified members of the eligible population. Previous experience has suggested that many individuals with basic skill deficiences are simply unable to take advantage of skills training.

Conclusions

The JTPA has made several important changes in the federal adult job training effort. Chief among these changes are: (1) an emphasis on training; (2) a new dislocated worker program; (3) an emphasis on performance standards; and, (4) an expanded role for the states and, especially, the private sector. Although the JTPA has been operating for only a relatively short time and accurate data are not yet available, early experiences suggest that program administrators and program operators have responded to these changes in such a way that measured performance (e.g., job placement rates) has improved relative to CETA. What is much less clear is whether these improvements in measured performance have resulted from better training, different types of training, changing economic and demographic conditions, and/or a focus on serving the most qualified of the eligible population.

References

Barth, M. and F. Resiner. *The Role of CETA in Providing Services to Non-Disadvantaged Displaced Workers*. Washington, D.C.: ICF, Inc., 1981.

Gordus, J., P. Jarley, and L. Ferman, *Plant Closings and Economic Dislocation*. Kalamazoo, Mich.: The W.E. Upjohn Institute for Employment Research.

Turnage, W.M., Cook, R.F., and R.J. *The Organization of Title III of the Job Training Partnership Act in Fifty States*. Rockville, Md., Westat, Inc. 1984.

SECTION III

REACHING OUT TO ADULT LEARNERS

Like every other postsecondary education endeavor in the United States, adult vocational education has evolved to serve special interests and needs. Consequently, there is no overall vocational education structure that sets policy for vocational education and directs operations. Similarly, there is not a single adult population, a captured audience, as there is with high school students going on to college. This diversity in organization and in the adult student population means that vocational educators must be creative in reaching out to adult learners and in organizing to develop effective programs.

This section focuses on what can be done and what should be done to promote better efforts at recruitment and retention of adult learners, in curriculum development, and in organizational structure.

Mary Ellen Kiss and Margaret A. Taibi describe a process model for assessment and counseling services for adult learners that addresses adults' particular concerns. This model is used at their community college.

Yvonne Ferguson examines the options open to adult vocational educators in recruiting adults into programs and describes the efforts that must be made to retain them once they are enrolled. She offers examples of successful programs in recruitment and retention.

Although vocational educators have always prepared their students for the world of work, David L. Goetsch observes that new approaches must be taken if students are to be adequately trained for the constantly changing workplace. He discusses curriculum proposals and new delivery systems, and recommends new cooperative efforts between private industry and vocational education to ensure that training meets market demands.

Alan B. Knox argues that adult education agencies should collaborate when collaboration is likely to improve the delivery of services to adult learners. He offers guidelines to follow in determining whether to launch a collaborative effort.

Clearly, adult vocational education's responsibilities are complex: vocational educators must constantly look in two directions: to the needs of the adult student and to the needs of the labor market. This section suggests how some of these responsibilities may be met.

SUPPORT SERVICES FOR ADULT LEARNERS

Mary Ellen Kiss and Margaret A. Taibi

This chapter presents a model of assessment and support services that has been developed to meet the unique needs of adults. The first section provides a description of the target populations for whom the model was developed. The second section presents the model and describes the process. The third section addresses the range of support systems needed to facilitate the job training/retraining process.

Adult Workers

Adult workers seeking training and retraining opportunities typically have short-term goals. They are concerned with getting the help they need to solve their immediate problem, whether it is clarification or redefinition of a career direction, identification of appropriate training opportunities, or placement. They tend to be highly motivated and impatient with procedures and programs that do not appear to be moving them toward their goal. The probability of successfully engaging adults in training programs can be increased if the program content and procedures are continually evaluated from a user perspective.

A target population(s) for services must be identified before assessment and counseling services can be developed, and an effective marketing effort can be made.

A number of categories of individuals have been identified as needing training or retraining so that they may enter or re-enter the workforce. Among these are the unemployed, under-employed, women, mid-career changers, and those with disabilities. In recognition of the problems confronting these groups of people, both the federal and state governments have passed legislation to help these groups. The following discussion will describe these classes of people and their unique needs.

Unemployed Workers
There are two primary groups within this category: those who possess skills and talents that can be utilized in the current job market and those whose skills are

obsolete. It is on the latter class of people, the dislocated worker, that this chapter and the proposed model focuses.

According to William H. Kohlberg, "Dislocated workers are identified as people who are unemployed and unlikely to return to their previous occupations because their skills have become obsolete or because of structural changes in the smokestack industries. The typical dislocated worker is male, 40 years old or older, a union member, and the head of a household. Although he usually has no more than a high school education, he has been able to maintain a middle-class salary status for most of his working life."

Title III of the Job Training Partnership Act (JTPA) of 1982 provides separate funding to states for the purpose of resolving the problems of structural unemployment. The House's draft version of the reauthorization for the Vocational Education Act, as of March 1984, also includes a separate entitlement for the dislocated worker. In states where industrial displacement has been particularly high, state monies have been appropriated for training and retraining.

Many of the affected industries have also formulated comprehensive policies to address the problem of dislocation. There is a recurring theme in these policies—the partnership concept. It is recognized that the problems of dislocation from the individual worker, the local economic system and industry are complex and require a commitment from multiple segments of the community. Some of the more critical components of the partnership concept will be addressed in the section on support systems.

Under-employed Workers

The Office of Management and Budget (OMB) defines an under-employed person as one whose family income does not exceed 70 percent of the Lower Living Standard established by the OMB, or is a member of a family receiving public assistance, including individuals who are recipients of Aid to Families of Dependent Children (AFDC). These people tend to be employed in dead-end, entry-level jobs or in the migrant labor market. They have unstable patterns of employment, tend to be uncommitted to work, and do not have a career identity.

Women

Two categories of women seeking employment present special challenges to vocational educators: (1) the re-entry woman; and (2), the displaced homemaker. The re-entry woman is one who enters or re-enters the workforce after a period of childbearing and/or childrearing. She may fall into one of several categories:

- Returns to work to maintain or increase the family's standard of living. In some cases, the additional income is "nice" to have. In others, the income is necessary to maintain at least a subsistence level of living;

- Returns to a career that was interrupted by childbearing;
- Enters the labor market as a new entrant for self- fulfillment and/or self-actualization;
- Enters or re-enters a former or new career because she must be self-supporting. In this category are those women who have been widowed or divorced or whose spouse is unable to or does not work. Depending on the family income level, and other financial criteria, women in this category could be identified as displaced homemakers.

A woman is considered a displaced homemaker if she:

- Has not worked in the labor force for a substantial number of years, but has worked in the home providing unpaid services for family members during those years; and
- Has been dependent on public assistance or on the income of another family member but is no longer supported by that income; or, is receiving public assistance on account of dependent children in the home, but that assistance will soon be terminated; and
- Is unemployed or under-employed and is experiencing difficulty in obtaining or upgrading employment.

The displaced homemaker is also defined under the Vocational Education Amendments of 1976 as male or female adults who are:

- Persons who have only been homemakers but who now, because of dissolution of marriage, must seek employment;
- Single heads of households;
- Homemakers and part-time workers seeking full-time jobs;
- Women and men in traditional jobs seeking employment in non-traditional areas.

It should be noted that a formal definition of displaced homemaker is not included in the JTPA legislation. The designers of the legislation felt that the economic criteria and the 10 percent window for economically ineligible persons sufficiently included service potential to displaced homemakers.

Mid-Career Changers

Three classes of people are contained in this category. These include mid-career changers, older workers, pre-retirees, and retirees. Only the mid-career changer will be addressed here. Applying a well-formulated definition to this population is difficult. A review of the literature yielded numerous characteristics of and motivations for mid-career changes.

The midlife career changers discussed here are those persons who need to define direction and/or acquire new worker behaviors and skills. Mid-life career changers may need as much support as those in other categories.

Disabled Persons

The federal government defines a disabled person as one who has a physical or mental impairment that substantially limits one or more major life activities, has a record of such an impairment, or is regarded as having such an impairment.

The individual who becomes disabled after entering a career track or occupation may be faced with similar career choice dilemmas as the dislocated worker, displaced homemaker and mid-career changer. Generally, the disability is unanticipated. Where job restructuring is not a viable option, the individual may be faced with a series of complex readjustments.

The causes and extent of disabilities in adults are diverse and differentially affect the responses that the individual has to career/occupational change. Support systems needed to facilitate labor market re-entry will vary considerably among individuals.

The Career Assessment and Planning Program

The process for assessment and counseling presented here is intended to provide flexible and comprehensive programmatic services to adults and to minimize certain difficulties that educators and counselors encounter. This model is used in Prince George's Community College (Prince George's County, Maryland). Often, adults' need for assessment, counseling and training differs from their perception of what their needs are. Many adults do not understand the difference between the short-term goal of getting a job and the long-term process goal of career planning. Often, they expect career counselors to give them a test to reveal "what they are good at" and to indicate the single job that will assure them success and job satisfaction. This lack of sophistication regarding career planning cuts across all socioeconomic levels, ages and racial groups. Even many professionals involved in vocational training programs fall into the "test 'em and tell 'em" trap or the equally dangerous attitude that there is no value in objective assessment.

Clearly, the trend in career counseling is away from objective assessment and toward teaching adults the career decision-making process so they can make satisfying career choices now and in the future. Any successful program for vocational training must emphasize the career decision-making process and make both objective and self assessments appropriate to the population served a critical element in the program as well.

Establishing a Climate for Service

First impressions count! Social scientists have shown that environmental conditions influence behavior; such variables as space, color, lighting, furniture arrangement, have a profound impact on behavior. Businesses have used this awareness successfully to influence consumer behavior.

Educational institutions need to be equally aware that they create an atmosphere for service through the character of the physical setting, the verbal and non-verbal behavior of the staff, and the procedures that are followed. Adults react to all of these factors and make decisions about the credibility of the program and the likelihood of benefits from participation.

Therefore, the physical setting should be consistent with the intent of the program and appropriate to the clientele served. The selection and arrangement of furnishings as well as use of color in the office and classrooms should be carefully considered so the client will feel welcomed and encouraged to use the facilities. A well-planned physical environment can make the client more relaxed, which will help support the learning process and increase client identification with the program.

Staff behavior also has a significant impact on establishing a positive climate for service. Human relations skills are important for all staff. An insensitive staff member can easily and unknowingly discourage an adult from using services that may be badly needed. Indeed, the behavior of the receptionist or secretary may impact greatly on the predisposition of students to enter the program and, further, on the attitude of students while in the program. Verbal and non-verbal behavior communicates the real level of staff concern about the adult learner. The staff member who keeps clients waiting while they finish a personal call, clearly engages in office gossip, or simply never establishes eye contact when talking to the client sends a clear message that the client is not really considered worthy of the staff person's time.

In situations where staff differ significantly from the population to be served in race, sex, age, or socioeconomic levels, staff must be particularly sensitive to client expectations. Clients may arrive anticipating staff reactions of indifference or hostility. Staff need to be aware of the potential misunderstandings and interact in such a way that will dispel these preconceptions and communicate their commitment to the adult learner.

When developing administrative procedures, staff need to be careful that they do not impose unnecessary barriers to the use of the program. While a certain amount of information is necessary to engage learners with a program, the staff should make the process as efficient as possible for the client. Asking for the same information on multiple forms or requiring the individual to shuffle papers from one office to another may be efficient for the organization, but from the perspective of the adult who may be giving up time on the job, it is wasted effort and another example of institutional insensitivity. Many programs require certification for eligibility and, again, it is important to identify all the information that will be required and find the most efficient procedure from the client's perspective for collecting this information.

The Client-Counselor Conference
The initial contact between the adult learner and the counselor should focus on understanding the client's perception of self as a worker. Counselors discuss the career areas of interest to the client, specific skills and knowledge that relate to interest areas, and relevant work experiences. In particular, counselors probe to find the client's degree of commitment to a particular occupational area, the clarity and accuracy of training and career goals, and evidence of planning in the career decisionmaking process.

This dialogue may invalidate the client's decisions about career direction. In many instances, however, the discussion may reveal that the individual has not adequately assessed abilities and interests to identify appropriate occupational areas, or has not carefully considered available options. The individual may have made too hasty a decision.

This initial conference is a first step in heightening awareness of the distinction between a career and a job, and learning the steps in the career planning process. At the end of the initial session, client and counselor should reach agreement on the client's subsequent steps. The counselor should stress that the assessments involved will provide information for decisions about the training program.

The initial session identifies two groups of clients: those committed to a clearly defined career objective (decided) and those who either are not committed to a specific objective or who show evidence of insufficient career decision-making efforts (undecided). Figure 1 shows the sequence of activities for each of these groups.

In all assessment phases, the counselor uses an integrative testing approach. The client is actively involved in identification of appropriate tests. Test results are discussed without technical jargon. The counselor uses the test information to react to client statements, to initiate new areas for discussion, and to assist the client's testing of the congruence between self-assessments and external measures. Note that in Assessment Phase I both groups are assessed for academic achievement and learning style. The achievement testing will encompass both global measures as well as career and occupation-specific measures when possible. Results are discussed with the client to determine placement in the training program or referral to Assessment Phase 2.

If clients decide on a particular occupational area but have insufficient academic skills to begin its training program, more in-depth assessment will provide them and their counselor with the information needed to plan a training program. Aptitude and interest assessments are necessary in order to establish that clients' preferred career direction is consistent with their aptitudes and interest areas. When clients and counselors review the results, the clients may very well decide that they wish to consider other career alternatives and then they would be placed in the career decision-making program for the undecided students. If the clients still maintain interest in the initial career area, an additional opportunity to test

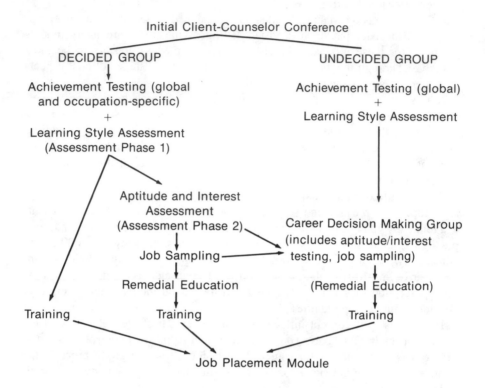

Figure 1. Career assessment and planning model at Prince George's Community College, Largo, Maryland.

the appropriateness of choice should be provided through job sampling. This allows clients to test the accuracy of their understanding of the occupation and affirm their choice. If the clients remain strongly committed to an occupation after exploring the real work situation, show the appropriate vocational interests, and have the requisite aptitudes, the clients can be confident that the investment of time in both remediation of basic academic skills and in training will be worthwhile.

For some clients, the job sampling will reveal that they had an inadequate understanding of the occupation and need to explore other alternatives. These individuals should be referred to the Career Decision Making workshop.

Career Decision Making Workshop

The Career Decision Making Workshop is designed to facilitate career exploration and decisionmaking in a group setting. While there are many models available for these groups, a highly experiential process appears to be most effective. Through this process, both the intellectual and the emotional aspects of career decisionmaking are addressed.

Adults can be led through the steps of career decisionmaking in a very intellectual and dispassionate manner, but such an approach is not sufficient considering the predictable crises that adults face. It is equally important to address the emotional component of career decisionmaking. Individuals may exclude occupations from consideration because they appear incompatible with their perceptions of self.

Linda Gottfredson has studied the effect on occupational choice of such factors as occupational prestige and sex-role typing of an occupation. She found that, at a relatively young age, individuals make a determination about an occupation's prestige level and its compatiblity with their sex-role. They are unlikely to consider any occupation that does not seem compatible. Many individuals unnecessarily limit career alternatives and need counselor assistance to see how their perception of self might be modified to expand their career options and consider training opportunities.

Individuals' self concept influences their perception of their ability to affect what happens in their lives. Too often, they feel helpless to control events and give others responsibility for career/life decisions. Using a group process, the counselor can help individuals become self-directed and self-empowered. Individuals can become more confident that they can make effective career/life decisions that will be satisfying and successful. Without this awareness, individuals will drift, allowing external forces to determine their career and will be on a course that involves job frustration or constant training and retraining.

A variety of assessment activities should be included in the workshop and the program should be flexible enough to allow differential assessment. Assessment activities for mid-life professional career changers are quite different from those appropriate for minimally skilled adults. Similarly, while the process of career decision-making cuts across occupational areas and levels, the types of resources necessary to support career exploration do differ depending on the type of population served.

Clients should leave the career workshop with a clear career direction and decision about the appropriate training program. They can enter remedial education activities and the training program, confident that the training will lead them toward a satisfying career.

They should also be aware that they have completed only the first phase of the career planning process. Implementation of their career plan requires completion of training, successful use of job search strategies, and satisfactory work adjustment. These topics can be covered in a Placement Module which can begin during the later phases of training. This Placement Module moves the individual from a global definition of career to a focused job search. Ancillary workshops can address work adjustment issues appropriate to the client population.

The Placement Module is intended to help clients understand their work style preferences and work values and needs so that the job search can be focused. Individuals often do not verbalize these preferences and needs, yet these factors affect job satisfaction. By identifying them prior to the job search, clients increase the likelihood of securing a job consistent with their goals and interests. Most adults need assistance in application and resume preparation, interviewing skills and job-hunting techniques. A variety of materials, and techniques are available to help develop skills in these areas.

Support Systems

In order for the process model described here to be responsive to the multiplicity of adult needs, a system of support services is essential. Though many of the support services listed below have been included in more traditional models, a number of them are less often considered and made available.

The support system presented in this chapter has two components. The first component includes support services directly related to the process model. These are programmatic services. The second component includes a number of ancillary services considered essential for adult workers.

Programmatic Services. There are three elements included in programmatic services: the Career Resource Center, the Job Placement Service and the Seminar Series. Some components of these services are currently in place at the College, while others are being developed and refined.

The Career Resource Center. A wide range of career guidance occupational information sources, and career related assessment tools need to be made available to the adult learner. The scope and type of resources utilized are defined by adult learners' needs and levels. Types of resources that should be made available include:

• computer mediated career guidance information systems such as DIS-COVER, SIGI and COIN;

- localized job listing information;
- multi-level print and non-print career and occupational training materials;
- paper and pencil assessments including life style, value clarification, learning style, occupational interest and aptitude, and achievement tests; and,
- performance based assessments such as commercial and locally developed work samples, APTICOM and MESA.

These resources should be used in a complementary, integrated way, focusing on continual self-assessment and definition of the range of options open to each individual. The services of the center should also be made available to other adult-oriented programs such as assessment of prior learning, job placement service, and business outreach.

The Job Placement Service. A second element of programmatic services is a job placement service. This service should be considered as complementary to the Career Resource Center. Three primary functions of this service are:

- maintaining and accessing local job listing information through internally developed business identification/tracking systems and external sources such as Job Service Employment Security Administration;
- utilizing the tracking system, contacting the work environment and analyzing job/worker requirements. Computerization of this information facilitates job to person matches. The applicant/student information is developed as part of the placement module previously described;
- providing follow-up services. These are considered essential for both the adult worker and as a program/service evaluation tool. Utilization of a computerized tracking system allows flexible scheduling of follow-up services. Follow-up services should be determined according to the needs of the adult worker. Initial follow-up may occur weekly, bi-weekly, monthly or quarterly. All program participants should be followed semi- annually and annually for the first year and annually every year thereafter for five years. Follow-up services may be conducted through on-site visits, individual counseling sessions, phone contact and/or surveys.

The Seminar Series. A number of related seminars, workshops, and conferences should be offered on an on-going basis. The adult learner/worker should be able to sign up for these programs at any time in the sequence of the program model, during training and while employed. These seminars should be offered at times convenient to the adult student. Among the topics to be included in this series are single parenting, financial planning, accessing community re-sources, work place conflicts, career image building, and time management.

The seminar series is most easily coordinated through the Career Resource Center. Seminar notifications should be sent to all individuals who have participated in the program as well as to selected organizations and agencies in the community at large.

Ancillary Services

While programmatic services are vital to the successful adjustment of the adult entrant or re-entrant to work, other services may be necessary to eliminate the barriers to training and placement. Among these services are day care, needs-based payment, transportation and assistance in accessing information about the community.

Child care is often cited as the most common barrier to successful work adjustment for women. Availability, location, quality of care and cost are common concerns and often present insurmountable obstacles to the woman wishing to upgrade her skills and to secure satisfying employment. A Center for Adult Learners or a Women's Center may serve as a catalyst for moving the community at large in becoming more responsive to the need for this type of service. Babysitting services, such as those made available by businesses, may be an interim solution. Church or YMCA sponsored child care programs may offer alternative options. Flexible and adaptive scheduling is another mechanism for encouraging participation by persons with children.

Needs-based payments are another factor. Often, program participation requires an individual to terminate supplementary income sources. Additionally, the cost of transportation, child care, purchase of appropriate clothing and other costs associated with training and initial employment can be prohibitive. JTPA eligible clients, depending on the priorities established by the Service Delivery Area, may be entitled to support payments. Other mechanisms that may be used include scholarships from community-based organizations, an institution's financial aid office, special benefits provided to the disabled and to veterans, and union programs.

Transportation is an issue that often eludes solution. Rural and suburban residents are often confronted with the unavailability of public transportation or exceedingly lengthy commuting times. If economic disadvantages or a disability compounds the situation, private transportation, such as automobile, may also be out of the question.

Often, there are alternative community resources that can be tapped. These may include coordinating efforts with senior citizen programs, services for the handicapped and public and/or private school transportation systems. Specially funded programs may include vans or other transportation options. Civic organizations can also be enlisted to assist with this problem. In some cases, a civic organization may donate a van or bus to the program, or make arrangements for door to door service on an as needed basis.

Referral services must also be an integral part of the ancillary service system. Updated sources for child care, financial assistance, transportation assistance and other resources should be included. A help line that provides information about campus and community services could be a viable tool in assisting the entering or re-entering adult to acquire "need to know right now" information. Staff could be available to provide more in-depth information on a scheduled basis.

This support service system may have many variations and options depending on who is the primary provider of adult occupational services and the extent to which funding is available. In any case, the program and services must be designed in such a way as to minimize traditional barriers and to facilitate the career/vocational process.

Conclusion

All adults, regardless of ability level and degree of career decisiveness, possess a wealth of experiences upon which program staff can draw. While the ultimate training and placement goals are important, the process of career/occupational selection is a priority.

The model presented here builds a support system that begins upon initial contact through the placement and follow-up processes. The Career Resource Center could as easily be called an Adult Service Center. The resources of this center are designed to be available on an on-going basis. The unique needs of each adult served are taken into account at each step of the process. The strength of this model is its flexibility and ability to draw upon all resources available— both within the community college structure and externally, in the community at large.

References

Benjamin, Libby and Walz, Garry. *Enhancing the Adult Experience: Counseling Approaches and Activities*. Ann Arbor, MI: ERIC/CAPS, 1982.

Borchard, David C., Kelly, John J., and Weaver, Nancy Pat K. *Your Career: Choices, Chances, Changes*, 2nd Edition. Dubuque, Iowa: Kendall/Hunt, 1982.

Briggs, James I. "Career/Life Planning in Groups." In Montross, David H. and Shinkman, Christopher J. (eds.) *Career Development in the 1980's*. Springfield, IL: Charles C. Thomas, Publisher, 1981.

Comprehensive Employment and Training Act, 1979, Section 301 (b)(1)(A) 20 CFR 675.4.

Crites, John O. "Integrative Test Interpretation." In Montross, David H. and Shinkman, Christopher J. (eds.) *Career Development in the 1980's*. Springfield, IL: Charles C. Thomas, Publisher, 1981.

Entine, A. "Counseling for Mid-life and Beyond," *Vocational Guidance Quarterly*. 25 (June 1977):332-336.

George, Calvin, Knight, Robert, and Wurzburg, Gregory. *Guide to the Transition from the Comprehensive Employment* and *Training Act to the Job Training Partnership Act*. Washington, DC: National Association of Private Industry Councils and Youthwork, 1982.

Gottfredson, Linda. "Circumscription and Compromise: A developmental theory of occupational aspirations. *Journal of Counseling Psychology Monograph*, (28), 1981:545-579.

Herr, Edwin and Cramer, Stanley. *Career Guidance Through the Life- Span*. Boston: Little, Brown, 1979.

Kohlberg, William H. (Ed), *The Dislocated Worker*. Washington, DC: Seven Locks Press, 1983.

Nondiscrimination on Basis of Handicap, *Federal Register*, Vol. 42 No. 86, May 1977.

Vocational Education Act of 1963, as amended. P.L. 94-482.

Walz, Garry R. and Benjamin, Libby. *Programs and Practices in Adult Counseling*. Ann Arbor, MI: ERIC/CAPS, 1981.

RECRUITMENT AND RETENTION OF ADULT LEARNERS

Yvonne Ferguson

All vocational educators have an important role to play in the recruitment and retention of adult students. They must cooperate in talking to adults about the opportunities vocational education can provide. Such a cooperative effort and a common philosophy among the county or district administrative staff, vocational administrative staff, adult education staff and the classroom teacher are real assets in the recruitment and retention of adult students. Their efforts may be reflected in administrative staff budget decisions, adult coordinators' extra effort to see that a specific strategy is carried out, or teachers' detailed lesson planning.

Recruitment

General marketing principles are also important in recruitment. The basic Ps of product, price, place, promotion, and people must be considered. Successful recruitment also includes planning, control, implementation, and evaluation. A sound plan is essential to the successful marketing of adult vocational programs. This plan needs to be comprehensive and based on the target audience. Programs and services offered should be planned to satisfy specific needs and wants. Before promotion techniques are decided upon, the market audience should be analyzed. It may be segmented in a number of ways: geographic, demographic, psychographic or behavioristic.

The recruitment plan is then developed based on this information. Personalize the promotion as much as possible and focus the message on the needs of the target audience. Benefits should be stressed. It is important that the potential student visualize the benefits that will result from participation in the vocational program.

The key to success in promotion is effective communication. To be effective in communicating with the public, educators must choose their medium carefully; place the message in the right context; and, carefully avoid conflict with audience biases.

Successful Techniques

Since recruitment is an on-going process, the techniques used may change as changes occur in lifestyles, available technology, and perceived needs of the target population. Very few successful recruitment programs rely on only one method; the utilization of a variety of techniques is usually more effective. When developing the recruitment plan, many methods should be explored. For organizational purposes, the techniques discussed here are divided into three categories: (1) printed media; (2) broadcast media; and, (3) people media.

Printed Media

The printed word is the old standby of adult recruitment. A few years ago, a brief advertisement in the local newspaper was all that was required to fill a class in many localities. This technique is still successful in some areas, but more and more educators have turned to other means to reach the adult student effectively. Some of the most common printed recruitment materials include newspaper articles and ads, brochures and handouts, flyers, posters, and direct mail. Distribution and placement are extremely important in this medium.

Poster. Since posters only hold the reader's attention for a few seconds, they must be simple, memorable, and clearly identified. These materials do not explain, elaborate, justify or clarify. Instead, they announce; they grab attention; they declare basic facts and, it is hoped, they do two other crucial things. First, they cause the reader to have positive feelings. Secondly, they cause the reader to remember the entity which sponsored the message so someone else doesn't get the credit. Posters should capture the passer-by's attention; identify the sponsor; and, give the basic message at a glance.

There are drawbacks. Posters have a limited readership and may generate a low-budget, non-professional image.

Flyers. Flyers should be simple. The design and copy should be clean and straightforward. This technique is low cost, and its impact is minimal. Knowledge of the target population helps determine the most effective method of distribution. While some adult coordinators would find it effective to send flyers home through elementary students to reach a particular audience, others might find it more effective to have the flyers stuffed in grocery bags at the check out counter of the local grocery store.

Direct Mail. Direct mailing allows for very selective contacts. It permits zeroing in on specific individuals who have been identified as potential recruits. The computerized equipment on the market today provides the opportunity to personalize messages and salutations. Even though there is a high unit cost per addressee, and sometimes problems with delivery by the postal service, this method has had some success in recruitment efforts.

Computer. As the microcomputer becomes commonplace and the telephone modem is used throughout an area, the potential for adult recruitment through the bulletin board, mail by computer, etc., will be utilized by the creative recruiter.

Newspapers. Newspaper coverage is a standard recruitment technique. Advertisements can be keyed to certain sections of the paper that have a specific focus and reach a specific audience. Much detail can be presented and the reader can clip information for further reference. However, newspapers are generally discarded, and those reading them often do so hastily and superficially. The percentage of adults reading newspapers regularly has declined in the last few years.

Broadcast Media

Radio. Radio announcements and recorded Public Service Announcements can be very powerful if they are done well. Production costs are relatively inexpensive and very little lead time is required for airing. Radio is very flexible and reaches large audiences, although it may be difficult to get announcements placed on the air.

Television. Television is an extremley powerful media. It reaches the masses and promotes a prestigious image. However, television production requires professional preparation. Television is costly, and air time is difficult to get.

People Media

Presentations. Presentations at clubs, committees, agency meetings, open houses, or any other gathering allow good, personal, two-way communication. They require a lot of effort, but the pay-off may be well worth the effort if the target group is reached effectively.

Personal Contact. Personal contact is the most effective type of communication. One-on-one, whether it be in person or by telephone allows for two way communication. The prospective student's response is immediately evident. The feedback may help the recruiter improve strategies used in dealing with others. This method of recruitment is extremely time-consuming, and time restraints may prevent its use.

Adults' Special Needs

Adults have some special needs that affect the techniques chosen for marketing adult programs. As a recruitment plan segments the population into target audience, factors beyond geography and social groupings should also be considered.

Older students are different from those who have recently graduated from high school. They are generally highly motivated, more mature in judgment and wiser because of their life experiences. Many students are married with family responsibilities; others are divorced and seeking the means to support their children.

They may also have unresolved fears, conflicts and needs which hinder learning. The older student is often fearful of failure and ability to learn. The student who took math and science years ago has forgotten many facts or may never have mastered the basic skills.

Older women may have some special problems dealing with the image they developed as a child, an image that tells them that it is not an acceptable feminine role to be too intellectual or have a higher career status than the male.

The displaced worker may not only have financial problems but some very keen personal conflicts that result from displacement. Reaching this group calls for great tact and understanding.

Some adults may have individual needs for personal growth and development that can be satisfied by vocational education. These needs can be difficult to identify yet are very important to the recruitment process.

Unemployment has given rise to some very basic financial needs in recruitment activities. It is especially important not to oversell or undersell programs to adults with financial needs.

Employers may also seek out vocational education. Some training may provide opportunities for advancement on the job, while other training may be required by employers. It is relatively easy to focus on these needs when planning promotional strategies.

Successful Recruitment

There have been many successful marketing and recruitment campaigns that have resulted in increased enrollment in adult courses. Some examples follow.

- In Monongalia County, West Virginia, adult coordinators working with a small budget have put together an effective recruitment effort. Long range planning is based on a careful analysis of target groups. The coordinators identify the habits of potential adults in the various geographic locations of the county. They look for things such as economic status, educational status, recreational choices, restaurant choices, service station choices, and shopping preferences. Next, they design strategies to reach potential students using as many methods of advertising as possible. They set up a schedule that includes two or three months pre-advertising and seven weeks actual recruitment followed by implementation and evaluation.
- In one district in West Virginia, instructors of part-time adult classes are paid a percentage of the tuition, and are responsible for recruitment of students for their individual program. The main recruitment tool appears to

be personal contacts. The adult enrollment has risen, at least in the initial stages, using this approach.

- One regional coordinator has taken the time to set up a series of meeting with several agencies and organizations that deal with the adult population. Some of the agencies include: Employment Security, Department of Welfare, Red Cross, Rehabilitation, and Social Service Interagency Council. As communications have improved and each group understands what the other agencies and organizations do, a referral service has evolved. Persons in need of vocational education are referred to the local vocational programs. This type of recruitment is on-going.
- New programs that meet needs or programs that follow current trends need very little in recruitment efforts. For example, classes in the use of microcomputers have been filled very quickly because it is the "in" thing. The work and family program in Minnesota also fits in this category. As industry recognizes the correlation between productivity and family, offering training becomes a positive option for industry rather than a massive recruitment activity for vocational education.
- New programs in new locations, such as "The Training Place" at the Charleston, West Virginia, Town Center Mall, provide unique programs in a unique setting and utilize recruitment methods in a different way. This program allows potential students to shop for classes as they would shop for other products, and it meets employment training needs of businesses within the mall.

All the successful recruitment programs I have observed have one thing in common—an enthusiastic and dedicated coordinator, who believes in what is being offered and is willing to put in the extra hours to make sure potential students have the opportunity to become a part of the program.

Reaching adults through creative recruitment pays off in many localities. A short message printed by computer on the local bank statement reaches many; invitations for husbands and children to a family night will help them understand that it's okay for the wife of a laid-off miner to return to school. Recruitment is the link between programs and people.

Retention of Adult Students

There are many factors that affect retention of students in adult programs. To reduce the drop-out rate or to encourage returning for additional training, three major areas must receive consideration: placement in program, program quality, and related services.

Placement in Program
It is extremely important to place adult students in the vocational program for which they have the ability and aptitude necessary for successful program completion and job placement. Mismatching of students to programs leads to higher drop-out rates, lower job placement, added retraining and recruiting costs, waste, lower productivity and general job dissatisfaction.

Predicting the vocational potential of adult students has become essential. This prediction should not be left to chance but made through utilization of a variety of assessment systems. Many are available today. A comprehensive assessment can assist in placing an individual in an appropriate program and in determining the individual's basic needs in order to become "job ready." Laura Wilcox conducted a survey of adult programs in West Virginia. Her results clearly indicated that there is improvement in program selection, retention and job placement where assessment systems are being utilized.

Adults come to the learning environment to reach specific goals. The vocational system owes it to these students to place them appropriately and efficiently in programs where the highest possibility of success is insured.

Program Quality
A quality program is essential to retraining adult students in a vocational program. Students who attend classes on a voluntary basis have a tendency to quit if the class is not meeting their perceived need. Poor quality is the main factor that causes an adult learner to drop out of a class or not return to an institution or agency for additional training.

To promote quality, credibility of instructors is extremely important. Adult students expect and deserve an instructor with expertise and experience in the area taught. The presentation must be relevant, interesting and factual. An unprepared instructor will drive away students who will not return. Adults will not sit through incompetence or busy work.

If students are to return to educational programs, the programs offered must also meet their expectations, and that means instruction must be relevant to the job, based on industry needs.

For many, a quality program will include job seeking and job keeping skills as well as work skills, so this training must also be made available.

Related Services
Retention of adult students may depend upon related support services that meet the needs of individual students. Support services provided must be based on the needs of the adults in the target population.

The lack of child care services becomes a deterrent to education for many adults. Since children are a primary responsibility and that responsibility is constant, attending a class or two for three hours a day, even for a short period of time may be impossible. Some schools do have child care services available to their adult students. These services are usually a part of an occupational child care training program.

Just getting to class can be a formidable task for some people. Provisions for transportation, such as a travel stipend or bus services, may be required of the school system in order to retain students.

A school that provides flexibility in scheduling will be able to serve adults whose responsibilities prevent school attendance during the regular school day and year, which has become too sacred in many systems. Persons with family, work, or personal responsibilities should not be eliminated from vocational education simply because they are not available at a specific time each and every school day. The open-entry open-exit concept should also become a reality if vocational educators are to serve adult students better.

Adults may need counseling or family services. For example, in an area where the men have always carried the work burden, such as coal mining, a lot of resentment toward the wife who is going to school and work may develop. Family nights and other activities designed to help the family understand that the changes they are experiencing will assist the family and also help retain students in school. Counseling services can also make a real difference with adults. These services should be available at convenient times and sites.

Other adults may need assistance with basic skills during or prior to participation in occupational training; and, some adults may need a little personal encouragement to return to school. For these individuals a phone call can make the difference.

Focusing on Adults

The key to successful recruitment and retention of adult students is to focus on what they want and need to make their educational experience successful. Adults must be recruited through methods that reach them where they live and work. They must be retained in programs by addressing their educational needs and providing support systems that make their educational experiences possible.

References

Cole, Lauretta F., *Academic and Selected Variables Related to Performances on the State Board Test Pool Examination for Graduates of Schools of Practical Nursing in the State of West Virginia*, State College, PA: Pennsylvania State University, November 1981.

Communication by Design, A Public Relations Handbook. Macomb, IL: Illinois State Board of Education, Curriculum Publications Clearing house, Western Illinois University, 1981.

Lovelock, Christopher and Weinberg, Charles, *Marketing for Public and Non-profit Managers.* New York: John Wiley, 1984.

Malarkey, Louise, "The Older Student - Stress or Success on Campus" *Journal of Nursing Education.* 18 (February, 1979):

Wilcox, Laura B., *Vocational Education Assessment for Adult Programs*, Marshall University, May 1984.

IMPACT OF TECHNOLOGY ON CURRICULUM AND DELIVERY STRATEGIES IN VOCATIONAL EDUCATION

David L. Goetsch

Preparing adults for employment has always been, and will continue to be, an important mission for vocational education. In fact, this mission is becoming even more important as advances in technology cause adults' needs to multiply, and demographic trends continue to increase the size of the working adult population.

Technological developments are having a significant impact on the world of work. The functional lifetime of a person's job skills is being shortened in many occupations. Traditional workers are being replaced by computers and robots. Manual tasks in many occupations are being automated, thus requiring less skill on the part of workers. New occupations are springing up rapidly; existing occupations are being altered significantly; and, many occupations are becoming outdated and eliminated.

Meeting the training needs of the adult population during a technological age means: delivering job preparatory training that is continuously updated and abreast of the latest technology; delivering skills updating training on a continuous basis; and, providing retraining for adults whose skills have become obsolete due to advances in technology or who, for personal reasons, wish to make career changes.

The challenges confronting vocational education in meeting the needs of adult learners during the next two decades are immense. People are living and working longer. The average age of the population is now 31, by the turn of the century, it will have risen to 41. Women are entering the labor force in large numbers, selecting careers, and planning to practice these careers until retirement; and, many of these entering the labor force during the next two decades will be single heads of households and displaced homemakers who will represent the sole source of income for their families. The retirement age is also sure to increase.

Challenges to Vocational Education

These parallel demographic and technological trends mean that more adults will need more training more frequently over the next two decades. For adult learners, vocational education will become a lifelong process. Although the challenges facing vocational education between now and the turn of the century are immense, there is also great potential for growth and expanded service.

To meet these challenges, and to realize the potential that exists, vocational educators must understand the impact technology will have over the next two decades and respond accordingly. Five critical questions must be answered:

- What Is Technology?
- What Is High Technology?
- How Is Technology Affecting the Workplace?
- What Impact Will Technology Have on Curriculum Strategies In Vocational Education?
- What Impact Will Technology Have on Delivery Strategies In Vocational Education?

This chapter addresses the first three briefly for background purposes and the final two in more depth.

What Is Technology?

Technology is the application of scientific principles and innovations to the solution of problems. Stated more simply, technology is applied science. Devices such as computers, robots, and satellites are the products through which science is applied to the solution of problems.

An ever increasing reliance on technology, especially to improve productivity, has marked the history of economic and industrial development in this country.

With the Industrial Revolution, technological developments continued to bring major changes. Americans learned early that in order to compete in business, industry, and commerce, maximum productivity on the job was essential. Increasing demands for improved productivity fueled the flames of technological development and a long series of "man is replaced by machines" situations ensued.

The technological developments which brought major changes to American society included: the concept of interchangeability of parts in manufacturing, Elias Howe's sewing machine, Cyrus McCormick's wheat reaper, electricity, Samuel F.B. Morse's telegraph, the railroad, the automobile, Alexander Graham Bell's telephone, and the typewriter.

Technology quickly became so important to continued economic development and growth in this country that technological innovation became an institutionalized concept. Government and private sector sources continually fund major scientific research projects at top universities and colleges. Industrial research and development laboratories have become a critical component of private enterprise.

The institutionalization of scientific research and innovation resulted in quantum leaps forward in technological development in this country. With the invention in the late 1950's of the programmable integrated circuit, an invention that took place at the Massachusetts Institute of Technology, this country took the first step into the age of high technology. Less than 30 years later, it is in the midst of a high technology revolution.

What Is High Technology?

In recent years, "high technology" has become a favorite buzzword. But even those agencies and individuals that have sought to define "high technology" do not always agree on its definition. The Florida Department of Education defines it as "the application of new technological developments causing pronounced changes in manufacturing, communications, transportation, marketing, health care delivery, and agriculture." The key words in this definition are "causing pronounced changes." But every major technological development over the years has caused pronounced changes.

James P. Fenton III, executive director of Connecticut's High Technology Council defines high technology industry as "any industry that is going to create jobs in the 1980's and 1990's." The Bureau of Labor Statistics classifies industries as high technology using such criteria as: the percentage of expenditures on research and development and the percentage of total employees classified as technicians. All of these definitions provide a working basis for separating high technology from technology. But they also share a common shortcoming. They do not get to the heart of what really separates the two concepts.

Charles A. Schuler, a noted expert in the field of high technology, defined high technology as "the application of programmable integrated circuits and systems based on programmable integrated circuits to areas including, but not limited to, data processing, manufacturing, information management and transmission, education, national defense, entertainment, energy management, pollution control, safety, communications, and efficient utilization of material and human resources."

A simple definition of high technology is the application of programmable integrated circuits to any form of human endeavor. This definition works well for two reasons. First, it correlates, as it should, with the definition of technology. This is important because high technology is a subset of technology in general. It is technology on a higher plane. And second, it speaks to what fundamentally separates the concepts of technology and high technology: the programmable integrated circuit.

This scientific invention launched the high technology revolution, and it is still the revolution's focal point. The programmable integrated circuit is a critical element in high technology devices such as the computer, industrial robots, laser beam devices, satellite communications equipment, and bio-medical equipment.

Other technological developments in areas such as mechanics, hydraulics, and pneumatics are also important aspects of the development of many high technology devices and systems, but the programmable integrated circuit is the one common element without which none of the devices or systems would work. Since this invention, technological development has accelerated exponentially, and this acceleration is having a significant impact on the workplace.

How Is Technology Affecting The Workplace?

Advances in technology have always brought corresponding changes in the workplace. For example, the concept of interchangeability of parts paved the way for assembly line production, thereby changing, forever, the nature of manufacturing from benchwork to mass production.

More recent technological developments are continuing this tradition of bringing major changes to the workplace. Technology is having a three-fold impact on the world of work: some manually-oriented occupations are becoming outdated and being eliminated; the skills required in many remaining jobs are being altered significantly; and, new jobs are being created in occupations that did not exist before the high technology revolution.

Occupations Which Are Becoming Outdated. Computer controlled automation of work processes are becoming more widely used in occupations that have traditionally been labor intensive. Signs of obsolescence can already be seen in the steel, automobile, textile, and manufacturing industries. General Motors, for example, plans to install approximately 14,000 robots in its automobile plants by 1990. Other automobile manufacturers will, of course, follow suit. These robots will perform tasks that have traditionally been performed by human workers.

New Occupations Created. Technological advances will also create new occupations. For example:

- As the nation's energy demands continue to increase, a corresponding increase will occur in the number of alternative energy sources that must be tapped. Energy Technician will become a high demand occupation. Over 1.5 million jobs will become available in this occupation by 1990.
- Technological advances in the processes used for collecting, storing, handling, shipping, and disposing of hazardous waste material will increase the need for Hazardous Waste Technician dramatically. Over 1.5 million new jobs will become available in this occupation by 1990.
- As manufacturing companies continue the transition from manual to automated operations, computer directed robots will replace numerous traditional factory workers. The proliferation of robotics in the workplace will create thousands of new jobs for Robot Technicians. These skilled workers

will be employed in the production, maintenance, and repair of industrial and, even, domestic robots.

Occupations Altered By Technology. Many occupations are being altered by technological developments. Jobs in these occupations will remain in demand, but the skills required to perform them will change. For example:

- Drafting and design technicians are beginning to exchange their pencils, scales, triangles, and other manual tools for computer-aided design and drafting systems (CADD) consisting of such components as processors, graphics terminals, text displays, digitizers, pucks, plotters, and printers.
- Supermarket cashiers will be able to simply pass grocery items across an electronic beam rather than pressing buttons on a cash register. This new high technology checkout system is tied into a computer which automatically takes a continuous inventory and places orders when a stock item is running low.
- Auto-mechanics are becoming more and more oriented to electronics in order to cope with the complex electronic systems found in modern automobiles. Computerized diagnosis and troubleshooting are becoming the norm in this traditional occupation.

High Technology's Impact on Curriculum Strategies in Vocational Education

The high technology revolution will present vocational education with major challenges. Vocational education will have to gear up to train the people who will design, develop, install, maintain, troubleshoot, and repair high technology devices, equipment, and systems. These are people who will be classified as high tech workers or "super techs." Training "super techs" will involve both job preparatory vocational programs and retraining programs.

Vocational education will also have to upgrade traditional jobs affected by high tech developments so that people already working in these fields will have opportunities to upgrade themselves and people wishing to enter these fields can receive up-to-date training that will make them employable.

How will these challenges affect curriculum strategies in vocational education? The answer lies in three major areas: in curriculum planning; in curriculum content; and, in curriculum evaluation.

Curriculum Planning
The most significant change in curriculum planning will be in who makes decisions. Traditionally, vocational educators have shouldered the bulk of the

responsibility for curriculum planning. They have looked to advisory committees, labor, and professional groups for guidance but, in reality, educators have made the decisions. This will not be the case in the age of high technology.

The traditional limited partnership of industry and education, characterized by such events as occasional advisory committee meetings and field visits, will not suffice in the age of technology. Representatives of the private sector will have to become equal partners in the decision making process as it relates to curriculum planning.

In order for this to become reality, two things will have to happen. First, local education/private sector councils will have to be established. These councils will be made up of top level managers and leaders from education, industry, and business. Such a council will not be an advisory committee. It will be a decision making committee with clout. Educators will have a vote on the council, but at least 51 percent of the voting members will need to be from the private sector. These local education/private sector councils can be adjunct councils of the chamber of commerce or autonomous committees. Such councils will serve institutions rather than individual vocational programs.

Vocational programs will still have advisory committees, but these committees will also have to have more of a voice in curriculum planning than in the past. Committee members will need to have a real voice in such matters as hiring instructors, developing and updating courses, approving courses, selecting textbooks, and purchasing equipment and expendable supplies. Advisory committes will make recommendations to the education/private sector councils through their chairpersons, who will be members of the councils, and the councils will, in turn, make the decisions. Giving the private sector a majority vote in making curriculum decisions will bring about the real education/private sector partnerships that are a must in the age of technology.

Further, some occupations, in the age of high technology will change by as much as 50 percent every three or four years. The planning models used by schools offering vocational education will not only have to allow for change, but will actually have to facilitate it.

This means two major changes for most schools. Needs assessment data will have to be collected and kept up-to-date much more frequently than in the past. Collecting needs assessment data yearly, quarterly, or even monthly will not suffice in the age of high technology. Data will have to be collected continuously and kept up-to-date constantly. This difficult task will be made easier by advances in technology.

The types of data collected will not change significantly, just the frequency of collection and use of the data. Such data as program placement rates, program retention rates, program dropout rates, student interest data, completer/leaver follow-up data, employer follow-up data, enrollment data, enrollment projections, employment source projections, labor supply and demand projections, and program cost data will still be crucial to the decision making process. In fact, these things will be even more important than in the past. Additionally, with the rapidity of change, projected data will become as important as existing documented data.

Curriculum Content

The high technology revolution will have a major impact on vocational education's curriculum.

Additions will be made to the technical aspects of the curriculum, to provide state-of-the-art training in new occupations; traditional programs will be adjusted to stay on the cutting edge of the latest developments in technology; and, programs that have become obsolete will have to be cancelled. But, then, these adaptations have always been the case in vocational education; only the rapidity of occurrence has changed.

The greatest changes to vocational education's curriculum will take place in the area of general education. General education has always been a fundamental part of vocational education's curriculum. In the technological age, it will become even more important. The key to lifelong productivity and employment for skilled workers will be flexibility, and the general education part of the curriculum will provide students with the intellectual foundation they need to grow and change continuously.

The purpose of general education in the curriculum is to help students develop the fundamental intellectual skills of reading, writing, speaking, listening, reasoning, and computing. This purpose will remain the same. What will change is the level of intellectual skills needed and, correspondingly, the level of general education required.

The high tech revolution is elevating the level of intellectual skills required to function in day-to-day life, both on the job and in general, especially in the areas of math and science. This means major changes to vocational education's curriculum.

The Center For Occupational Research and Development (CORD) in Waco, Texas, recommends a common core of general education courses in vocational education's curriculum. All vocational students would complete the common core of general education courses and then branch out for specialized technical training in their occuptional areas.

The core consists of courses in the areas of math, science, communications, computer literacy, and socioeconomics. Within each of these core areas, there is a list of courses that students would take depending on their field of study. For example, in math the list of courses includes business math, algebra, trigonometry, analytical geometry, and precalculus. A student studying electronics would be required to complete the entire sequence of courses. A secretarial student, on the other hand, would complete only business math, algebra, and trigonometry. In science, CORD recommends applied biology, applied physics, and applied chemistry. In communications, CORD recommends technical writing and technical speaking. Under computer literacy, CORD recommends keyboarding, computer use, and introductory level programming. Finally, in socioeconomics, CORD recommends courses in industrial relations and economics.

This general education core is much more difficult than would normally be found in traditional vocational programs. However, this is the type of core that will be needed to give students adequate preparation for success and survival in the age of technology.

Curriculum Evaluation

The two most significant changes that the age of technology will bring to curriculum evaluation will be the frequency of evaluations and the degree of involvement of the private sector in conducting evaluations. The workplace will change constantly, and so must vocational education's curriculum. Thus, in order to ensure quality and relevance, curriculum evaluation will have to be a continuous process.

Traditional evaluation methodologies such as student evaluation of instruction, student evaluation of curriculum materials, feedback from graduates, feedback from employers of graduates, and advisory committee reviews of curriculum content and materials will still work. But only if they are conducted constantly and the results are fed to the education and private sector councils. The councils will interpret the results, with assistance from advisory committees, and ensure that the necessary changes are made.

In addition to these traditional methodologies, new and different evaluation procedures will be needed. One of the most effective uses of federal funding for vocational education in the age of technology will be in the area of curriculum evaluation. Federal funds will need to be used to defray the costs of periodic on-site visits from evaluation teams made up of private sector representatives from the local, state, and national communities. These teams will need to be composed of a broad cross-section of personnel representing all aspects of a given occupation. For auto mechanics, an evaluation team would include hands-on mechanics, research and development personnel who are working on the latest innovations in the field, customer service agents, people who market the latest tools and equipment to the field, and management representatives. Feedback from these teams, like all other evaluation feedback, will be fed to the education/private sector council for verification and action.

Delivery Strategies in Vocational Education

Competency-based vocational education will finally come of age because advances in teaching technology will finally make it feasible. CBIM—competency-based, individualized and multimediated instruction—will become the norm. CBIM offers several advantages over traditional teaching strategies. First, it allows students to pre-test prior to beginning learning. This means that each student can begin learning at his or her own level. Second, it helps students develop specific industry and business approved competencies that can be measured against prescribed standards. Third, it offers learners the advantage of maximum time on task. And, finally, it allows students to progress at their own rate.

Computers and video technology will not be limited to the teaching of cognitive skills. Hands-on skills will also be taught using modern technology. Students will learn to operate complicated equipment and systems through self-teaching/learning systems that are actually part of the equipment. More technology, particularly the microcomputer, will be used to teach students how to use technology.

Bausch and Lomb Corporation is already experimenting with such a training package for clients who purchase one of their computer-aided design and drafting systems. Along with the actual system, buyers also receive a self-paced learning package on video tape and training workbooks that allow people totally unfamiliar with Bausch and Lomb's systems to develop operational skills quickly on the job. The combination microcomputer/video system will be an integral part of the delivery of vocational education.

Numerous other technologies that will have an impact on delivery strategies in vocational education are also being developed. Advances in such technologies as electronic cameras, home video cassette recorders, video disk players, programmable television receivers, teleconferencing equipment, and satellite dishes will affect the way vocational education is delivered and where it is delivered. Several of these innovations will allow more and more learning to take place in non-traditional locations such as home or work.

Interactive voice recognition is the next frontier to be developed in terms of modern teaching technology. Once this concept is perfected, students will actually be able to converse with computers. This will maximize the amount of time actually spent learning by decreasing the amount of time devoted to necessary, but non-learning oriented activities such as keying in commands, activating responses, and selecting menu options.

The role of the vocational instructor in the automated classroom will be new and different. It will be more a role of learning manager than teacher. As a learning manager, the instructor will coordinate learning, assess progress, and evaluate knowledge and skills development. Such traditional teaching duties as lecturing and presenting demonstrations will become less and less necessary, although they will not disappear completely. They will still be done, but more frequently in front of a video camera than in a classroom.

Far-reaching Impact

This chapter began with a definition of the word "technology." It was stated that technology is simply applied science. Using this definition, a distinction was drawn between technology and high technology. It was stated that high technology was any technology that relies fundamentally on the programmable integrated circuit. Technology, especially high technology, is having a marked impact on the world of work, and, in turn, on curriculum and delivery strategies in vocational education. Technology is affecting the vocational curriculum in the areas of planning, content, and evaluation. More private sector input will occur in both curriculum planning and evaluation. Technology will become the watchword for delivering instruction. Consequently, the vocational education instructor will become a learning manager. The instructor's primary duties will be coordination, assessment, and evaluation.

The challenges presented by technology are immense, but so are the opportunities. Over the next two decades, more adult learners will need more training more frequently. For adult learners, vocational education will become a lifelong process. This presents vocational education with an unparalleled opportunity for growth and expanded service.

References

"America Rushes To High Tech For Growth." *Business Week*, March 28, 1983, p. 84.

Cetron, Marvin and O'Tolle, Thomas. "Careers With A Future: Where Jobs Will Be In The 1990's," *Careers Tomorrow: The Outlook For Work In A Changing World,* (ed.) Edward Cornish. Bethesda, MD: World Future Society, 1982.

High Technology Vocational Resources Guide. Waco, Texas: Center for Occupational Research and Development, 1983.

Purcell, Curroll W., Jr. *Technology In America: A History Of Individuals And Ideas*. Cambridge, Mass: *The MIT Press*, 1981.

COLLABORATION AMONG ADULT EDUCATION AGENCIES

Alan B. Knox

The agencies that provide vocational education and training programs for adults should collaborate with each other when collaboration promises to benefit learners, agencies, or society and should proceed independently when it does not. These agencies include divisions of continuing education in community colleges and universities, departments of adult education in school systems, and training departments in business and industry.

The experience of a director of continuing education and community services at a community college illustrates the distinction between costs and benefits. Each year, many of his adult vocational education courses and workshops are conducted with little cooperation from other providers because the college seems to be responding well to a strong demand for offerings not available elsewhere. By contrast, some programs are co-sponsored with school systems, employers, and labor unions in the region because each co-sponsor benefits from the program results and makes important contributions, such as instructors, materials, equipment and, especially, encouraging learner participation.

There are, of course many ways in which collaborative arrangements can strengthen adult vocational education offerings. This chapter provides a rationale to help adult vocational education practitioners recognize trends likely to influence cooperation among various types of providers; identify examples of how collaboration strengthens adult education; consider the costs as well as the benefits of collaboration; and, explore roles and guidelines for deciding when and when not to collaborate.

Effective collaboration should benefit adult learners, agencies, and society. Practitioners can use these suggestions for decisionmaking in their provider agencies and in associations such as the American Vocational Association.

Influence on Collaboration

The agencies that provide adult vocational education in the United States vary greatly. Many are described earlier in this Yearbook in the section on "Delivery Systems for Adult Education." Providers' characteristics should be considered in relation to the distinctive contribution each can make to a collaborative effort.

For example, adult education agencies that are part of a school system or postsecondary education institutions that coordinate educational activities for adults on behalf of educational institutions (such as public schools, community colleges, proprietary schools, and universities) typically have facilities, libraries, and faculty members with subject matter expertise. By contrast, other providers (such as those associated with employers, labor unions, the military, penal institutions, and associations) typically have members or constituencies with educational needs to be met. What better basis for a partnership than an agency with adult learners interested in being served teaming up with an agency with instructors able to help them learn?

Several major trends that affect adult vocational education help explain the increasing importance of collaboration. Until recently, each type of provider proceeded quite independently, due to separate traditions, unfamiliarity with most other types of providers, and a sense that distinctive missions and unmet educational needs that far exceeded program offerings made needless duplication unlikely and collaboration unnecessary.

During this century, there has been a steady but dramatic increase in participation in adult education, along with the number and size of adult education providers, and the diversity and availability of program opportunities. The increasing rate of social and technological change has encouraged adults to use part-time and short-term educational activities to cope with change and advancement, and has encouraged adult education providers to be responsive to societal trends and learner needs. Workers now cope with major occupational changes in less than a decade that used to occur gradually over several generations. Also, there is increasing recognition of relations between occupational and non-occupational domains as interdependent parts of a total career.

As a result, each type of adult education provider (educational institution, employer, labor union, other) has evolved its own tradition, with specialized terminology, associations, and publications. Adult education practitioners' primary allegiance has been to their segment of the field, and especially to relations with their parent organization—the labor union, employer or educational institution. Practitioners strived for concerted efforts to conduct effective adult vocational education programs and found it necessary to be persuasive advocates for their program, especially within their own parent organization. There have been fewer incentives to collaborate with other types of providers, or to address program areas that are socially significant but unprofitable. One exception to this pattern is cooperative efforts on behalf of unemployed adults under the Job Training Partnership Act and its predecessors.

Increasingly, adult education practitioners are recognizing that collaborative and independent leadership can be enhanced by attention to strategic planning. Such planning entails making decisions about organizational priorities and ways to achieve goals, based on both internal and external information. Internal information includes trends (such as economic conditions, occupational opportunities, and job requirements in an information society), and relations with other adult education providers. Attention to provider goals and community relationships is also fundamental to effective collaboration.

Reasons for Collaboration

Stronger collaboration benefits individual learners, adult education providers, and the larger society. Cooperation among providers can benefit adult learners by offering access, equity, range, convenience, lower expense, quality, relevance, and application. For example, when providers cooperate by supporting and providing timely program information to community-based inquiry centers, the center staff can perform an educational brokering function that increases clients' accessibility to a wide range of educational opportunities. Clients can then select the programs they prefer based on program emphasis and level, convenient time and location, and satisfactory cost. Also, when an educational institution cooperates with an employer or community agency to co-sponsor a program at a satellite location, possible client benefits include higher program quality, relevance, and assistance in applying new knowledge. Equity can be increased and sometimes costs reduced by co-sponsoring programs with organizations which are associated with underserved adults.

Collaboration can benefit providers in various ways, such as, complementarity, resource sharing, in-kind contributions, and marketing. For example, when an educational institution—with faculty members and educational materials—cooperates with an employer or association—with members with educational needs—each co-sponsor can contribute what the other lacks. Also, co-sponsors can provide in-kind contributions, such as free use of facilities or provision of materials, and can encourage participation by adults who already identify with the co-sponsor as members, employees, or recipients of service.

Collaboration can benefit the community or larger society by reducing duplication, filling gaps, increasing public understanding, and increasing the impact on performance. For example, a local adult education council made up of representatives from continuing education programs, can help identify similar offerings with low enrollments and reduce needless duplication to minimize cancellations and keep costs down; can encourage providers to fill gaps in program offerings and meet unmet needs; and can counteract fragmentation and increase public understanding. Similarly, cooperation between a community college and an employer can improve performance, and cooperation between a university and a school can strengthen materials and staff development.

Costs and Benefits

Whenever collaboration is considered as an alternative to the unilateral provision
of a program, practitioners should weigh the benefits and costs of a cooperative
effort. Because specific benefits and costs vary, it is helpful to assess trade-offs
to decide whether collaborative arrangements are desirable in a particular instance.

Benefits

Most successful collaborative efforts among adult education providers are sustained by one or more of four types of benefits—complementarity, coordination,
marketing, and subsidy. The benefits of complementarity have already been
noted. Sometimes, coordinated efforts by multiple providers produce better results for the investment than unilateral efforts. This is illustrated by consortia,
councils, and associations. A typical example is agency level program development, such as needs assessment, in which findings from a joint study are
shared with multiple providers who fund the cost. Another example is professional development for adult education practitioners, in which interaction with
people from other providers helps broaden perspectives, introduces new ideas
and establishes networks in ways that a single provider would have difficulty
achieving.

Marketing efforts to increase support and cooperation can sometimes be
strengthened through collaboration. Multiple providers can work together to
prepare a newspaper supplement on their adult program offerings, to use a
common logo and slogan along with different examples as part of a periodic
media campaign to increase public understanding of educational programs for
adults generally. They can also conduct legislative luncheons and letter writing
as part of a concerted effort to be persuasive advocates for adult education when
legislators and other policy makers consider legislation or other actions that
affect educational programs for adults.

Costs

There are costs as well as benefits of collaboration. Most collaborative efforts
experience one or more of four types of costs—differing goals, time and money,
slow response, and restricted opportunities.

Each adult education provider has a particular image and high priority goals
that are reflected in the relative emphasis placed on subject matter content, special
populations served, adult life roles, and attention to outcomes such as productivity

or personal development. Co-sponsorship can blunt that image by combining differing goals.

Cooperation by two or more providers takes time and money to sustain the partnership: arranging for meetings; keeping each other informed; gaining agreement; and coordinating separate efforts. In unilateral efforts, these resources could be used for programs.

The time entailed in sustaining cooperative efforts also tends to slow down the response time regarding requests for assistance. If this is the case, each partner may pay a price in a less positive public image of the provider's responsiveness.

Collaboration may restrict educational opportunities so that the public has fewer choices. In the private sector, such efforts to restrict competition are considered collusion in constraint of trade. In such instances in adult education, the public may pay the price in the form of fewer opportunities or higher fees.

When practitioners are considering or reconsidering collaboration, the foregoing types of benefits and costs can be used as criteria to evaluate the specific proposal. This analysis can enable a practitioner to collaborate in those instances in which the benefits outweigh the costs.

Roles and Guidelines

How can practitioners decide the desirability of collaboration in a specific case? This section suggests some guidelines and a rationale for deciding when to and when not to collaborate.

A practitioner can more readily decide on the desirability of collaboration within the context of strategic planning and priority setting. In general, collaboration should be considered when it promises to benefit individual learners, provider agencies, or the larger society of community or service area.

For an adult education agency, strategic planning entails setting and achieving desirable goals in a turbulent environment. The agency considers societal trends and issues and ways to achieve goals, using information and participatory methods. Thus, strategic planning combines internal and external information to help achieve desirable future outcomes.

Several societal trends are likely to make collaborative approaches increasingly desirable: rapid rates of social and technological change, with resulting dislocations for individuals and communities; increased appreciation of the importance of career development, expanded efforts to assess and enhance basic proficiencies that enable adults to function in an information age; and, heightened recognition of international interdependence.

The individual adult learner is one focus of planning for collaboration. The majority of adult learning projects are informal, self-directed efforts. Collaborative efforts among adult education providers can provide information and support for community-based educational brokering centers. Such inquiry centers can help adults to become more effective consumers of educational and career development programs, to clarify educational and career goals, and to discover pertinent resources.

The provider agency is another focus for planning related to collaboration. Effective practitioners engaged in adult vocational education want to attract resources to provide high quality programs to serve adult learners. Collaborative arrangements are desirable to the extent to which they are means to such ends. Co-sponsorship with a complementary type of provider can help attract, retain, and serve adults more effectively by reducing unit costs and increasing the numbers of hard-to-reach adults who are served. Cooperative arrangements can increase program quality be sharing resources such as experts, facilities, equipment, and materials. Joint advocacy can increase public understanding and support. However, before initiating or continuing such collaborative arrangements, practitioners should decide how desirable it is for their agency to strengthen such aspects, and which agency they should choose to strengthen those aspects.

The broad field of adult and continuing education as it relates to the larger society must also be considered. Collaboration is desirable to the extent to which it helps more adults gain insight into and make sounder choices about the relationship between work and life and society and become active agents in their own career development. Professional associations that include practitioners engaged in adult vocational education and human resource development can be especially useful in promoting collaboration. These include: the American Vocational Association, the American Society for Training and Development, the American Association of Community and Junior Colleges, and the National University Continuing Education Association. Each seeks to address relevant trends and issues in the larger society and to encourage members to discover practitioners from other providers with whom collaboration would be mutually beneficial. The American Association for Adult and Continuing Education is especially useful in this regard since it includes members from all types of provider agencies.

Strategic planning concepts can help practitioners approach collaboration with agencies or associations with a sense of direction and commitment, instead of mainly reacting to outside forces. Such planning considers internal influences—traditions, strengths and weaknesses, leadership —as well as external influences—trends, market directions, competitive situation.

The essential ingredient in successful collaboration, however, is supporters in the cooperating provider agencies who have a sense of direction that should be strengthened and a commitment to a collaborative strategy to do so. Participatory planning methods are important because they can attract and encourage such supporters, without whose leadership even very desirable plans tend not to get implemented.

Successful collaboration among providers, as with any partnership, depends on commitment to shared goals, complementary contributions, and equitable benefits to all partners. To initiate and sustain such cooperation, practitioners must be willing to negotiate and renegotiate mutually satisfactory arrangements. The emerging realities of adult vocational education make such collaborative approaches increasingly central to effective leadership. But they need committed practitioners to make it work.

Enhancing Benefits

In effective collaboration, everyone can benefit. The cooperating providers can use complementary contributions to enhance program quality and impact. The adult learners can receive more varied programs of higher quality at lower cost. Society can have more comprehensive programs with fewer gaps and greater access and equity.

However, such benefits are not automatic. Self-serving cooperation among providers could reduce opportunities and increase costs, as providers seek to divide the market and enjoy monopolies. Much depends on the professional commitment of providers to serve adult learners and society. The available literature on collaboration can enable practitioners to cooperate with other providers in ways that truly benefit all.

References

American Vocational Association. *Collaboration: Vocational Education and the Private Sector*. (1984 Yearbook) Arlington, VA: American Vocational Association, 1984.

Aslanian, Carol B. and Bricknell, Henry M. *Americans in Transition: Life Changes as Reasons for Adult Learning*. New York: College Board, 1980.

Darkenwald, Gordon and Larson, Gordon A. (eds.) *New Directions for Continuing Education: Reaching Hard-to-Reach Adults, No. 8*. San Francisco: Jossey-Bass, 1980.

———— and Merriam, Sharon D. *Adult Education: Foundations of Practice*. New York: Harper & Row, 1982.

DiSilvestro, Frank R. (ed.) *New Directions for Continuing Education: Advising and Counseling Adult Learners, No. 10*. San Francisco: Jossey-Bass, 1981.

Grabowski, Stanley M. (ed.) *New Directions for Continuing Education: Strength-*

ening Connections Between Education and Performance, No. 18. San Francisco: Jossey-Bass, 1983.

Heffernan, James M. *Educational and Career Services for Adults.* Lexington, MA: D. C. Heath, 1981.

Houle, Carol O. *The Design of Education.* San Francisco: Jossey-Bass, 1972.

_____ . *Continuing Learning in the Professions.* San Francisco: Jossey-Bass, 1980.

Kasworm, Carol E. (ed.) *New Directions for Continuing Education: Educational Outreach to Select Adult Populations, No. 20.* San Francisco: Jossey-Bass, 1983.

Keller, George. *Academic Strategy: The Management Revolution in American Higher Education.* Baltimore, MD: The Johns Hopkins University Press, 1983.

Knox, Alan B. "New Realities in the Administration of Continuing Higher Education." *The NUCEA Spectator*, 39 (December 1975): 6.

_____ . *New Directions for Continuing Education: Leadership Strategies for Meeting New Challenges. No. 13.* San Francisco: Jossey-Bass, 1980.

_____ and Associates. *Developing, Administering and Evaluating Adult Education.* San Francisco: Jossey-Bass, 1980.

_____ and Farmer, Helen S. "Overview of Counseling and Information Services for Adult Learners." *International Review of Education*, 23 (1977): 387-414

Kotler, Phillip. *Marketing for Non-Profit Organizations.* Englewood Cliffs, NJ: Prentice Hall, 1974.

Smith, Wendell L. (ed.) *Collaboration in Lifelong Learning.* A Report on the Airlie House Lifelong Learning Leaders Retreat. Washington, DC: American Association for Adult and Continuing Education, 1983.

Votruba, James D. (ed.) *New Directions for Continuing Education: Strengthening Internal Support for Continuing Education. No. 9.* San Francisco: Jossey-Bass, 1981.

SECTION IV

EDUCATING SPECIAL POPULATIONS

Vocational educators have always been concerned about providing programs that will enable their students to respond to labor market demands. In addition, vocational educators need to examine the special needs of new groups that are becoming an increasingly important segment of the adult vocational education population.

The National Council on the Future of Women in the Workplace reports that women make up a growing and significant proportion of the workforce. By 1990, nearly half of the projected 128 million workers in the workforce will be women. It predicts that they will seek out better-paying and more satisfying employment in occupations traditionally reserved to men. Many of these women will turn to vocational education, and vocational educators must be prepared to meet their needs.

Minority groups need education of better quality in order to participate effectively in a technological economy, according to Roy G. Phillips. He discusses trends in participation in education among minority groups that impair their opportunities for employment. He also describes a new effort in Florida to improve standards in public education.

Disabled adults do not participate in vocational education in proportion to their share in the population. George Travis discusses the barriers to education that face adults disabled as children and those faced by adults who become disabled after reaching maturity. This background is a necessary prelude to meeting the vocational education needs of disabled adult learners.

Until recently, displaced or dislocated workers would not have been considered a special population. But the growing number of such workers is a serious policy issue for the nation and presents a new challenge to vocational education. Robert G. Wegmann discusses the forces influencing the development of a large group of dislocated workers and the role of vocational education in dealing with this issue.

These chapters provide vocational educators with the background information they need to begin to understand how to meet the needs of special groups in the adult labor force.

WOMEN AND VOCATIONAL EDUCATION

The National Council on the Future of Women in the Workplace

During the last three decades, 60 percent of the nation's new workers have been women. In 1950, women comprised slightly more than one-quarter of the labor force. Today, they make up 43 percent of all workers and by 1990, it is projected that out of 128 million workers, 60 million will be women.

Women's growing influx into the workplace has been driven by economic necessity. Two-thirds of all women who work are either single, widowed, divorced, separated or have husbands who earn less than $15,000. The number of female-headed households has more than doubled in the past 20 years, up from 4.5 million in 1960 to 9.4 million in 1981. And, poor families are increasingly maintained by women. In 1981, 70 percent of poor Black families, 50 percent of poor Hispanic families and 39 percent of poor White families were headed by women. These families had the responsibility for nurturing 7 million children. Thus, the earnings of women workers are crucial to sustaining a decent standard of living for the American family.

While women have increased their numbers in the labor force, they continue to be tracked into a limited number of occupations. According to the Census Bureau, women were concentrated in only 60 out of 441 major occupations in 1981. Nearly 80 percent of women workers are employed in the lowest-paying occupations—clerical, sales, service, and unskilled factory jobs. Women comprise 80 percent of clerical workers, 86 percent of librarians, 97 percent of registered nurses, 64 percent of social workers, and 84 percent of elementary teachers. On the other hand, women are only four percent of engineers, 14 percent of lawyers, 14 percent of medical doctors and osteopathic physicians, five percent of dentists, and five percent of clergy.

This occupational segregation is one of the most important labor and social issues of the 1980's. If women are going to be full participants in the workforce, it is crucial that they obtain adequate training and education in order to qualify for jobs within all occupational categories.

Career Choices

Women are concentrated in low-paying jobs for complex reasons. But certainly, the way they are encouraged to make career choices is a significant factor.

Traditionally, women choose or have been encouraged to choose careers in which other women predominate. One study by the American Institute of Research found that one-fourth of women taking courses "unusual to their sex" had been advised against enrolling. Another 14 percent had considered taking non-traditional courses but were dissuaded by counselors.

Enrollments in vocational education programs reflect the same patterns. According to the Vocational Education Data System (VEDS), most programs that prepare students for traditionally "female" jobs have overwhelming female enrollments. For the school year 1979-80, 91 percent of nursing assistant students were female, as were 92 percent of cosmetology students and 92 percent of secretarial students. However, women were only five percent of the students in electrical technology; four percent of auto mechanics students; and four percent of those studying small engine repair. Clearly, the result of these patterns will be the continued segregation of women into low-paying occupations with limited career mobility. Therefore, any consideration of women's concerns in vocational education must include the role of vocational counseling.

In 1983, the Business and Professional Women's Foundation commissioned a study of the state of the art in women's career counseling, at the request of the National Council on the Future of Women in the Workplace. Elaine Reuben, a researcher in the area of women and education, found that many good "models" for counseling girls and women exist, but that the potential "consumers" of such counseling are too often unaware of the need for career planning. Dr. Reuben concluded that programs are needed to educate girls and women about career planning. She also found a need for vocational counseling that focuses on long-range planning information and skills that take into account changes in the workplace; adequate structures to link girls and women with mentors and role models; and a commitment to educational and vocational equity for women.

Career Mobility and Retraining

Career mobility will also be an important issue for the future of vocational education. The American economy is shifting from a manufacturing or goods-producing society to one that produces information and services. At the same time, automation is altering the way work is performed. For women to move out of dead-end, low-status jobs, as well as those that might become obsolete, further career training and retraining will be essential.

When many policymakers speak of retraining programs for displaced workers, they think of the typical displaced worker as a male blue-collar worker from the declining "smokestack" industries. But women workers, because they are clustered at the bottom of the job ladder, are particularly vulnerable to job loss from automation.

Many office jobs in the female "ghetto" —stenographers, insurance clerks, banktellers, keypunch operators — have disappeared. For example, since 1970, the number of telephone operators has been reduced by 30 percent as a result of the introduction of computerized equipment.

Women workers in the industrial sector have also experienced job losses. The textile industry, which is over 62 percent female, has suffered the the loss of over 150,000 jobs because of automation and foreign competition.

Another displaced worker too often ignored is the displaced homemaker. Many women who have spent their twenties and thirties at home raising their families, suddenly find in middle age that they have the major responsibility for the financial support of their families. They are thus "displaced" from their role as homemaker and must join the paid labor force. Unlike many displaced male workers, displaced homemakers have little, if any, paid work experience. They may have little or no awareness of the career options available to them, or even how to go about job hunting. Therefore, in addition to teaching specific technical skills, adult education programs for women must help them develop increased self-confidence and career planning skills, such as self-assessment.

Family Responsibilities

Because of traditional family responsibilities, women are more likely to leave and then return to the labor force. This pattern poses questions about how vocational education deals with the adult learner.

Many vocational education programs require a period of apprenticeship, and many apprenticeship programs have an age limit of 25-27 years. Yet, most adult learners are over 25 years old. This is especially true of women, or career changers. If traditional vocational education programs are not the answer, what are the alternatives?

Women's traditional family responsibilities also pose other questions for vocational education. Working women today face a great problem in getting access to adequate care for family dependents. With women's increasing participation in the labor force, their availability as traditional care providers is reduced at the same time as the cost of paid care for dependents is rising.

Fifty-nine percent of the mothers with children under age 18 are in the workforce. Fifty percent of the mothers of the nation's preschoolers work for pay. But available child care is so inadequate that an estimated 7 million of the nation's children are caring for themselves during a substantial part of the day.

The increased need for child care comes at a time when another segment of the population is requiring increased care as well. American society is growing older. The responsibility for care of the elderly will fall primarily on family members, as it always has. Women have a special stake in these problems. The disproportionate number of women in the elderly population means that women are most likely to be the elderly persons in need of care. In addition, since women are the traditional care providers for the elderly, they are more likely to have to supply such care to others. The "woman in the middle"—facing her own aging simultaneously with the care of aging relatives—will bear most of the burdens of an aging America.

These women in the middle are often the persons most in need of vocational training. Increasingly, they must support their own families—perhaps children and parents at the same time—and assure their own economic security in both work and retirement. Despite their need, they find it more difficult than those without family responsbilities to attend classes, pay tuition and systematically plan careers.

Vocational education programs must help meet the needs of this group by helping to identify and, if possible, support dependent care programs; constructing flexible course schedules and providing convenient class locations; setting affordable tuition rates; and, steering students toward training and education that can help them assure their own economic security.

Recommendations

Women will be a growing "market" for vocational education in coming years. Their rapid entry into the workforce, their current ghettoization in low-paid, dead-end jobs, and their increasing responsibility for support of their families all mean that women will be looking for new and alternative careers. They will be seeking to upgrade their skills. They will be re-entering the job market after gaps in their work experience. And they will be trying to enter occupations and positions that are not traditionally "women's work."

Vocational education programs and institutions must be prepared to meet the needs of women. They can do so by:
- Providing guidance and counseling that encourage women to seek non-traditional careers and creating programs to attract women into non- traditional areas of training;
- Helping to overcome attitudinal barriers to women's entry into non-traditional occupations;
- Emphasizing training and skills that will be useful in emerging fields (such as high-technology occupations), and encouraging long-range career planning for women;

- Targeting employees from traditional female occupations for retraining programs;
- Developing programs that target displaced homemakers for vocational training and education;
- Developing supplemental programs that help meet the dependent care needs of vocational education students;
- Constructing flexible course schedules and choosing convenient locations, to allow students to meet their family responsibilities while taking courses;
- Including the development of career skills (resume writing, job hunting) as part of the vocational education curriculum; and
- Supporting legislative and programmatic initiatives with the goal of educational and vocational equity for women (such as the Vocational Education Reauthorization Act).

These measures will help make vocational education programs more appropriate to the needs of all adult learners. They will also help integrate women more fully into the vocational education curriculum and into the work force.

References

Bluestone, Barry, Harrison, Bennett, and Gorham, Lucy. *Storm Clouds on the Horizon: Labor Market Crisis and Industrial Policy*. Brookline, Mass.: Economic Education Project, May 1984.

National Advisory Council on Women's Educational Programs. *Title IX, The Half Full Half Empty Glass*. Washington, D.C.: Government Printing Office, Fall 1984.

National Council on the Future of Women in the Workplace. *The Invisible Worker in a Troubled Economy: Women and the Industrial Policy Debate*. Washington, D.C.: National Federation of Business and Professional Women's Clubs, 1984.

Reuben, Elaine, "Current Practices and Needs in Career Counseling of Girls and Women." Unpublished report to the Business and Professional Women's Foundation. Washington, D.C., 1983.

U.S. Dept. of Labor, Women's Bureau, "Economic Responsibilities of Working Women," Washington, D.C., 1982 (Mimeo).

ISSUES AND TRENDS INFLUENCING THE EDUCATION AND TRAINING OF MINORITY GROUPS

Roy G. Phillips

The character and make-up of minority groups is important to understanding the problems and issues they face as this nation moves toward the 21st century. First, minority groups in America are classified into four major population groups: Blacks, Hispanics, Asian/Pacific Islanders, and American Indians/Alaskan natives. Blacks are the largest minority group, constituting approximately 11.7 percent of the nation's population. The Hispanic category includes several subgroups of Spanish origin: Chicanos (Mexican origin), Puerto Ricans, Cubans, and Central/South Americans and constitutes the second largest minority group— 6.4 percent. However, Hispanics are expected to constitute the largest American minority group by the beginning of the 21st century due to: the increasingly large influx of immigrants and refugees from Central/South America and the Caribbean Basin, and a relatively high birth rate. The Asian category—1.5 percent of the population is also composed of a number of sub-groups, with the two largest being Chinese- and Japanese- Americans. American Indians (native Americans) constitute .6 percent of the population.

Second, on the average, American minority groups tend to be younger and have a faster rate of increase than the majority White American population. Indeed, Blacks and the other minority groups are projected to account for slightly more than 21 percent of the additions to the labor force during the 1982-1990 period, increasing to nearly 28 percent in the 1990-1995 period. The rapid growth of the majority group population has significant implications for the education and training of the emerging adult workforce.

Third, a disproportionate number of minorities live in poverty, especially an increasingly large number of minority female heads of household. The mean income of minorities continues to lag far behind that of White Americans, and this condition alone places a heavy burden upon the group's ability to break the cycle of poverty.

It should be noted, however, that all minority groups do not share the same disadvantages. As a group, Asian Americans have the highest level of education attainment comparable to, and in some cases, exceeding the educational attainment of White Americans. Because of this fact, the discussion in this paper is confined to the most disadvantaged groups: Blacks, Hispanics and Native Americans.

217

Trends and Special Challenges

The psychological impact of poverty, accompanied by other disabling factors, tend to isolate individuals and groups from mainstream participation in American life. Thus, the critical challenge now facing the American educational community is to develop a massive, well-planned effort to increase and to enhance the participation of minority and disadvantaged students in the education and training programs.

America's credentialing process places a high value upon education as the means for assuring upward mobility. Minority group children, who are born into poverty, face extraordinary odds in moving through the educational hierarchy. More than ever before, advanced education and training is required for the vast majority of persons to function in a society based upon technology, which increasingly requires new ideas and skills.

There is growing difficulty in providing more access for a larger proportion of minority and disadvantaged student. Several trends have added to an anti-affirmative action mood of some White Americans toward the advancement of minority Americans. First, the energy crisis brought on by the Arab oil embargo of 1973 made this nation realize that our domestic fossil fuels are a limited and non-renewable stock. Moreover, the high dependence upon foreign oil and other key minerals to fuel our technological society has accelerated a shift to more energy conservation and the development of alternate energy sources that are not sensitive to the moods of international producers. The increasingly high cost of energy and a corresponding high rate of inflation has brought about a decline in spending in the public sector, which has reduced funds for public education.

Second, structural changes are taking place in the American economy. There has been a shift from blue collar to white collar jobs as old line manufacturing industries—high energy users—in steel, automobiles, textiles and rubber have declined. Since 1978, more than a million jobs have vanished permanently. The transition to the new technologies has witnessed large scale unemployment among minority workers, especially Blacks and Hispanics, who have occupied jobs at the lower rung of the declining industries.

Historically, Blacks and other disadvantaged minorities have found their greatest opportunities in the dynamic sectors of the economy, in expanding industries during the periods of most rapid growth. They have had little success in breaking into stable or declining industries, particularly where the White workers have been well organized. Thus, the critical problem that faces minorities during the next decade is a need to prepare themselves educationally to move into the new jobs that are being created during this period of transition.

Third, the American economy is increasingly global. This nation no longer wields the dominant economic power that it once did during the 1950's and

1960's. It faces intense international competition. Jobs have shifted from the American economy to emerging third world nations that are able to produce the same quality and quantity of goods at a lesser cost.

Fourth, government-funded programs for adult training are being reduced. The Reagan Administration reduced funding for the old CETA program from $9 billion in fiscal year 1981 to $3.6 billion for the new Job Training Partnership Act program which replaced CETA. The Republican Administration's new policy direction has had the effect of reducing expenditures for support services and needs-based payment; strictly curtailing stipends for living expenses and other services, such as child care and counseling; and, mandating program performance standards that emphasize job placement as a basis for refunding. Coupled with these reductions, the lack of enthusiasm by the private sector for government sponsored training programs has created a void for increasing the level of participation of unemployed minorities in adult training programs.

The multiplying effect of these trends has accelerated a fifth trend that emerged during the mid 1970's. Increased emphasis upon quality at all levels, including more efficient machines and other products, has spilled over into education. The message has been clearly articulated that education and training not only must be more available, but must be enhanced as well. Quality education is important.

Higher standards are required to ensure that all students have the skills to succeed economically and socially in a changing world, and higher expectations do inspire better performance. Students can achieve in an educational environment where teachers, counselors, administrators, and parents communicate positive expectations to students regarding their ability to learn. However, the focus upon quality, when defined only by high standards for student performance, can reduce the participation of minority and disadvantaged students in education and training. Special action must accompany increased higher educational expectations so that more students may succeed. Efforts must also be made to enhance professional quality so that students will be taught how to meet higher standards.

Participation in Education and Adult Training Programs

Minority groups' participation in education and adult training programs is severely impaired by their ability to move through the educational hierarchy. As minority group members move up the educational hierarchy, their numbers decline through attrition, which results from the lack of educational and economic opportunities, and residual institutional racism. Alexander Austin, a noted expert on retention, has identified three major "leakage points" along the educational continuum: high school completion, college entry, and college completion (undergraduate-graduate).

High School Completion

Generally, Blacks, Chicanos, Native Americans and Puerto Ricans have a much higher high school dropout rate than Whites. According to a recent report by the American Council on Education, the high school completion rate for Blacks has increased dramatically over the past thirty years, from a low of 10 percent in 1940 to approximately 70 percent today. This compares with 83 percent for Whites and 54 percent for Hispanics. The data on high school completion rates for Native Americans are insufficient.

In terms of high school preparation, Blacks, Chicanos, Native Americans, and Puerto Ricans tend to be more heavily enrolled in a vocational or general high school curriculum, than in a college preparatory curriculum. Recent surveys show that less than 50 percent of all students have taken math or science beyond the tenth grade. This figure is even worse for Blacks and other disadvantaged minorities, virtually eliminating them from entry into careers requiring a background in science and math. Furthermore, Asians and Whites enroll more frequently in the science and math college preparatory curricula which are prerequisites for the growth fields of medicine, engineering, computers, and other science-related careers.

College Entry

Even though the number of Black and Hispanic high school graduates has increased, serious concerns still exist about the rate of Black and Hispanic college enrollments as a percent of high school graduates.

During the 1960's and early 1970's minority participation in higher education and adult training programs showed significant gains. However, there was a decline in minority enrollment from the mid 1970's to the early 1980's. The earlier efforts rather quickly drew into postsecondary education those students who clearly had the skills to benefit from higher education. Early identification, recruitment, and special educational and financial assistance resulted in increased participation. The affirmative action demands to increase minority participation in higher education and other training programs during the 1960's fared poorly after the Baake decision, and as the nation moved toward a more conservative mood.

Higher education census data for 1982 show that in almost all occupational categories requiring some degree of postsecondary education and training, minority groups are significantly under-represented. Black Americans constitute approximately 9 percent of all students enrolled in higher education. Hispanics represent 4 percent, while Asians and Native Americans represent 2.9 percent and 0.7 percent, respectively. As a group, minority Americans tend to be concentrated in two-year community colleges and public institutions of higher learning. Blacks represent between 95 and 100 percent of the student body in the historically Black colleges. Blackwell reported that it is rare to find historically White institutions with more than 6 to 7 percent Black enrollment, despite litigation and Supreme Court decisions.

Hispanic students are concentrated in fewer than 2 percent of the 3100 collegiate institutions in the country: 21 colleges in the continental United States enroll 24 percent of all mainland Hispanic students.

College Completion

The completion rates for various groups in college are drawn from conflicting data. The rates for Blacks and Whites are more accurate than for Hispanics and Native Americans. The American Council on Education reports that in 1981, the most recent data available, the completion rate for White students was 17.8 percent, Blacks, 8.2 percent, and Hispanics, 7.7 percent. These data, however, are not consistent with data from other sources.

Graduate Enrollment

Because of attrition that had already occurred, minorities' enrollment at the graduate level is miniscule compared to their distribution in the general population.

Minority group enrollment in graduate schools shows the same pattern as evidenced in undergraduate enrollment during the 1960's and 1970's. James B. Blackwell reported to the American Council on Education that Black enrollment increased from 4.2 percent of the graduate school population in 1960 to 6.2 percent in 1978. However, that proportion declined to 5.9 percent in 1980. The enrollment trends for Blacks and other minorities in professional schools—medicine, law and engineering—have experienced similar declines.

The persistence of minority groups as they move up the educational hierarchy is due to several factors that have been widely researched in the literature.

Factors Influencing the Retention of Minorities

Astin has identified several factors that influence the persistence of all groups, including minorities, in education and training. These include: academic preparation, demographic characteristics, career and study plans, personal characteristics, and environmental factors.

Students who demonstrate the greatest degree of success in college are those with good high school grades, good study habits and a positive self-concept regarding their ability to succeed. Students who have taken a strong college preparatory curriculum, including well-balanced offerings in science, math, foreign languages, and communication skills, are more likely to succeed than those enrolled in the vocational or the general education curriculum. Among Blacks especially, the achievement of high standardized test scores, also tends to be an accurate indicator of success.

Demographically, college success is highly correlated with family income and educational background.

Environmental factors, particularly attendance at a four-year college or university rather than attendance at a two-year community college, appear to be a strong factor for persistence. Living on campus rather than at home and having adequate financial aid in the form of a grant or scholarship also appear to be strong factors for success.

One of the strongest indicators for success is the minority student's career choice at the time of college entry. Minority students who persist in delaying a career choice tend to be less likely to succeed. These factors have broad policy implications for policymakers in education and training, especially as they relate to the development of programs to assist disadvantaged minority students in moving successfully through the educational hierarchy.

Improving Retention Policy Issues Relating To Participation

There is a clear need for educational policymakers to arrest the decline in minority group participation in education at each point along the educational continuum. The economic future of America depends upon educating all Americans for more active and equal participation in the economy.

In recognition of this need, some states have begun to make policy decisions to improve the quality of education and training for the increasing minority population within American secondary and postsecondary institutions.

The State of Florida, through its Postsecondary Education Planning Commission, has embarked upon a bold state-wide program to improve the quality of education for minority and disadvantaged students at each level of the educational hierarchy. It addresses the need for programs to help under-prepared students to qualify for the next educational step in order to improve their level of success before proceeding to the next level. In doing so, Florida has attached two major

conditions to support programs that are designed to enhance minority participation. The first condition is accountability. Support dollars are tied to the specific
number of underachieving students served and the success of this program is
measured by the students' progress. Student eligibility is determined by statewide
procedures and criteria.

Each program is identified and funded as a separate entity in order to trace
the students, faculty and educational outcomes to the funds provided for these
services. Second, Florida has established a system for monitoring the activities
and results of these programs on a statewide basis. The Florida Institute for
Education was created to assist in this effort as it relates to Blacks within the
State system of secondary and postsecondary education.

The specific policy issues that are addressed in Florida's legislation are:
* the academic preparation in secondary schools of Black, Hispanic and disadvantaged students, and specifically, the preparation of such students in
  high school college preparatory courses and programs;
* the counseling of Black, Hispanic and disadvantaged students concerning
  postsecondary education opportunities and necessary preparation;
* the validity of tests as an indication of a student's academic ability, with
  specific attention to any disparity in test score results and completion rates
  of Black and Hispanic students in postsecondary education;
* the disproportionate number of Black students failing the teacher certification
  examination, and the performance of Black, Hispanic and disadvantaged
  students in the College Level Academic Skills test and other testing programs;
* the admission of Black and Hispanic students into professional and graduate
  programs; and
* the role of remedial education at the postsecondary educational level.

A statewide response to these key policy issues and a well-defined program
designed to achieve parity of minority groups in American education training is
a step in the right direction.

References

"A New Direction for Economic Growth," *Black Enterprise*, Editorial, Vol.
14, No. 11, June, 1984.

American Council on Education. *Demographic Imperatives. Implications for
Educational Policy*, Washington, D.C., ACE, 1983.

Astin, Alexander W. *Minorities in American Higher Education*. San Francisco:
Jossey-Bass, 1982.

Boyle, Ross. "New Directions for Economic Development in an Information-Based Economy," *Economic Development Review*, 2 (Winter 1984):57-63.

Johnson, Berman. "Counseling Black Americans for High Technology." (Paper presented at Southern Regional Council on Black American Affairs, February 4, 1984).

Killingworth, Charles. "Jobs and Income for Negroes." *Race and the Social Sciences*. Irwin Katz and Patricia Gurin (eds.) New York: Basic Books, 1969.

Policy Papers. South Florida Employment and Training Consortium, 1984.

The Postsecondary Education Planning Commission. "Enhancing the Participation of Minority and Disadvantaged Students in Postsecondary Education." Tallahassee: PPEC, 1984.

Ross, Arthur and Hill, Herbert. *Employment, Race and Poverty*. New York: Harcourt, Brace, 1967.

"Unfinished Business" (Editorial), 11 *Change* (October 1979).

IMMIGRANTS AND REFUGEES

William P. Reich

Several million newcomers—immigrants, illegal aliens, refugees—have arrived in the United States over the past ten years. Approximately 3.6 million of these immigrants are from countries where the United States has diplomatic missions. The number of illegal aliens who came from Latin America during this period is difficult to determine but has been estimated in the millions. Since 1975, there have been about 700,000 people classified as "refugees" from Southeast Asia, and another 10,000 from Eastern Europe, Africa, and the Middle East. In addition, approximately 125,000 Cubans and Haitians who came in 1981 were classified as "entrants."

This newcomer population needs self-sufficiency, which is something beyond employment. It includes cultural skills for survival both in the workplace and in the American community.

New immigrants and refugees in general need to survive and become self-sufficient—to work, to use public transportation, to rent an apartment, to open a checking account, to accomplish the activities and tasks that constitute life in the United States.

Inability to interview for a job, inability to ask directions or request information, get a driver's license, or buy a car are all barriers to the newcomers' success. These barriers can be removed one by one through good English as a second language (ESL) training. This chapter examines the instruction available to the newcomer population in ESL training.

Acclimatization Through ESL

Good ESL training incorporates culture as an integral part of the curriculum. America holds many curious surprises for the newcomer. The newcomer needs cultural orientation to avoid making the mistake of seeing events through the eyes of another culture. Without training, people tend to project and impose their own values, misunderstand and make mistakes. For example, going for a job interview is a different process in this country. In a job interview, Americans have very distinct expectations that reflect their values and their culture. Newcomers must learn, sometimes through painful trial-and-error, that Americans think differently and act differently than people in the home country. Training can facilitate this change.

Things did not work out for newcomers in the old country, and it can be assumed that most of them feel some guilt or failure to a greater or lesser extent. Adult educators must recognize this feeling and make every attempt to turn their perception of failure into success.

The entire gamut of resettlement needs must be considered when giving ESL training. The goal of self-sufficiency is a goal both for resettlement activities themselves and for ESL classes. Language/cultural training is the key to resettlement. Although language/cultural training is often a minor activity, perhaps relegated to a back shelf; it is, ultimately, language skills that will make the refugees self-sufficient and able to live in this country on their own.

ESL Training

Ethnic differences among newcomers do not warrant different kinds of ESL training. Experience has shown that there is no real need to provide ESL/Employment services for Cubans as a distinct group, or ESL/Employment services for Vietnamese or Indochinese.

For training needs in the United States, the real differences are differences in the amount of education that people have had. College graduates and professionals need a different type of training than do non-literate students. Students in a multi-ethnic classroom have in common the need to become self-sufficient new Americans. In this, they are virtually all the same. They have a common goal, a similar motivation, and a need for the same language and cultural training. The experiences they share as adult learners in a new environment also give them a common understanding of the successes and failures that occur with people in trying to achieve a common goal.

Limited to a focus on grammar and language structures in the past, ESL training today also includes language practice and communication activities. Good ESL training anticipates the cultural needs of newcomers.

For example, some come here with the attitude that job applicants are subservient in an interview. ESL training wants to adjust this behavior. Students practice asserting themselves and initiating questions, appropriate behavior in an American job interview.

Students rarely open books. They are more likely to work with objects and perform tasks such as taking a flashlight apart, operating a machine, and filling out job applications for local businesses. Students practice language in real-life contexts.

Role-playing is another common activity in ESL classes. Students become driver and passengers on a bus; landlord and tenant with faulty plumbing; manager and applicant in a job interview; or, employee asking the boss for a day off.

ESL programs take mental health needs of adult newcomers into account. They recognize the psychological dimensions of learners who, perhaps,have come through a series of traumas and have new fears, such as not being able to contribute anything to the life of the community; rejection by Americans; the loss of self; and fear of change itself. If these fears are dealt with, learning can be facilitated and attempt to remove psychological barriers to learning. Teachers today take on the role of counselor-facilitator-friend and achieve broader goals than the grammar-bound teachers of yesterday.

ESL looks to the resettlement and survival needs of individuals and translates these into objectives or competencies. This approach provides a better outcome and one that is measurable. The better ESL programs take an integrated, holistic, and humanitarian approach toward the training of adult newcomers. Programs today answer the need for individuals in their own community and the relevance of this training is a tremendous force in motivating students to learn.

Delivery Systems

Since 1981, the United States Department of State has funded very innovative language and cultural orientation programs for refugees coming from Southeast Asia. The Department funds a five-month intensive ESL and Cultural Orientation program in centers in Indonesia, Thailand, and the Philippines for refugees delayed in Asia by the immigration and sponsorship process. The actual training is done by the Experiment in International Living, Save the Children, World Education Association, and the International Catholic Migration Commission.

These programs offer ESL, cultural orientation and some pre-employment training for approximately 25,000 newcomers per year. Though affecting only a portion of the many newcomers who come here every year, their high quality has every professional looking in these programs' direction. They are also exploring ways to meet the needs of students who are illiterate in their own languages. They are giving new dimensions to teacher training, curriculum development, supervision and evaluation. They have been at the forefront of survival language training, native language literacy training, and competency-based instruction.

As a result of these programs, some refugees now come to this country with training that really makes a difference in terms of initial adjustments. And, the development of these very creative programs is leading the language training profession in curriculum and methodology.

Another development in delivery systems is ESL in the workplace, provided by the employer. Recognizing that value of staff development and training industry is also beginning to offer English classes and cultural orientation in the workplace. Usually conducted in cafeterias, conference rooms, or at actual work stations, both group classes and tutorial sessions enhance the English language skills of immigrant and refugee employees. Teachers in these programs offer language relating to specific jobs, safety language and informal language for interaction in the workplace. This instruction assists newcomers in improving their relationships with supervisors and coworkers and gives employees an opportunity to upgrade their positions. Since ESL in the workplace is just beginning to develop, questions have been raised concerning quality of instruction and curriculum development.

This country has seen a dramatic increase in Volunteer ESL Programs since 1982. This voluntary support has been the public's response to a decrease in funding for ESL and other resettlement services. Thousands of volunteers organized into more than 100 programs have emerged all over the country to help newcomers with ESL and cultural orientation and some of these programs are quite successful. Though training and professional input are minimal, the personal and psychological investment of both volunteer teachers and their students have succeeded in language learning and cultural adjustment. The best programs have a trained ESL professional as volunteer coordinator and have anywhere from ten to 100 active ESL volunteers.

County adult education programs continue to be one of the mainstays of ESL in the United States. Funding that formerly came directly from federal agencies such as the Department of Health and Human Services (HHS) and the Department of Education (ED) has diminished and is now dispersed mostly at the state level. Exceptions are: targeted assistance funds from HHS, funds for demonstration projects from ED, and the HHS Mainstream English Language Training Project, which attempts to adjust stateside training to the overseas curriculum.

Challenges for the 80s

The future of ESL training depends heavily on research and the development of new programs with emphases in the following areas:
  • employment-related language training and curriculum development for ESL in the workplace; guidelines for assisting industry
  • the ramifications of first and second languages in vocational training
  • literacy needs of newcomers; the benefits of native-language literacy training; special English literacy training; how native language literacy impacts on second language learning (or ESL) and all other learning, including basic skills and vocational training
  • student-initiated language learning; learning strategies that enable newcom-

ers to acquire language and cultural skills on their own; the lifelong training needs of newcomers
- teacher training and especially the training of volunteers to upgrade programs; the role of the teacher as a facilitator
- coordination between programs; dissemination of curricula; development of new funding sources, especially foundations and industries; guidelines for program design and evaluation
- testing in both English as a second language and cultural orientation

During the next decade, though resources are limited, ESL will be meeting the training needs of newcomers to the United States with improved sophistication and greater effectiveness.

VOCATIONAL EDUCATION FOR DISABLED ADULTS

George Travis

Educators face serious problems in meeting the needs of adults who are disabled. Disabled adults do not easily make their way into the classroom. Statistics show that about 12 percent of the adult population is disabled, yet disabled individuals are not distributed uniformly in vocational programs. They represent only 5.7 percent of the students in secondary area vocational centers, 2.6 percent of students in occupational programs in comprehensive high schools, and 2.2 percent of the students in post-secondary area vocational centers. Disabled students constitute only 2.6 percent of the freshman class in higher education.

Disabled Populations

There are three distinct populations among disabled adults who are potential participants in vocational education. In the first category are adults with limited formal education:

Adults who were disabled as children (used here to identify those congenitally disabled or who became disabled in childhood) and did not attend school, thus lacking formal education as well as vocational skills. There are an estimated one million disabled children and youth not enrolled in school.

Adults who were disabled as children and dropped out of school, thus lacking formal education credentials as well as vocational skills. The high school dropout rate for disabled youth is five to six times greater than for nondisabled youth.

Second, there are an estimated 625,000 disabled youth who graduate from high school or terminate school eligibility annually because of age. Among this group are: Adults who were disabled as children but did not participate in career and/or vocational education, and who are lacking in vocational skills. Well over 90 percent of disabled high school graduates fall into this category.

Adults who were disabled as children and who participated in career and/ or vocational education, and who need to continue and further develop

231

vocational skills. Ten percent or less of disabled high school graduates fall into this category.

And third, there are those who became disabled after becoming adults. This population far outnumbers those who were congenitally disabled or who became disabled as children or youth. Exact numbers are difficult to determine, but it has been estimated that less than one person in six was born with a disability. Moreover, there are four to six times as many adults disabled as children. When did these disabilities occur?

The President's Committee on Employment of the Handicapped reports that disability strikes primarily in adult years, "Eighty-two percent of the disabled age 18-64 acquire their disability after age 17. By this time they had already received their basic education and had acquired normal work aspirations." Of these adults who became disabled after age 17, 32 percent became disabled during early career years (18-34), 41 percent became disabled between age 35-54, nine percent became disabled after age 54.

Those who become disabled as adults are in many ways a unique population. Their disability often causes a temporary, and possibly a permanent loss of skills and abilities experienced throughout a lifetime. When hospitalization is required, the disability restricts movement. The adult must adjust psychologically to a loss of mobility. With loss of mobility often comes a loss of employment and income which, in turn, causes a change in social and family roles. Stress results, and the longer the disability lasts, the greater the stress becomes.

Vocational education has the potential to provide a means of returning to work and income, and to previous social and family roles. Vocational education often becomes a part of the therapeutic process.

Vocational Education's Role

Vocational adult educators must take into account the age at which the disability occurred, the student's educational and life experiences, including his or her background or formal and vocational education. Moreover, vocational adult educators must consider the principles of adult education that acknowledge the learner's status as an adult, while making necessary allowances for the disabling condition.

Teaching adults in vocational education, or in general education, differs from the teaching of children. Malcolm Knowles used the term "androgogy" to distinguish the teaching of adults from the term "pedagogy," the teaching of children. Knowles identified four concepts in which the difference becomes clear: Concept of the Learner, Learner's Experience, Readiness to Learn and Time Orientation.

Concept of the Learner

The concept of the learner as a child is that of a dependent learner with a teacher who is responsible for what is learned, when it is learned, how it is learned, and if it has been learned. The child has no part in these decisions. As the child matures into adulthood, an independent learner emerges. Adults are capable of self-direction, and of determining what they want to learn, when they want to learn it, and how learning will take place. Independence in vocational education is demonstrated in an adult's selection of a vocation as reflected by his or her interest abilities, selecting one school over another, selecting part or full-time study, and determining, in part, whether individual or group study will be used.

An individual disabled as a child may, according to the kind of disability, not achieve the same degree of independence as one who is not disabled. A developmentally disabled child's independence may be modified by having fewer educational options. Parents and educators play major roles in making decisions which affect the child. Children with visual or hearing impairments may become relatively independent, but may also learn to avoid educational situations in which their disability poses major problems. They may, in fact, avoid vocational education entirely unless programs are designed to meet their special need.

An adult who becomes disabled as an adult will at least temporarily be returned to the state of a dependent learner. If vocational retraining is necessary, the newly disabled adult will start from a relatively inexperienced knowledge base, and others will again be making many decisions for him or her. Vocational adult educators must be aware that these adults may face an uncomfortable return to dependency, and that some degree of resistance or rebellion may occur. The wise vocational adult educator will recognize the potential problem and make special efforts to make the disabled adult learner as independent as possible in the learning process.

The Learner's Experience

Children bring little or no direct experience to the learning situation. Whatever experience they may have serves only as a starting point. As children mature into adulthood, an experimental base is developed. As adults, learners often have experience equal to or beyond that of their teacher.

Adult educators become adept at learning about an adult's prior experience, and at finding ways to use prior experience as a base for further learning. Experience is a key factor in the initial selection of an area of vocational study, in both children and adults.

Adults who are developmentally disabled, including those who have been institutionalized, have developed a lifetime of potentially valuable experience. Years of living and interacting with other humans, and exposure to television, cannot help but contribute to a learner's experience. Vocational adult educators can build on the interests and observational experience of developmentally disabled adult learners in determining appropriate vocational goals.

Other adults who experienced childhood while disabled will similarly have accumulated vast experience. One who grew up with a speech, hearing, or visual defect will have accumulated different kinds of experiences than a nondisabled counterpart. It is important for the vocational educator to gain insight and understanding into the different kinds of experience the learner brings to vocational education, and to use those experiences to advantage.

Newly disabled adults may find that much of their previous experience has now become useless to them. An adult who has become a paraplegic and achieves mobility in a wheelchair must re-evaluate life experiences based on a different kind of mobility. An adult who has lost vision or hearing may have some advantages that one who has never experienced vision or sound may not have, but the newly disabled adult will still feel a loss. An adult who becomes blind can place limited value on the experience of having driven a car. It will become necessary for the disabled adult to acquire new experiences of a different kind, which can potentially aid in vocational education.

Most vocational adult educators are familiar with the experiential base that adults bring to learning situations, and use it to their mutual advantage in the instructional process.

Readiness to Learn

Society determines children's readiness to learn in formal (school) situations. Children start school at approximately the same age across the nation. Throughout the elementary school, and to a lesser degree in secondary school, a standard curriculum is established, with most students progressing in uniform step through grades, or subject sequences.

Adults, on the other hand, most often decide to come to a formal learning situation because of their individual needs. They begin when they want to begin, and often select their own courses and course sequence. Alan Tough has documented adults' tendency to undertake individual learning without enrolling in degree courses and programs.

Adults who are developmentally disabled remain largely other-directed rather than self-directed as they progress through educational programs. Fewer options are available to them than to nondisabled students. Education has been slow to recognize that with maturation, these adults become increasingly capable of self-direction, and are able to exercise options if options are made available to them. They are able to select among vocations that are of interest to them, and to respond to education as needs arise in their lives. Independent living skills are approached differently by one living in an independent situation than one in school who is learning for future needs. One who is living independently has an immediate need to know.

Other adults who were disabled as children may be ready to learn in vocational education programs earlier than nondisabled counterparts. Hearing impaired youth have had to learn signing, even as visually impaired children may have been literally forced to learn Braille and mobility skills. If carried over, this practical orientation to learning can be a valuable asset in learning vocational skills.

Adults who become disabled as adults may have lost some degree of independent readiness when they became disabled, and return to a child-like dependency on others to determine appropriate courses, course sequences and even content. As they become adjusted to their disability, they may be capable of resuming control and return to dealing with their needs themselves. Vocational adult educators must recognize this emerging readiness to assume control.

Time Orientation to Learning

Education for children is a future-oriented process. Children learn subject matter as part of a sequence for learning more subject matter. Addition is followed by subtraction, multiplication and division, and arithmetic precedes algebra and geometry. Knowledge is gathered for use later in life, in the real world as an adult. Most adult education, on the other hand, is focused on short-term goals and immediate pay-off for what is learned. Even in technical areas of vocational education covering long periods of study, learning has a practical focus.

For adults who are developmentally disabled, education has always had a practical focus. Self-help, independent living skills, and vocational education are studied and explored in lower school grades. Practical vocational skills may have been taught in junior high and high school, in contrast to focusing on programs leading to a post-secondary career and vocational education.

Other adults who were disabled during childhood will vary in their now/future orientation according to the kind and duration of the disability. Some disabled children make an early commitment to college preparatory courses and graduate study because of their scholastic ability and their awareness that some kinds of work may be closed to them. Others may decide that their disability would preclude extended higher education, and make an early commitment to vocational education. As noted earlier, the majority of disabled students do not make a commitment to vocational education while in high school.

Recently disabled adults may, because of their disability, be forced into job and career changes. They need to learn new job skills, or relearn previously learned skills. Adults who become disabled are often in financial difficulty, and may be greatly motivated to learn vocational skills which will make them employable. Once a reasonable return to independence is achieved, the disabled adult may readjust to a future orientation to learning. Abraham Maslow's theory that basic needs must be met before higher, more abstract needs are a concern, is illustrated in how disabled adults prioritize needs.

Meeting Disabled Adults' Needs

One possible explanation for the low rate of participation by disabled adults in vocational education may be that disabled adults fear that if they return to vocational education they will be treated as children. Their concern is logical, considering that their total educational experience has been as a child.

Vocational education for adults is most successful when vocational educators are knowledgeable about adult education and conduct their classes for adults, design programs for adults, and treat adult learners as adults.

Vocational adult educators who come in contact with disabled adults need to go beyond their understanding of adult education and know something about the impact of a disability on an adult, regardless of the time of life at which the disability occurred. A twenty-five year old male or female who became a paraplegic at age twenty-five presents a different challenge than a twenty-five year old who was congenitally disabled and has spent twenty-five years adapting to the disability. A middle-aged retarded adult who has lived a lifetime in the community has different vocational needs than a middle-aged retarded adult who has been recently deinstitutionalized. A hearing-impaired adult who dropped out of high school has different educational needs than a similar adult who graduated from a vocational high school.

It is the uniqueness of these individuals as adults that presents the greatest challenge, and the greatest opportunity to adult educators.

Cheryl Hansen observed that "By far the most common thread throughout the entire history of vocational habilitation is optimism." Vocational adult educators must remain optimistic in learning the skills necessary to meet the vocational needs of disabled adults.

References

Blueprint for Action, President's Committee on Employability of the Handicapped, Washington, D.C.: Government Printing Office, (n.d.).

The Disabled College Freshman. President's Committee on Employability of the Handicapped, Washington, D.C.: Government Printing Office, 1980.

Expanding Opportunities: Vocational Education for the Handicapped. (ed.) Cheryl L. Hansen. Seattle: University of Washington, October, 1980.

Facts About Handicapped People, President's Committee on Employability of the Handicapped, Washington, D.C.: Government Printing Office, (n.d.).

Ferris, Richard J., "Editorial Opinion", *Mainliner*, [United Airlines], (January, 1981):6.

Knowles, Malcolm. *Modern Practice of Adult Education*. New York: Follett Co., 1970.

Riffel, Rodney, "Articulating Secondary Special Needs Groups into Post-secondary Programs: Some Directions for Future Research", *Career Development for Exceptional Individuals*. 1 (Summer), 1981:83-89

Shworles, Thomas and Wang, Paul, "Education for Handicapped Adults," *Serving Personal and Community Needs Through Adult Education*. San Francisco: Jossey-Bass, 1980.

Tough, Alan. *The Adults' Learning Projects*. Toronto Ontario Institute for Studies in Education, 1979.

GROUPS AT RISK

Robert G. Wegmann

One of the major political and social problems facing the United States today is how to assist the large number of workers who have lost jobs, particularly in manufacturing, and who are having difficulty finding new employment. These individuals are commonly referred to as "displaced" or "dislocated" workers.

A careful examination of the reemployment problems they face suggests that three major factors have contributed to their plight, which has emerged with particular strength over the past decade: an increase in the number of persons seeking employment; economic trends which have depressed the number of jobs being created and maintained; and, a change in the mix of available jobs (and the pay which accompanies these jobs), so that the economy now has a higher proportion of low-paying positions than it did previously.

As a result of these trends, displaced workers have difficulty in finding new employment; and, even when they do, they often face painful adjustments to a lower standard of living.

Labor Force Increases

Table 1 gives the size of the American labor force at five year intervals from 1950 through 1980, the most recent data for 1983, and the projections of the Bureau of Labor Statistics for 1990 and 1995. This table shows clearly that the labor force has grown with extraordinary rapidity during the postwar period; in fact, between 1950 and 1983 it almost doubled.

There are at least three major factors which have played key roles in this labor force growth. The first is the "baby boom" generation, born during the period of very high birth rates (approximately 1945 to 1960), and entering the labor market in search of full time jobs twenty years later, between 1965 and 1980. The second is the steady increase in the proportion of adult women seeking paid employment outside the home. A third factor, much harder to measure accurately but undoubtedly involved, is the impact of immigration, both legal and illegal. These three factors, occurring simultaneously, generated very rapid labor force growth, particularly between 1965 and 1980.

Today, the baby boom generation has largely entered the labor market, and the growth in the proportion of women seeking employment seems to be slowing.

Table 1

Postwar Labor Force Growth
(in millions of persons)

Year	Civilian Labor Force	Employed	Unemployed	Unemployment Rate
1950	62	59	3.4	5.3%
1955	65	62	2.9	4.4
1960	70	66	3.9	5.5
1965	74	71	3.4	4.5
1970	83	79	4.1	4.9
1975	94	86	7.9	8.5
1980	107	99	7.6	7.1
1983	112	101	10.7	9.6
1990 est.	125	117	7.9	6.3
1995 est.	131	124	7.9	6.0

Source: Bureau of Labor Statistics data. See, especially, "The U.S. Economy in 1995." *Monthly Labor Review* 106 (November 1983): 3-58 [Special Issue]. Details may not always add to totals due to rounding.

Nonetheless, the Bureau of Labor Statistics expects continued, if somewhat slower, increases in the number of people seeking work through 1995.

Table 1 also makes clear that the ability of the American economy to create enough new jobs to meet the needs of this rapidly growing labor force changed for the worse about 1975. From about 1950 to 1975, the unemployment rate went up and down within a rather narrow range of approximately four to six percent. Since 1975, however, the unemployment rate has gone below 6 percent only once (5.8 percent in 1979), and the federal government does not expect it to do so again before 1995.

Why is the American economy no longer able to create enough jobs for those who seek them?

Pressures Reducing New Job Creation

While there have been many factors which have tended to keep the number of available jobs below the number of persons seeking employment, greatly increased energy costs and unprecedented foreign trade expansion between 1975 and 1984 both played key roles. In 1950, the goods portion of the American gross national product was $162.4 billion. The value of American merchandise exports was $10.2 billion, a modest 6.3 percent of this goods segment of the gross national product. In other words, the United States shipped only a relatively small proportion of what was produced in its mines and factories to other countries. Twenty years later, in 1970, this percentage had grown somewhat, to 9.2 percent. In 1975, however, it ballooned upward to 15.4 percent and by 1980, it had increased again, to 19.6 percent. In the space of only a few years, the proportion of American goods shipped to other countries more than doubled while the proportion of goods sold in this country but produced abroad increased at a similar pace.

In trying to gauge the impact of this much increased involvement in foreign trade on American employment, one critical fact must be kept in mind. On average, the goods this country buys are much more labor-intensive than are the goods it sells. To give a concrete example: when South Korea needs an airliner, it is not able to make one itself. A modern airliner is a very complex product, and can be constructed by only a small number of highly industrialized countries. South Korea is much more likely to turn to the United States for such a purchase, buying the airliner from a company such as Boeing. The United States, in turn, can then take the money spent by South Korea on that airliner (say, $50 million), and use these funds to buy $50 million worth of shirts made in South Korea. In dollars, this is an equal trade.

It is not an equal trade in jobs, however. It takes significantly more people to make $50 million worth of shirts than it does to make a $50 million dollar airliner. Selling an airliner creates jobs in the United States for engineers, machinists, electronics technicians, and all of those whom Boeing hires to design, build and test the airliner. Buying shirts means that jobs which might have existed in this country making shirts are not needed, since the shirts are coming from abroad. Thus, jobs are both gained and lost for American workers in this $50 million exchange, and more jobs are lost than are gained.

The merchandise which the United States sells to other countries is, on average, considerably more capital-intensive than is the merchandise it buys, which is more labor-intensive. As a result, even when this country sells somewhat more merchandise than it buys (measured in dollars), it still loses jobs at approximately a 4 to 3 ratio. That is, for every four jobs lost because of imports, only three jobs are generated by exports. While this 4/3 ratio might not be very important if the great bulk of the goods produced in this country stayed here, it becomes a significant factor when a fifth of all that is made here is shipped to other countries, with an equivalent amount coming back here in the form of imports.

This would be a difficult enough situation under any circumstances. In the last few years, however, it has been made much more difficult by the fact that the dollar value of the imported merchandise has greatly exceeded the dollar value of American exports. During 1983, the United States bought $69 billion more merchandise than it sold, and this negative trade balance alone is estimated to have cost the United States approximately 1.5 million jobs. (When the merchandise trade balance becomes negative, this country continues to lose the four jobs due to imports displacing American workers, but it does not gain the three jobs that would otherwise have been generated by exports.) This situation is now worsening; the negative merchandise trade balance for 1984 is estimated at over $100 billion.

Unemployment Overhang

The net effect of all the trends discussed so far is that, particularly since 1975, a growing number of persons seeking employment have moved into a labor market where very strong forces are acting to decrease the number of available jobs. This has created an "unemployment overhang" of individuals seeking work, and anxious to accept employment (even, if necessary, at lower wages than those paid in the past). During the recent Greyhound strike, for example, it was widely publicized that management threatened to replace the 12,700 striking workers if a settlement (involving lowered wages) could not be reached. As a result of this publicity, Greyhound received over 65,000 applications from persons willing to accept the positions that these discharges would open. Greyhound could have replaced its entire workforce five times over!

The Changing Mix of Available Jobs

Not only are there an insufficient *number* of jobs but, equally important, the *mix* of available jobs (and the mix of incomes attached to them) is changing in important and striking ways.

Table 2 divides the nation's payroll employment (farmers and the self-employed are excluded in these figures) into four major groups: those in the goods-producing sector (primarily manufacturing, but also construction and mining), trade (wholesale and retail), other service (medical, business services, consumer services, finance, real estate, and so on), and government (federal, state, county, city, school districts, and all other government units).

These figures show clearly that the proportion of the working population employed in producing goods, and particularly in manufacturing, has been dropping steadily (although the Bureau of Labor Statistics believes that this decline has now bottomed out) while the proportion employed in services has been rising, and is expected to continue to do so. This pattern has been widely discussed by those who believe the nation is entering the era of a service or information economy.

Equally important in understanding this change in the mix of available jobs, however, is the much less discussed fact that government employment, which played a major role in absorbing the workers being displaced from manufacturing during the 1950-1975 period, is now falling rather than rising in its share of the

Table 2

Nonagricultural Payroll Employment
by Major Industry Division

Year	Goods Producing	Trade	Other Service	Govern- ment	Total
1950	41%	21%	25%	13%	100%
1955	41	21	25	14	100
1960	38	21	26	15	100
1965	36	21	26	17	100
1970	33	21	28	18	100
1975	29	22	29	19	100
1980	28	22	31	18	100
1983	26	23	33	17	100
1990 est.	26	23	35	16	100
1995 est.	26	23	36	15	100

Source: Bureau of Labor Statistics data. See especially, "The U.S. Economy in 1995." *Monthly Labor Review* 106 (November 1983): 3-58 [Special Issue]. Details may not always add to totals due to rounding.

workforce. Since employment in both the government and goods-producing sectors typically offered steady work at good pay to many individuals who did not have high levels of formal education, drops in these two sectors have had a major impact on income levels, particularly for the less educated.

This situation can be understood most easily by examining the average hourly pay of workers in the non-governmental sectors of the economy during 1983. The average nonsupervisory worker in manufacturing earned $8.84 an hour, or approximately $18,400 per year on a full-time basis. The average for the services area was significantly lower ($7.26 an hour or $15,100 a year), and trade incomes were lower still ($6.49 an hour or $13,500). Clearly, if the proportion employed in the goods-producing sectors falls, while more and more people are employed in trade and service jobs, then average income is going to keep declining. In fact, average incomes, adjusted for inflation, have been falling steadily during the post-1975 period, both for the general population and for men over 25 years of age. Family incomes, however, have not fallen to the same degree because of the large number of wives who have newly entered the paid labor force.

The Displaced Worker

The person who has worked for many years in a factory which has now closed faces, therefore, a very difficult situation. He or she must enter a labor market where the number of manufacturing jobs has been falling as a proportion of the total jobs available, so that the competition for such positions is intense. It is significant that the 1983 Fortune 500 figures show that, despite the considerable increase in the total number of persons employed between 1973 and 1983, the number employed by the 500 largest manufacturing corporations actually decreased by 10 percent over this same period.

Such an individual also soon discovers that, of the jobs that are more easily available, usually in the trade or service sectors, many pay much less than the position which was lost when the factory closed. There may be a high level of competition even for these jobs, despite their lower pay. If the worker is older (over 55 years of age, particularly), he or she can also expect to encounter significant age discrimination, no small factor when employers have many younger workers from whom they can choose.

Implications for Vocational Education

In this situation, what can be done by vocational educators? Is retraining the solution for these problems? Is it vocational education to which the nation should primarily turn to answer the problem of the displaced worker?

The evidence suggests that the answer to these questions is, on the whole, negative. There are no longer a significant number of jobs sitting empty because no one has the training to fill them. The fundamental problem which the nation faces today is not a lack of training; the fundamental problem is that there are too few jobs, with even the jobs which are available paying significantly less than was previously the case.

This is not to deny, of course, that wisely chosen vocational training might help a specific person get a good job. But very large-scale training would only intensify the already fierce competition for the declining number of wellpaid positions.

What are the implications for anyone who does offer vocational training to displaced workers?

First of all, it is absolutely essential that such training not be offered without first conducting a careful review of the jobs available in the local labor market. The local situation may differ significantly from the national pattern, and the training which is offered must make it possible for displaced workers to compete for local jobs. The natural tendency of any educational institution is to offer courses in areas where the faculty feel competent and for which the school has equipment. Both, unfortunately, have a tendency to lag behind the market. While this tendency causes problems under any circumstances, it is a particularly tragic course of action when dealing with those displaced by factory closings.

It would be cruel and unfair to take persons who have lost steady, well-paying positions (many of whom may not have attended classes of any kind for many years) and put them through weeks and months of training without reasonable certainty that the skills being acquired are needed locally, and can command an adequate income.

Moreover, even when the skills being taught are needed, it should be expected that the graduates of this skill training will inevitably face competition when applying for the jobs that will use their newly acquired skills. Facing such competition is, in today's labor market, an inevitable part of the job search process.

These conditions imply several things. It is even more important than it used to be that the skills taught be founded on a natural aptitude for the work involved. In a highly competitive labor market, the worker has to be good at what he or she does. In addition, they suggest that job search training should be a part of any such vocational program from day one.

There are, in other words, two sets of skills that now have to be mastered in order to prepare displaced workers for success in this highly competitive labor market. The first set is the skills to do the job being sought—skills well taught, thoroughly mastered, up to date, and built on a natural aptitude for the work involved. The second set is the skills necessary to obtain a position—knowing how to use the telephone as a key job search tool; how not be be screened out by a job application form; understanding how the labor market operates; being able to present oneself effectively in a job interview.

Both sets of skills can be learned, both can be taught, and both need to be seen as essential parts of any program which attempts to prepare the displaced worker for new employment.

SECTION V

PUTTING THEORY INTO PRACTICE

Across the nation, rapid technological change and worker displacement have often resulted in high unemployment and poor economies. Cities, counties, states, and the federal government have tried to respond to these conditions by providing education and training to those who need and seek it. These efforts draw upon knowledge about labor market conditions, theories of adult learning, and new collaborative approaches between education and industry.

In this section, authors who have been directly involved in these ventures describe how they operate. Their projects' approaches demonstrate how to put theory into practice.

In Cincinnati, all levels of government as well as private industry came together to sponsor a training program. Robert E. Scarborough describes their efforts, formally organized into a non-profit corporation, "The Greater Cincinnati Industrial Training Corporation." The program trains several different groups of workers in industrial machining and fabrication skills.

Robert W. Rupert discusses the special case of the Los Angeles Unified School District, the second largest school district and the largest urban adult education program in the nation. The adults served are a majority of minorities—only 22 percent are Caucasian. And they represent different languages, cultures, levels of education, and work experience.

Michigan has depended on the American automobile industry for a large part of its economic well-being. Gale King and William Weisgerber report on how that industry faltered during the 1970's and on Michigan's State Department of Education's effort to redress the problem through vocational programs, in co-operation with both the United Auto Workers and automobile management.

In Virginia, marketing and distributive education leaders, in cooperation with the state's Department of Education Marketing and Distributive Education Service, developed a new delivery system. Barry Reece discusses how "Operation

1000'' was put together to stem and reverse the decline in enrollments in public school sponsored adult vocational education.

And, finally, Rosemary F. Kolde explains how the Center for Employment Resources, in Cincinnati, Ohio, brings together the multitude of services that employed, underemployed, and dissatisfied adults need to find satisfying employment. Business and industry also use the Center in identifying workers who will be successful employees.

COLLABORATIVE EFFORTS WITH INDUSTRY, GOVERNMENT AND EDUCATION

Robert E. Scarborough

In a unique public/private joint venture among industrial machining and fabrication industries, the Greater Cincinnati Area Private Industry Councils, vocational education planning districts, JTP Ohio, and the United States Department of Labor, formed a partnership to develop high quality, video-based instructional material that can be used by industry and vocational schools to train people in industrial machining and fabrication skills. These public/private entities formed a non-profit corporation, "The Greater Cincinnati Industrial Training Corporation" (GCITC) to administer the experimental effort, which is called the "National Pilot Program." Representatives from each entity sit on the GCITC Board of Directors.

Substantial financial support has been provided for the National Pilot Project. The Department of Labor awarded a $1.1 million grant to GCITC on September 28, 1983; The General Electric Aircraft Engine Business Group (GEAEBG) in Cincinnati, Ohio, is contributing $2 million over the two-year period; three area Private Industry Councils and five service delivery areas are contributing $261,000; and, JTP Ohio has committed $195,000. Target groups for the program are: dislocated workers; JTPA-eligible adults; disadvantaged youth; and under-employed individuals.

Developing the Project

The National Pilot Program was developed at the GEAEBG Educational Services Center by Jerry Haynes, Director, and Penn Ansorg, Manager of Instructional Design, and is administered by the Greater Cincinnati Industrial Training Corporation. GEAEBG faced the twin challenges of providing a means of upgrading the hourly workforce to maintain qualified workers in state-of-the-art technology and of devising a mechanism to assure standardized preparation for entry-level employees to fill vacant positions. GEAEBG projects growth in its own employment requirements by the end of this decade, and it is anticipated there will be an overall national shortage of qualified workers, given America's defense

249

needs and the labor market, which will see a thirty percent reduction of entry-level job candidates by 1990.

It was determined that a standardized set of instructional materials could be used by those already on the job, as well as by those desiring to enter industrial machining and fabrication, and that such materials would be the most effective and efficient means of expanding opportunities for minority groups and women. And, it was determined that high quality audio-visual materials would be the most appropriate teaching tools, particularly for individuals with lower reading skills.

As one of the largest industrial employers in the Greater Cincinnati area as well as a leader in the field of design, development and production of aircraft engines, GEAEBG presented the training partnership concept to the local community, which also was seeking a means of upgrading the existing hourly workforce and standardizing preparation for entry-level employees.

Until recently, it has been the responsibility of business and industry to train their own employees in the high technology skill areas that are commonplace in today's industrial community. Big businesses have been practically the only source of highly technical job training because only they can afford the incredibly expensive machinery that is becoming essential in the extremely competitive international marketplace. Even if educational institutions had the money, most of them are not as close to the leading edge of technology as are companies such as General Electric, Cincinnati Milacron, Meyer Tool, Planet Products Corporation, Xtek, LeBlond/Makino Machine Tool Company, and General Tool Company. Now, with the advent of the National Pilot Program, sophisticated training efforts can be shared in a community. The National Pilot Program can serve as a paradigm for others to adopt in order to create new training opportunities for workers in other parts of the country.

Training Materials

The selection of twelve initial courses for the National Pilot Program was based on GEAEBG's research, consultation with other local companies, vocational educators, and data from the U.S. government. The twelve courses are: Standard Gages; Cutting Tools, Tool Geometry, Fixturing; Conventional Turning Processes; Conventional Milling Processes; Conventional Drilling Processes; Conventional Grinding Processes; Numerical Control Machining; Packaging; Horizontal Boring Mill; Vertical Turret Lathe; Tungsten Inert Gas Welding; and, Resistance Welding.

The training materials include video tapes, student guides and, in some courses, interactive video programs. Each course will include an instructor's guide which provides information on how to administer the course, lesson plans, etc. The amount of time for each of the courses varies from six to sixty hours, depending on the complexity of the topic.

The inclusion of interactive video programs reflects the National Pilot Program's commitment to state-of-the-art training methods. Interactive video lets a learner use a computer to control a video-based instructional program in terms of variables such as pace and sequence. Interactive video-disc training technology is still in its infancy, but is expected to be a $25 billion industry by 1990. By employing these cost-effective, high-tech educational methodologies, the National Pilot Program hopes to affect a wide spectrum of schools and businesses.

The Greater Cincinnati Industrial Training Corporation will assist in: developing, using and validating materials; creating an integrated job identification system in the machining and fabrication field, in partnership with the vocational education centers; and, putting into place and supervising a national information dissemination mechanism related to the assessment and availability of the materials. This dissemination effort will use established clearinghouses.

Program Delivery System

Assessment. The collaborating vocational education planning district's assessment center personnel contributed significantly to the design and implementation of the comprehensive assessment package. The assessment process is used to evaluate the adult's current abilities, rather than relying on a previous record, and an attempt is made to match past skills with those needed for success in a training program. By utilizing the Dictionary of Occupational Titles, candidates are tested only in the categories for that particular occupation.

All training sites adopted this process:

Step 1 - Career interest:
- System for Assessment and Group Evaluation (SAGE) - Vocational Interest Inventory
- Career Orientation Placement & Evaluation Survey (COPS)
- Holland Self-Directed Search

Step 2 - Test of Adult Basic Education (TABE)

Step 3 - Aptitude tests:
- Career Ability Placement Survey (CAPS)
- System for Assessment and Group Evaluation (SAGE) - Vocational Aptitude Battery
- Bennett Mechanical
- Bennett Hand Tool Dexterity
- Valpar Component Work Samples
- Crawford Small Test

Since the Vocational Education Planning District's (VEPD) assessment centers did not have all the same assessment components, the GCITC selected similar components at each site. Upon successful completion of the battery of tests, each candidate is required to go through an interview process. The candidate is interviewed by a panel with representatives from: industry, local service delivery areas; the VEPD and GCITC.

Length of Program. The proposed length of the training program is approximately 9-12 months (900-1200 hrs.). The student will spend approximately 75 percent of that time in the shop utilizing hands-on training; the remaining 25 percent will be spent in related classroom study.

Certificate of Achievement. A key feature of the training program is the awarding of a certificate to prospective and current industrial machining and fabrication workers, following satisfactory completion of courses. The certificate will be accepted by GEAEBG and the other private sector partners as evidence that the individual, in terms of skills, may be an "eligible candidate" for hiring. The certificate is considered a vital part of the National Pilot Program, since it can provide critically needed "credentials" for previously unskilled and semi-skilled JTPA-eligible men and women, dislocated workers and out-of-school youth. Credentials are important elements in determining whether or not people in the target groups are hired. In addition, the certificate provides standardization of demonstrated job skills which could be the basis for establishing a system of nationally accepted skills.

Research Studies

The University of Cincinnati designed research studies to provide data on two issues: the validity of the courses; and, the value of the competency certificate to JTPA eligible adults, dislocated workers, and youth.

A series of independent empirical studies will be conducted to determine whether or not training provided through the National Pilot Program is valid. The empirical evidence will be complemented by a separate ethnographic study. The ethnographic study will provide insight into why a training program is effective or ineffective, and will describe and document the effects of a "Certificate of Competence" upon the relative job-getting ability of the JTPA adult, dislocated workers, and youth population of the program. Structured interviews with students, instructors and employers, observational checklists, and other unobtrusive measures will be used in collecting data.

Partnership

Private Sector Partners. An excellent cross-section of businesses in the field of industrial machining and fabrication was brought together for technological expertise, endorsement of the National Pilot Program, and to serve on the Board of Directors of GCITC. The industrial representatives are:

Company	Business
Cincinnati Milacron, Inc. 4701 Marburg Avenue Cincinnati, OH 45209	Manufacture machine tools, industrial robots, plastics, machinery, industrial specialty products and electronic models
General Electric Company Aircraft Engine Business Group Educational Services Center 1 Neumann Way/Box 6301 Cincinnati, OH 45215-6301	Research, design, development, manufacture and provide logistic support of propulsion systems for military, commercial and business aircraft and for marine and industrial applications
General Tool Company, Inc. Landy Lane Cincinnati, OH 45215	Manufacture tools, jigs, fixtures, custom machine building and fabrication, precision machining
LeBlond/Makino Machine Tool Co. Madison & Edwards Road Cincinnati, OH 45208	Manufacture machine tools and related products
Meyer Tool & Die Company 3064 Colerain Avenue Cincinnati, OH 45225	Manufacture turbine engine components and associated fixturing, gaging and machine tools
Planet Products Corporation 4200 Malsbary Road Cincinnati, OH 45242	Manufacture food processing equipment, plastic thermoforming packaging machinery, hydraulic equipment components, and robots
Xtek, Inc. 211 Township Avenue Cincinnati, OH 45216	Manufacture hardened steel gears, pinions, forged steel rolls, track wheels and custom gears

George Wile, Planet Products Corporation CEO, was elected Chairperson of GCITC. Robert Scarborough serves as President and Susan Conway as Vice-President of GCITC.

Education Partners. For many years, vocational education in the Greater Cincinnati area has been the cornerstone for training local young people and adults for careers in business and industry. Leaders in vocational education agreed to serve on the Board of GCITC and utilize the training materials in their machine shop adult vocational programs. The partners in education include: James Boyd, Superintendent, D. Russel Lee Joint Vocational School; he is also the GCITC Corporate Treasurer and a Trustee; Rosemary Kolde, Associate Superintendent, Great Oaks Joint Vocational School District; Willis Holloway, Assistant Superintendent, Cincinnati Public Schools. Fernando Cress, Superintendent of Warren County Career Center, has agreed to adopt the training materials in the adult machine trades program at that site.

The "Partners in Education" have had an excellent rapport with industry in developing and maintaining successful occupational skills training programs that:
- provide graduates with skill levels required by industry;
- are responsive to industry's immediate and future needs;
- maintain industrial structure and oversight;
- demonstrate outstanding results in longitudinal studies of long-term job retention; and
- demonstrate cost efficiency.

Private Industry Councils/Service Delivery Areas.
Members include:

Gerald S. Hammond, Chairman
Private Industry Council of Butler
County

Gordon Hullan, Chairman
Private Industry Council of
Cincinnati and Hamilton County

Vern Bradley, Chairman
Clermont/Warren Private Industry
Council

Stephen G. Brooks, Director
Clermont/Warren County Manpower
Consortium

George Estes, Executive Director
Butler County Private Industry
Council/ETA

Henry L. Christmon, Executive
Director
Employment Training Division
City of Cincinatti

David R. Schweir, Director
Hamilton County Employment
Training Agency

Lifelong Education

Technological changes have, more than ever, caused vast numbers of youth and adults to seek educational opportunities that offer training and upgrading to meet job competency requirements. Statistics show that the average worker will face four to eight employment changes during his or her working life. This nation must leverage all financial, technological, and training resources in order to develop an industry-wide standard set of competency-based instructional materials that will be utilized by the current and future workforce in industrial training and in vocational education.

Since business and industry spend over $35 billion annually in various training activities and an educational system costs the nation $120 billion annually, I feel that the joint venture in the National Pilot Program in the Greater Cincinnati area could be a breakthrough. This concept must come under the guidance of experts in manpower from business and industry, labor, and educators in combating the ever-increasing shortage of matching newly emerging occupations with dislocated workers, under-employed, unemployed and the youth of our nation. The leadership role must come from the private sector in breaking the barriers that have arisen in the past concerning the pre-employment deficiencies among secondary school graduates and non-graduates entering or attempting to enter the workforce. This collaboration will:

- open lines of communication between the private sector and educational systems regarding the quality of academic skills required on the job
- target ways of alleviating basic skill deficiencies
- develop curricula that meets industry standards
- design vocational education programs that will train people for tomorrow's jobs
- design vocational education programs that are consistent with industrial standards
- design vocational education programs where there are jobs

Vocational education must continue to play a vital role in training, retraining and upgrading the American workforce, but it must maintain its partnership with the private sector and labor in order to have a positive impact on putting America back to work.

ADULT EDUCATION IN AN URBAN ENVIRONMENT

Robert W. Rupert

The second largest school district in the United States also supports the largest, single, urban adult education program in the nation. In fact, the scope and number of the Los Angeles Unified School District's adult schools and vocational center are not matched anywhere in the world.

The 710 square miles that is the Los Angeles school district is also served by the nation's largest community college district; the nation's largest university extension program; five state universities, each with a continuing education program; three major private university continuing education systems, and several smaller ones; and, private or proprietary schools whose listings fill many yellow pages in the telephone book. Have the Los Angeles Unified School District, Los Angeles Community College District, the University of California at Los Angeles Extension, the California State University system, and the private colleges and schools ever approached the idea of coordinating adult education activities? Only loosely, through informal linkages. There is enough adult education demand in Los Angeles for all these institutions.

California, along with Florida and Texas, had 22 percent of all job opportunities in the country in 1982. In the same year, California, with Florida and Texas, had 38 percent of the nation's population increase. The same three states also demonstrated the greatest population mobility, within and across borders, in the United States. Los Angeles, and the area which surrounds it, share in these demographics. The adult education systems which serve greater Los Angeles are hard-pressed to keep up with the job needs, increases in population, and the movement of people that are occurring.

Adult Populations Compared

Figure 1 compares the adult education populations served, the providing institutions, and the type of adult education offered. There is a definite hierarchial trend.

The many different adult education providers in Los Angeles have long understood this hierarchy, each carving out its "piece of the action" over time.

Figure 1
Comparison of Adult Education Offerings in Los Angeles

Institutions	Population Served	Vocational Training	General Continuing Education
University Extension and Continuing Education	Professionals and degree holders	Higher-tech professional up-grading	Advanced academic education, global and life-issues
Community Colleges and Proprietary Schools	High school graduates, blue and white collar workers	High-tech technician up-grading, entry level training	Freshman, sophomore academic education, remedial education, community service classes
Public School System Adult Education	Illiterates, high school drop-outs, high school graduates, entry level and blue collar workers	Entry level training, low-tech	Basic Education, Life-coping skills

This chapter deals expressly with the lower end of the hierarchy—the public school system of adult education in the Los Angeles Unified School District.

Public School System Adult Education

Since 1972, the Los Angeles Unified School District has provided literacy education, job training, and general adult education to both high school dropouts and adults under one major division. Each year since 1981, this division has served an average of 335,000 students. Of this number, 25,000 have been secondary school youth and 310,000 have been adults. Thirty percent of the total enrollments have been in job training, 60 percent in literacy education, and 10 percent in general adult and continuing education. This last category addresses special adult populations (handicapped and senior citizens) and special adult needs (parenting, home/consumer economics, health and safety).

Job Training

Adult job training, literacy education, and general adult and continuing education classes are located in many places. Currently, five regional occupational centers (ROC) enroll a mix of 80 percent adults and 20 percent youth, with one goal — job placement — established for the end of training, which lasts one year or less. Recent records indicate that goal is accomplished with adults about 75 percent of the time, and youth about 50 percent. Since many high school youth use center training as an exploratory experience, the difference in placement rates is understandable.

In addition to the ROC's, high school youth may participate in regional occupational programs (ROP). These after-school and Saturday job training classes are offered in specially-equipped high school shops and laboratories or in community classrooms located at business and industrial sites and taught by workers. The State of California has provided special funds to support both ROC and ROP. These programs have become a model for job training in California.

Another job training network available to Los Angeles adults is a system of six Job Training Partnership Act (JTPA) skills centers. Located in six manpower areas defined by the Los Angeles City Council, these centers have their roots in the Comprehensive Employment Training Act (CETA) and Manpower Development Training Act (MDTA). Job training in these small centers, which enroll about 5,000 adults yearly, is targeted at the disadvantaged population, as was the case under MDTA and CETA.

Adult and Continuing Education

The largest network of adult and continuing education classes is composed of twenty-five traditional evening high schools, which share late afternoon and evening space on high school sites, and the Evans Community School, for adults only, which operates from 8 a.m. to 10 p.m., Monday through Friday. These twenty-six schools enroll over 80 percent of the Los Angeles Unified School District adult student clientele. Of this number, the Evans Community Adult School enrolls over 6,000 average daily attendees (ADA) yearly. (One ADA equals 525 instructional hours.)

The term "traditional evening high schools" conjures up a picture of the struggling drop-out trying to earn a high school diploma at night after a hard day's work. The Los Angeles situation is quite different. In most cases, more classes are offered off campus in neighborhood locations than on the high school site, and more classes are offered during the day than at night. There are more than 700 branch locations of the twenty-six adult schools each year. The curriculum is still highly oriented to literacy education, but it includes all of the adult education curriculum currently supported by state funds.

Fiscal Resources

The Los Angeles Schools' Adult Regional Occupational and Center and Regional Occupational Programs Education Division combine federal and state funding to offer a variety of job training and adult education services with a yearly budget that totals $71,000,000. Ten percent of this amount comes from federal sources. The other 90 percent comes from state and local taxes, and it is driven by the previous year's average daily attendance (ADA) on a per ADA support basis. During the 1983-84 school year, the statewide average ADA reimbursement rate for ROC and ROP was $1,735, while the rate for adult education was $1,034.

The Curriculum

The California legislature has limited the adult education curriculum for which it will provide ADA reimbursement to ten areas. These are: elementary and secondary basic skills, English as a Second Language, citizenship, short-term vocational training with high employment potential, apprenticeship, parent education, home economics, health and safety, classes for senior citizens, and classes for the handicapped. Figure 2 illustrates the scope and location of these classes within the Los Angeles Unified School District System.

Populations Served

The Greater Los Angeles Area presents an enormous multi-ethnic and multinational mix. A recent journal termed the city, "Ellis Island - West," and rightfully so. Los Angeles has more Mexicans than any place but Mexico City, more Samoans than on American Samoa, almost 200,000 Koreans, and significant Filipino and other Hispanic populations. The unified school districts' racial and ethnic statistics for 1981-82 are: American Indian - 4 percent, Asian/Filipino - 7.5 percent, Black - 22.2 percent, Hispanic - 47.4 percent, and White - 22.5 percent. Los Angeles schools are a majority of minorities, as are its adult schools, but percentages do not tell the whole story.

The categories "Asian/Filipino" and "Hispanic" are very broad. "Asian/Filipino" includes Korean, Chinese and Filipino people who have three distinct languages and three different cultures. The Chinese may further be subdivided into Indo-Chinese, Cambodian, Mong, and other groups. Although ethnic Chinese may be a common bond, the cultures attributed to each and native educational levels, are vastly different.

The same hold true for "Hispanic." Spanish is the common language, but significant differences exist among Cubans, Hondurans, Columbians, Mex-

Figure 2
Adult Education Classes Receiving ADA Reimbursements

Citizenship	Where Offered	% of Total Attendance (April, 1984)
Literacy Education		60%
Elementary Basic Skills	Adult Schools	
Secondary Basic Skills	Skills Centers	
English as a Second Language		
Citizenship		
Job Training		28%
Short-term vocational	ROC/ROP	
Apprenticeship	Adult Schools	
	Skills Centers	
General Adult/Continuing Education		12%
Handicapped	Adult Schools	
Health and Safety		
Home Economics		
Parent Education		
Senior Citizens		

icans, and others. Their cultures, type and levels of education at "home" range from total illiteracy, to some schooling, to college degrees.

The adult population that immigrates to Los Angeles has two common goals—to learn the language and to get a job. Faced with this diverse population mix, the public school's adult system has an enormous challenge to meet the literacy and job training needs of its clientele.

Solutions to Urban Adult Education Problems

Despite its share of the hard times created by less fiscal support and more public criticism for all schools during the past ten years, adult and continuing education is alive and well in Los Angeles. There are, however, four problem areas that must be continually dealt with. The areas are: meeting diverse and multi-ethnic adult education needs; creating communication links between the adult education system and the business, industrial, and social community; gaining recognition from the local, state, and national political structure; and, ensuring quality in job training and adult/continuing education teaching. To deal with these problems, the Los Angeles Unified School District continually seeks and gives information, networks, and coordinates fiscal and human resources.

Meeting Multi-Enthic Adult Education Needs

Big city people tend to be open and accepting in their approaches to people problems. Thank goodness! It takes an enlightened group of professionals to develop a curriculum which takes into consideration the language, culture and personal needs of adult learners who want to become literate in a new language and achieve academically, or who need to develop a job skill. It helps to have 100 years of passed-on experience (adult education began in Los Angeles around 1887) at the disposal of curriculum developers.

Through the use of teacher committees, formal community advisory committees and school and staff expertise, the language literacy curriculum (English as a Second Language or ESL) has become stable, transferable, and more standardized over the past several years. In addition, a competency-based high school diploma program for adults, called "Diploma Plus," is in place at each adult school and regional occupational center. Los Angeles Mayor Tom Bradley has commended these efforts publicly and likes to talk about them when out of his own city.

Constantly in need of change and fine tuning, both the ESL and the diploma curriculum have established a reputation for excellence and are well known in the community. Through community involvement, information, networking and evaluation, more of the community are made aware of what is available in adult schools. Because of the highly mobile nature of the urban dweller, networking is essential to keep people informed.

Creating Communication Links

With a constantly changing job market, curriculum needs in the ROC's, ROP's and skills centers need to be adjusted almost annually. Community advisory councils, trade advisory councils for each area of occupational education, and communicating links with the business/industrial community are essential to quality job training, too. By working with local coordinating councils, the employment department, and the social service department, education-to-work transitions are made easier. A newly organized Los Angeles Business Labor Council contributes. LABLC was created by the state legislature to bridge the education-to-work gap, and it has produced an effective 2-year track record.

Political Recognition

To paraphrase California State Treasurer Jesse Unruh's famous quote, "Money is the mother's milk of education." Without a share of public funds, adult education systems in California would not have survived over the years. Constant information-sharing efforts with local school boards and city and county governmental bodies is required to keep this support. Local support and understanding of the role of adult and continuing education is essential if programs are to survive in an educational milieu primarily concerned with children and youth.

In California, recent political events have shifted the purse strings for education from the local to the state taxpayer. The California legislature, in fact, controls the dollars channeled to local school districts. As this phenomenon came about, adult and vocational educators were compelled to develop a strong information base capable of lobbying from afar. Primarily through the efforts of professional organizations with both local and state lobbying capabilities, most legislators more clearly understand and are aware of the need for adult job training, literary and continuing education. Since one-third of the legislature changes each election year, this informational effort has become on-going and a way of life for leaders in vocational and adult education.

The national legislative scene is even more remote. Were it not for organizations like the American Vocational Association and the American Association for Adult and Continuing Education, little would be known or be done when the time came to secure federal financial support. A Los Angeles adult education network has been developed to keep representatives and senators aware of problems and needs. Congress often calls upon the network to provide information needed to make the right decisions in policy and appropriation bills.

Insuring Quality

Although literacy education and general adult/continuing education is primarily a part-time learning endeavor and job training is still largely so, the recent trend is for adult and vocational teachers to be less part-time and more full-time. The trend has been led by those involved with job training, who find it nearly impossible to compete in the job market for teachers and instructors unless teachers can be assured of a living wage. Auto mechanics, business, electrical, nursing instructors, and others, can be employed more easily on a full-time basis.

With the recent curricular stabilization and standardization of the ESL and "Diploma Plus" programs, it has been found that part-time and partially committed teachers cannot handle the pressure of new material and new methodology. They wish to continue in the same old ways, which do not fit the new systems. Thus, it has been necessary to recruit and train full-time teachers who have become a professional cadre and train other teachers at their jobs. Since teacher training and development is the key to success in vocational and adult education classrooms, extra fiscal resources need to be applied to that task if change, and acceptance of change, are to occur.

Today's Necessity

Adult education in an urban environment is one of today's most exciting educational challenges. Those involved in the process, whether teaching, counseling, coordinating or administering, face a variety of jobs and tasks. And, adult educators are not the kind of people who are satisfied with pat answers or solutions. Particularly in the urban environment, the necessity for change is always present. Unfortunately, many traditional educators still ignore this fact whenever possible.

The number of colleges and universities involved with the education of those who wish to study or to practice adult education is on the rise. Reports from legislative bodies, foundations, and research indicate that lifelong learning is not tomorrow's necessity, but today's. Adult and continuing education will be three times longer than the eighteen years of childhood learning. The adult education profession will be looking for, actively recruiting, and better rewarding those individuals who are flexible, open, and knowledgeable about the skills necessary to deal with the lifelong learner.

Come. Join the battle!

MICHIGAN'S EFFORTS TO ADDRESS LABOR MARKET CHALLENGES

Gale King and William Weisgerber

Vocational education in the State of Michigan has entered an exciting new era. This new era is characterized by increased cooperation between the auto industry and vocational education. There is a new insistence on results, not just the reporting of training hours and numbers. It would be glorious to say that the new era was carefully planned and orchestrated by clear thinkers from vocational education and the auto industry. The truth is, the new vocational education needs were thrust upon Michigan. Fortunately, efforts to respond have produced thoughtful and long-range results—results may provide a recipe, or at least a starting point, for solutions to similar problems in other areas of the nation.

This article discusses: three phases in modern auto industry history; responses to the current phase; impact of this phase on jobs in the auto industry; the expanding need for vocational training; how the joint effort between vocational education and the auto industry was initiated; the action produced by the joint effort; and, the significance of this effort.

This auto industry analysis, could be entitled, "Impressions From Within," but with the hope that the authors will not appear as the eighth blind man attempting to describe the configuration of the elephant from within the stygian blackness of the creature's stomach. Some historical perspectives are required. Solutions are meaningful only in terms of the problems that were being addressed.

Modern History

Those within the auto industry feel they have lived through three relatively distinct phases since World War II. They feel that movement through these phases has rivaled in peril the passage of early sailing vessels around Cape Horn. And to carry the analogy a step further, the snug harbor at journey's end is still a long way over the horizon.

Post War - 1973

The period from 1946 to 1973 could be called "the good old days." Workers, salaried and hourly, skilled and non-skilled, were comfortable in the illusion that their jobs, except for brief, disquieting periods, would be permanent and would remain relatively unchanged for their entire career. Management jobs, in retrospect, were fun because there were so few outside interferences. Management-union relationships were essentially adversarial. There were, however, ample opportunities for heroes and knights in shining armor on both sides of the bargaining table.

Traditional practices and wisdom could be applied again and again. Management and technical wisdom were essentially pragmatic: what worked in a similar situation last time should be tried again. Take on a little "fat" in good times; pare some off to weather the brief hard times. Develop some good slogans. Give good benefits. Work hard for productivity gains to match cost increases, but remember that, ultimately, increased costs could be reflected in price. Don't worry too much about training programs. Needed skills can be taught in plenty of time through apprenticeship programs, on-the-job training programs, or just on the job. Management training programs were developed. And they were accepted, except when they taught concepts which differed from those held by current managers.

Psychology 101 teaches that an organism in a state of balance, of comfortableness, of complacency, of homeostasis, if you will, will not cry out for change nor respond to the cries of others. And so it was in this period.

1973 - 1979

Out of the unrest of the early 1970's, came a growing awareness on the part of the managers of the auto industry that they and the government (at several levels), were slowly moving into a close-knit partnership. This partnership would manage the auto industry in almost every aspect—employees, customers, the product, energy usage, and the environment.

A list of specific programs/areas shows the automobile industry was forming a partnership with the government and education:

- Occupational Safety and Health programs at the federal and state level (OSHA)
- Federal Motor Vehicle Safety Standards (MOSS) which require certification that established standards of manufacture and performance have been met.
- Federally-established goals, with penalties for failure to meet them, for fuel consumption across the fleet of models produced by a given maker.
- Federally-established standards for exhaust emissions.
- Federally-established standards protecting the air, water, and land surrounding the manufacturing facilities.
- Federally-established standards for the safety of occupants within the motor vehicle.

- Federally-established standards relating to the recruitment, selection, hiring, development, and employment of persons who would work in the industry.

While some within the industry might question specific requirements under these standards and specific procedures by which they would be enforced, few disagreed with the actual need for the requirements themselves.

Of special interest, is the fact that those requirements added significantly to the cost of the vehicle and as such represented an attack upon the comfortable and expensive institutions of the "good old days."

The tendency from within the industry was to continue to hope against hope that those comfortable institutions could, however, endure. And they might have, except for the combined one-two punch that developed fully towards the end of the decade. Economic recession and the long-developing effects of foreign competition eroded profits to the point where complacency, balance, and homeostasis no longer accurately described the nature of the organization. Survival instincts now clamor for change.

1979

In 1969, only Hawaii, California, and to a lesser degree, a few locations in the eastern United States, showed 25 percent or more market penetration by imported autos. By 1979, 17 states had 25 percent penetration or more and 26 states showed 15 percent to 25 percent penetration. Overall, by 1979, foreign competition, largely Japanese, had won almost 30 percent of the American market.

Why were people buying the foreign product in such large numbers? Because they cost less! And what's even worse, because the foreign product was perceived to be of better quality. At what point would the penetration level off? If the auto industry waited to see, it could go the way of bicycles and television—industries, which are overwhelmed by Japanese imports.

How could the Japanese pay the freight all the way to San Francisco and still enjoy up to an $1,800 price advantage? And did they own the only secret to being able to engineer a quality automobile and then being able to reproduce it exactly again and again?

Generally, these questions did have some answers. The Japanese did employ high, new, advanced technology to the fullest. Here the important word is robots. And they did fully utilize the valuable resource represented by employees at all levels. In addition, much has been made of use of statistical process controls which they learned from an American named Deming. A case could also be made for their system of managing and developing managers. And there are some obvious cultural and societal advantages which could be paraded in front of us as excuses for our own failure to compete.

So the phase that began in 1979, and which will continue forever, could be summed up in three words - *Competition* calling for the full use of *Technology*, and a maximum contribution on the part of the *Human Resource*. And from this must come increased productivity and high quality. The assault on the comfortable institutions of the good old days was now complete and the stage was set for change.

Responses

Competition being a relative matter, there are two ways for the auto industry to even things up: increase the effectiveness of the industry itself in productivity and quality, or decrease the ability of the Japanese to compete through import limitations, embargoes, and the enactment of domestic content laws. Lawmakers and industry leaders have mixed views about what, if anything, should be done to decrease the intensity of the foreign competition. Industry leaders leave no doubt, however, about their resolve to become more effective. It almost appears that the lawmakers are waiting to see how much help the domestic industry will still need after current programs to increase productivity and improve quality have had a chance to produce results. Because world markets involve two-way trade, well-intentioned, immediate solutions could have profound and undesirable long-range effects.

Auto industry efforts to become more effective have been profound and wide-sweeping. This list includes:

- Product redesign so as to have available the size and model the customer finds attractive.
- Improvement of manufacturing facilities.
- Development of design, engineering, and manufacturing concepts which make possible quicker responses to the market.
- Maximum use of high technology to produce consistent, repeatable quality at an acceptable rate of production.
- Reorganization of structure, systems, and management style.
- A full range of programs designed to increase employee involvement and more effectively utilize the human resource.

These efforts are obviously highly inter-related. All of them will impact vocational training needs. The two that have the most direct impact, however, are: the maximum use of high technology and programs for developing human resources.

High Technology

Every time a machine becomes worn out or obsolete and is replaced, the new machine will embody some form of high technology. Machines that are not replaced will probably have high technology retrofitted into them. The most dramatic changes have occurred in the area of advanced electronics. Hydraulics and pneumatics, to a lesser degree, are also critical areas for the use of high technology.

The new machine that draws most of the industry's attention is the robot. In terms of keeping it running, however, the repair person, if properly trained, is not overwhelmed by the robot technology because he or she realizes that the robot is nothing more than a complex machine involving specific applications of electronics, hydraulics, pneumatics, and mechanics.

High technology applications involve all classifications of skilled trades and machine operators in these areas:

* Mathematics, from basic to advanced, depending on the individual.
* Basic Industrial Electronics, Hydraulics, and Pneumatics.
* Equipment-specific trouble-shooting and/or operations training.

Human Resource Programs

Foreign competition gains an advantage by fully tapping the valuable resource represented by workers. Who could know more about how effective the manufacturing process is than the person who is actually doing the work?

It is paradoxical that in a country where individual worth is given such high importance, the individual's ability to make a thoughtful contribution to productivity and quality is essentially ignored. At some time in the past, this nation may have been misled into worshiping efficiency when it should have made effectiveness its goal and then strived for efficiency within that context. Human resource programs are attempting to move toward the latter approach.

The Japanese concept of "quality circles," under one guise or another, is sweeping across the auto industry. Every person, skilled and unskilled, hourly and salaried, supervisory and non-supervisory, is being offered the opportunity to become involved in quality circles, or similar mechanisms.

Effective involvement in work groups and in promoting the quality of worklife, calls for a set of basic skills and knowledge that include:

* Basic math and reading.
* Team involvement concepts.
* Data collection and analysis.
* Problem solving and decision-making.
* Action planning.
* Written and oral expression.
* Conducting/participating in effective meetings.
* Product and process information.

Needs Clarified

As these human resource programs develop, and they must, and as high technology totally invades design, engineering, tooling, and manufacturing processes, no job will be the same as it was in the "good old days." Both the company and the employees have needs and concerns which must be considered.

Company Needs and Concerns

Quality and productivity *must* come from industry efforts to become more effective. Where education and training are considered critical to the effectiveness of workers, results are all that count. If a program was designed and offered to develop a certain skill, the industry must know if it really did. Can the person who now has the skill apply it and thus enhance the industry's capacity to be productive and to manufacture quality products? No longer can the industry afford to be satisfied with a simple reporting of the number of people trained and the number of hours.

The fact that no job will ever be the same as it was speaks to the magnitude of the training need that is being thrust upon vocational education. Every operator, every skilled tradesperson, every unskilled worker (perhaps a bad term in the new era) will have unique educational needs.

Manufacturing organizations recognize, as never before, the critical nature of employee training. However, manufacturing organizations are good at manufacturing, not education. Assessment, counseling, training, and follow-up are matters for the professional educator; and, individuals' need for privacy can best be served by a professional third party. Professional educators and the facilities needed for training workers already exist in the communities that surround manufacturing organizations.

Every indicator points to a natural joining of efforts by industry and the educational community. The educational community has always been ready for such a joint effort, and joint efforts have been carried out in different locations. Never before, however, has industry in general felt such a critical need and sought help quite so enthusiastically.

Employee Needs and Concerns

As employees sense that new opportunities exist to make a thoughtful contribution on the job, more and more of them will join in self-development programs that are offered.

Employees are further motivated when they observe the impact such self-development programs can have on their roles as parents and members of their community.

Vocational Education and Change

The changes that vocational education has faced during the past decade have been no less significant than the changes that the automotive industry faced. While not as obvious as down-sized automobiles, increased overseas competition or high technology on the assembly line, there have been substantial challenges to vocational education. In previous years, a primary objective for vocational education was initial employment for youth and young adults. Now, the retraining of our adult workforce is a significant and growing objective. In the past, the relationship with business and industry was vague at times and, in some instances, even doubtful. Today, effectiveness depends on knowing the day-to-day changes in business and industry. In the past, programming for the job training programs was structured with class schedules at the same hours for all classes. Little consideration was given to one-time programs or the termination of an existing program. Programs of short duration tailored for specific job needs are now becoming commonplace. Cooperation in the form of articulation and joint planning between educational agencies, such as two community colleges, and educational levels, like secondary and postsecondary, is vital to serving the current and future needs of the labor market and must expand.

Local Vocational Programs

The rapidly changing job market has presented some unique challenges to vocational education. In Michigan, these challenges were seen as an opportunity to initiate significant program improvement activities in what is taught, when, where, and how. Today's and tomorrow's vocational educators must be able to communicate well and fully understand the situation and problems encountered at the workplace. To do this, they must develop and maintain good working relationships with business, industry, and labor. From these relationships, they will be able to identify the precise job requirements in both essential basic skills and job tasks. In addition, they must be able to provide trainee assessment services, whether for initial employment or retraining. Then, an individualized training plan can be developed that will include all needed educational outcomes, based on what a person already knows and what he or she needs to know to perform in a new job. These vocational services, whether in a community college, area vocational center, or vocational program in a high school, are located in the community in which the person to be trained lives and the business or industry is located. This location provides vocational education with good local and regional insight about the present and future direction of the business/industry and overall community development.

The State Agency Position

The state department of education should play an essential coordination role when the business/industry complex spans several regional educational agencies. When the Michigan Department of Education becomes aware of vocational education needs, a team of representatives from local educational agencies is assembled to lay out an educational program and then select the agency best suited to do each component. The state department acts as a referral or brokering agency, locating the various educational agencies and setting up meetings between business/industry/labor, and education to help identify the exact nature of the needs and the resources that are needed. In addition, the Michigan Department of Education has developed necessary liaisons with other state governmental agencies in an effort to identify and provide important supply/demand data and specific information concerning job task analysis, basic skills required on the job, working conditions, and physical requirements of the job. Also important is the allocation of special federal and state funding for training. In Michigan, federal vocational education funds, Job Training Partnership Act funds, and state appropriations have been distributed through the Departments of Labor, Commerce, and Education.

In Partnership

Organized Labor

The United Auto Workers have demonstrated their concern for education through their organization's staffing. They have a director of education who is willing to work with the education community, and a former U.A.W. education director, Carroll Hutton, was instrumental in the identification of several training needs throughout the State. Mr. Hutton has provided an excellent liaison between education and labor. He currently serves on the Michigan State Board of Education, is a member of the Governor's J.T.P.A. Council, and is the Director of the Ken Morris Labor Studies Center at Oakland University. In addition, the U.A.W. has been very cooperative in providing staff to serve on the State Advisory Council for Vocational Education and the Michigan Career Education Commission.

Organized labor is working with its members to help them understand their needs for training and retraining. It has sponsored, and will continue to sponsor, management-labor agreements which include educational improvements for its membership. It is essential that organized labor have a greater understanding of what education can provide so additional relationships can occur.

Management

The identification and initiation of training programs for product quality and productivity remains an important management function. When a good relationship with the educational community has been developed, a partnership will be formed which will insure that the newly identified job skills have been incorporated into both the ongoing and short-term vocational education programs.

An Industry Education Partnership

A recent partnership shows how the new labor-management system works. The Michigan Department of Education was approached by the Fisher Body Division of the General Motors Corporation concerning its educational needs in several plants located throughout the State. The Kalamazoo Fisher Body Plant was selected by General Motors to participate in a major tool room modernization project. This project required state-of-the-art computer-aided design. The training for this project was jointly provided by the companies which provided new manufacturing equipment, Kalamazoo Valley Community College, and Comstock Public Schools. Historically, many people in the business/industry community see education's role ending with its contribution to the apprenticeship program. The Kalamazoo Fisher Body Computer-Aided Design (CAD) training program initially designated education's role to be approximately 10 percent. Following joint planning and development sessions with Fisher Body, the United Auto Workers, Comstock Public Schools, and Kalamazoo Valley Community College, the share of training done by educational institutions was increased to 47 percent. The partners in this venture did not really understand each others needs or capabilities prior to this project. Management needs to know what education programs were available in their community, and to be able to make some judgments concerning the selection and implementation of these programs.

A staff member of the Michigan Department of Education, James Bebermeyer, developed a strategy identifying the important stages in the selection and implementation of an educational program for business and industry. This planning structure was extremely helpful to the Fisher Body Plant education coordinators and local union representatives as they developed and implemented the basic reading and math program, as follows:

BASIC MATH AND READING PROGRAM

Stage One   Decide generally how to implement the program.
- Who will provide the education?
- What will the education consist of?
- What will its general goals be?
- What should be offered, if anything, beyond math and reading?

Note: This step will certainly involve management and the local union and may involve the local educational agency.

Stage Two   Determine the basic concepts which will govern the ultimate program:
- Competency based?
- Individualized?
- Open entry?
- Adult level?
- Individual assessment?
- Learning prescriptions?
- Individual counseling, including individual preferences and concerns?

Note: The Department of Vocational Education can be of help in this area.

Stage Three   Select the local educational agency the plant will work with:
- The local educational agency will probably have been selected before this step. If not, it should be selected at this time.

Stage Four   Detailed planning - how the steps in the plan will be implemented. Typical steps are:
- Recruiting
- Assessing
- Counseling
- Individual learning prescriptions
- Facilities to be used
- Appropriate training given
- Evaluation: student progress and program
- Budget required (a given level of response to recruiting must be assumed; expect a slow start with buildup)
- Funding
- Approvals - management and local union

This information was available for educational contacts at each of the Fisher Body plants that participated in the program. It helped focus the objectives of the educational program and helped identify the educational process and potential students prior to the selection of a local educational agency.

As a result of the planning that has taken place in Michigan, there are four tool room modernization projects in operation in Fisher Body plants, each done in cooperation with educational agencies located in the plant cities. The four plants are located in Grand Rapids, Kalamazoo, Flint, and Grand Blanc, Michigan.

Cooperating educational agencies are: C. S. Mott Community College, Flint Community Schools, and Genesee Intermediate School District, all located in Flint; Grand Rapids Junior College, Grand Rapids; Kalamazoo Valley Community College, Kalamazoo; and Comstock Public Schools, Comstock.

In addition, 12 Fisher Body plants in the State of Michigan are working with educational agencies in the design and operation of basic skills programs. The Michigan Economic Development (Quick-Start) Program, which is funded with vocational education monies, has worked in 75 local business and industry sites. The local educational agencies have trained over 8,000 unemployed and under-employed adults. Interest in the program has expanded to a point where additional funding must be sought if vocational education can continue to respond to the requests.

What Needs To Be Done

The labor market challenges in education in any state will go unanswered without some type of organizational willingness to make them a priority. They become a priority when industrial and educational organizations assign staff to education and allocate resources to accomplish the educational mission. Educators at the state, regional, and local levels must see as part of their mission the identified educational needs in manufacturing plants, places of business, and union halls.

To do this, they need to make themselves accessible and take every opportunity to change their ongoing programs to encompass company needs. They must also help the community understand the full range of existing educational programming. Without serious commitment to coordination between educational agencies, this effort loses some of its potential in many communities. When educational jurisdictions overlap, the danger of unhealthy competition exists. This results in not only mixed signals to the business/industry community, but is a demonstration of poor use of tax revenues.

Conclusion

It should now be clear that: (1) from the 1970's into the 1980's, the automobile industry has faced rapid changes, bordering on turmoil; (2) the comfortable "good old days," are gone forever in many ways, but specifically in regard to vocational educational needs; (3) the changing nature of jobs and resulting critical needs in education have caused both industry and the educational community to change; (4) industry's urgent cry for help and education's new willingness to enter the rough and tumble world of industrial training and retraining have produced a positive partnership; and, (5) machinery for working together has been established and effective joint efforts are developing.

The partnership, so necessary and already begun, is ongoing and permanent, as future events will show.

PREPACKAGED ADULT PROGRAMS

Barry L. Reece

America's most successful companies stay "close to the customer," say the authors of *In Search of Excellence*. These companies learn from the people they serve. They provide unparalleled quality, service, and reliability—things that work and last. Good service is the rule, not the exception, among these excellent companies.

In the field of adult vocational education staying "close to the customer" is no less important. Many of the client groups vocational education seeks to serve today are becoming increasingly sophisticated consumers of training and development services. These client groups are doing more "comparison shopping" and quality, not price, is often the factor that influences their buying decisions.

Can Vocational Education Compete?

There is already some evidence that public school sponsored adult vocational education is not competing successfully in the marketplace. At a time of unprecedented demand for adult training and development services, adult vocational and technical education enrollments in many school divisions have either reached a plateau or actually declined. And some school divisions no longer attempt to serve adults.

Declining enrollment was one of the factors that prompted Virginia's marketing and distributive education (MDE) leaders to examine existing course offerings and study alternative delivery systems. In 1976, the State Department of Education MDE Service, under the leadership of James Horan, Jr. and Elwood Roche, established a task force to study the problem and develop a corrective plan. The task force cited three major factors that contributed to declining enrollment:

- *Quality of the instructional programs.* Too often, workshops, seminars, and short courses did not meet the training needs and expectations of client groups.
- *Availability of well-prepared adult instructors.* A major barrier to the expansion of the adult MDE program was the shortage of instructors who could effectively teach adults.
- *Ineffective program promotion.* In many cases, instructional programs of

277

the highest quality did not attract sufficient enrollment and had to be cancelled.

The task force agreed that more attention should be given to careful planning, development, and promotion of adult programs. The members also realized that very little additional funding would be available to support this effort.

Doing More with Less

In order to "do more with less," MDE leaders decided to develop and disseminate a series of prepackaged competency-based courses that would not only have broad appeal throughout the state, but would be designed with built-in quality controls. This new approach, labeled "Operation 1000," was initiated in Fall 1976, just a few months after the task force made its final report. A goal of enrolling 1,000 adult learners annually in each course was established. A small amount of money (less than $1,000) was budgeted to develop and field test the first prepackaged adult course.

At the outset, a decision was made to develop and offer adult courses that would exhibit excellent quality in both content and presentation and to design the elements of the program in a way that would ensure quality control. The planners also decided that the market potential of each course would be assessed carefully during the initial planning stages. Further, the new adult marketing education courses would have a strong market demand, feature current knowledge of the subject, and present information in accordance with modern adult learning and communication theory. When adults are the intended learners, the curriculum designers are faced with the special kinds of problems associated with teaching students who already have a broad informational and attitudinal base.

Operation 1000 Planning Model

Since 1976, a five-phase model has guided the planning and development of each Operation 1000 course. During Stage I, the specific competencies to be developed are identified. An advisory committee made up of volunteer adult marketing and distributive education specialists assists with identifying training needs. Committee members are selected by the State Supervisor for Marketing and Distributive Education.

Stage II involves the development of a comprehensive instructional package. The project director works cooperatively with the Virginia Tech Instructional Development Division staff to produce:

- a comprehensive instructor's manual
- a color slide presentation (about 80 slides) with accompanying audio cassette tape
- Overhead projector transparencies
- Learning activities that facilitate competency development
- Resource materials and handouts that support major concepts presented throughout the course
- Promotional materials (brochures, news releases, and lapel buttons) that can be used at the local level to develop interest in the course

Stage III represents perhaps the most important and unique dimension of the Operation 1000 adult education delivery system. Each person who volunteers to instruct an Operation 1000 course must complete a five-hour instructor training program. These train-the-trainer sessions are an essential part of the Operation 1000 concept. Persons attending these training sessions are introduced to the goals and purposes of the instructional module and then observe a demonstration which shows exactly how the materials should be used. Because the trainers learn the concepts from the demonstration, they become more convinced of its value as a teaching tool. This training session also features many tips on how to instruct adult learners. Enrollees are encouraged to read *Teaching Adults: A Guide for Vocational Instructors* which is published by the American Vocational Association.

At the conclusion of the instructor training session, the MDE teacher is encouraged to return home and organize classes in his or her local community. Stage IV of the planning model is therefore the responsibility of the local teacher. Stage V, Follow Up, is the responsibility of the project director.

Program Outcomes

To date, three Operation 1000 courses have been developed for use by school divisions throughout Virginia. The titles and a brief description of each course are:

Contact: Making Positive First Impressions. In a business setting, positive impressions are extremely important because they contribute to repeat business and greater customer loyalty. One goal of this course, offered for the first time in the Fall 1977, is to increase awareness of the importance of positive first impressions in building customer goodwill. A second major goal is to identify those factors that contribute to a positive first impression. Many of the concepts presented in this course appeared in *Contact - The First Four Minutes* by Leonard and Natalie Zunin.

Sales Effectiveness Training. This course emphasizes the development of selling practices used by America's most productive sales personnel. Offered for the first time in Fall of 1979, this course emphasizes those fundamentals of personal selling that have application in a wide range of personal selling positions, i.e., retail, wholesale, service and manufacturing settings.

Fundamentals of Effective Supervision. Introduced in Fall 1981, this course is designed to develop those skills that are essential to success in a supervisory position. The course emphasizes the development of those performance-related job behaviors which are displayed by supervisors recognized for their ability to maximize employee motivation and performance.

One way to assess the impact of Operation 1000 is to consider enrollment. Between 1977 and 1983, a total of 712 classes were offered throughout the state. Total enrollment during this period was 10,868 (1977-78: 661; 1978-79: 802; 1979-80: 1,602; 1980-81: 3, 628; 1981-82: 2,467; 1982-83: 1,708). Average class enrollment is approximately 15 students.

Another way to assess the Operation 1000 program is to consider evaluation forms completed by class members at the end of the course. Approximately 90 percent of those who completed these forms rated the instruction as "good" or "excellent" and would recommend the course to others.

At the end of the third year of the project, the Virginia Tech Instructional Development Division conducted a study to determine what personal and professional benefits were gained by secondary MDE teachers who instructed Operation 1000 adult courses. A questionnaire was mailed to 31 secondary MDE teachers who had taught one or more Operation 1000 courses in their community. Twenty-six usable responses (84 percent) were received.

Figure 1 shows a statistical comparison of selected items. The numbers in parentheses represent the percentages of total responses. The secondary teachers, who are provided with a prepackaged adult course, and in-service training to help them teach the course, can be effective as adult instructors. In addition, it appears that these teachers received a number of personal and professional benefits from their involvement in the Operation 1000 program.

Teacher Involvement
A major barrier, perhaps the most significant barrier to an expanded adult vocational education program, is the shortage of qualified persons who can effectively instruct adult learners. The success of an adult course depends upon the instructor to a very large degree. Operation 1000 is helping the state of Virginia develop a cadre of instructors who are successful in the adult classroom. Teachers find the prepackaged instructional materials easy to use and effective. With the

Figure 1
Summary of Selected Questionnaire Responses

Questionnaire Item	Number of Responses			
	A	AS	DS	D
Teaching Operation 1000 courses has given me a greater feeling of self-confidence.	18 (69)	7 (27)	1 (4)	
As a result of teaching Operation 1000 courses, I have acquired information that I can use in my secondary classes.	21 (81)	5 (19)		
I find teaching Operation 1000 courses professionally rewarding	20 (77)	6 (23)		
Adult learners enrolled in my Operation 1000 courses seem to find the instruction helpful.	22 (85)	3 (12)		
Teaching Operation 1000 courses has permitted me to achieve greater respect in the business community.	9 (35)	16 (62)	1 (4)	
I find the teaching of adults a pleasant alternative to teaching secondary students.	19 (73)	6 (23)	1 (4)	
Operation 1000 courses contribute to improved communication with the business community.	13 (50)	12 (46)	1 (4)	
Persons enrolled in my Operation 1000 classes do not seem to appreciate the instruction.			7 (27)	29 (73)

Note: A-Agree; AS-Agree Somewhat; DS-Disagree Somewhat; D-Disagree

aid of prepackaged training programs, local teachers are gaining more acceptance as professional trainers in the business community.

Future Directions

In the past few years, Operation 1000 has operated without state or federal funding. Without funding, it has been difficult to upgrade the training programs.

In order to maintain the quality of the materials, and insure that they will be available to local school divisions in the future, a decision was recently made to house them at the Interstate Distributive Education Curriculum Consortium (IDECC) center located on the Ohio State University campus. The IDECC center has agreed to revise and update the training programs and to develop a national dissemination plan. In the near future, Operation 1000 will become an adult training and development program available to all states.

References

Peters, Thomas, and Waterman, Robert H. *In Search of Excellence*. New York: Harper and Row, 1982.

Reece, Barry L. *Teaching Adults: A Guide for Vocational Instructors*. Arlington, VA: American Vocational Association.

Zemke, Ron, and Zemke, Susan. 30 things we know for sure about adult learning. *Training/Human Resources Development*, June 1981, pp. 45-46, 48, 52.

Zunin, Leonard, and Zunin, Natalie. *Contact - The First Four Minutes*. New York: Ballantine Books. 1972.

CENTER FOR EMPLOYMENT RESOURCES

Rosemary F. Kolde

Successful employment and individual productivity are important to personal fulfillment and to improving the quality of life for everyone in society. Human resource centers, or career resource centers, are becoming an essential stop for adults entering, reentering, retraining or upgrading their skills for the labor force. These adults are concerned with finding employment that will be personally satisfying. These centers provide career information, vocational assessment, employment planning, employment counseling, and referrals to appropriate community social service agencies and training programs.

Human resource centers also ameliorate many of the existing barriers to employment and job satisfaction experienced by high school dropouts and unskilled graduates. This large segment of the nation's adult population is untrained, unskilled and unemployable and many may be candidates for welfare rather than for productive jobs. Job information, counseling, and career planning are no longer easily accessible once an individual has left the formal school structure. Unemployment, underemployment, and job dissatisfaction in this population demand a high price in society.

High technology, fluctuating unemployment, displacement of workers, and the shifting age mix of our population also contribute to the need for additional support services provided through human resource centers. Barriers to employment such as age, lack of marketable skills, and poor knowledge of the world of work, are being encountered by a steadily increasing number of adults. Through human resource centers' services, thse individuals can be provided assistance which enables them to become or remain productive members of the nation's workforce.

The nation's economy has provided another avenue for services associated with human resource centers in recent years. Industrial assessment is rapidly growing as business and industry endeavor to ensure that shrinking operating budgets are optimally utilized. Pre-employment and pre-apprenticeship screening, pre-promotional assessment, and employment counseling and outplacement services are also a viable part of human resource centers.

The Mission

The Center for Employment Resources opened its doors on August 28, 1978. It is located north of Cincinnati, Ohio, and is an integral part of the total vocational education program provided by the Great Oaks Joint Vocational School District for the people and business and industry of Southwest Ohio.

The Center for Employment Resources provides a viable program to assist unemployed, underemployed, and dissatisfied adults in becoming successfully and satisfactorily employed. At its inception, the idea of a "total human resource center" was new in the United States. Various individual components of such a resource center have been used by community colleges and business and industry during the past five or ten years. However, the concept of providing individuals and industry with access to all of the components at one location is unique.

CARF Accreditation

The Center has been utilized as a model human resource center in Ohio as well as in many other states. The uniqueness of the Center revolves around its many available services as well as its linkage with over 45 cooperating community agencies. It has become noted for its "one-stop-shopping-center" approach - all necessary services and resources under one roof.

The linkage between the Center and community agencies has proved to be a valuable asset in the delivery of services to clients. In 1982, the Center decided to apply for accreditation through the Commission of Accreditation of Rehabilitation Facilities (CARF) to become an accredited institution providing assessment and skill training services for handicapped adults. Among the Center's clientele were many handicapped adults who had not been successfully integrated into the job market. The Great Oaks Joint Vocational School District was granted accreditation in 1983 and became the only vocational school in the United States to receive this accreditation.

A funding proposal was then initiated and submitted to the Ohio Department of Education for the expansion of services for the handicapped adult and out-of-school population. This project is currently underway and provides preassessment counseling, assessment, development of training and/or employment plans, vocational training alternatives with instructional support services, job placement and follow-up. Often, these services are provided in collaboration with referring community agencies which also financially assist the client.

Industrial Assessment and Related Services

Collaboration with business and industry and the recent recession have led to extensive utilization of the industrial assessment and related services provided through the Center for Employment Resources. Business and industry utilize the Center for a total development system, which identifies individuals with advancement potential, assesses their strengths and weaknesses, and provides assistance for individual growth. These services assist companies in saving time, effort, and financial resources in developing their personnel.

The Center has validated its testing instruments and established norms. It constantly reviews and updates the norms. The testing programs are individually designed to meet industry's specific requirements, and they are based on extensive research and development of effective industrial testing instruments. Currently, the center has over fifty occupational work samples to simulate field operations in specific vocational areas, a wide range of paper and pencil tests, and interest inventories which evaluate preferences and proficiences. Since successful and continual industrial relationships are better fostered by program flexibility, testing is provided either at the Center or at the industrial site.

Industrial services provided by the Center include:

Pre-employment screening reduces attrition and increases production; provides sound information for making personnel decisions; identifies potential employees who are appropriately skilled; and, assesses employees' capabilities to learn new skills.

Pre-apprenticeship screening identifies employees who have potential for success; provides an objective, non-biased assessment; aids in improving employees' performance; and, assists in meeting training objectives.

Pre-promotional assessment identifies supervisory skills and talents; evaluates job knowledge; determines decisiveness and organizational skills; and, assesses leadership potential.

Employment counseling initiates direct referral services to community agencies for employees' problems (i.e. alcoholism, family discord, and emotional difficulties); determines employees' educational growth possibilities; and, defines employees' career goals and skill upgrading.

Outplacement services define transferable employment skills; build self-esteem and confidence; investigate occupational interests and skill aptitudes; refine job seeking techniques; and, develop job placement leads.

Individual Assessment and Counseling

The great majority of people needing individual career counseling and assessment are outside the formal structure which normally provides career information and guidance - the traditional framework of school. Population changes — fewer youth, more adults and senior citizens — have brought about a societal transformation in the way job information and counseling are provided.

The increase in female participation in the labor market and increased divorce rates also have implications for the utilization of services provided by human resource centers. Many women are entering the labor force for the first time or after an extended period away from the job. Additional resources and services are needed to support their efforts to achieve successful and satisfactory employment.

A broad spectrum of the population also currently needs assistance in coping with mid-life career changes, rapidly advancing technology, a constantly changing job market, increased leisure time, and greater longevity. Evidence indicates that many more middle aged persons experience a "mid-life crisis" in their careers and will make career changes within and between their fields. The growth in the population increases the need for innovative career counseling and the development of new career or second career programs designed to ease their transition.

The Center for Employment Resources provides assessment services to individuals in a testing atmosphere that is conducive to optimum client performance. A comprehensive assessment program is designed for each individual to determine occupational interests, employability strengths, and barriers to employment—enabling each person to experience a better understanding of his or her employment potential. Clients are provided with up-to-date labor market information and pertinent knowledge of specific occupational requirements. An employability and/or career plan is prepared which coordinates an individual's aptitudes and interests with occupational requirements and the method to be utilized for implementation of the plan. Career counseling assists individuals in acquiring a more precise understanding of their employment potential and options and leads to a more successful and rewarding career path.

Personnel

The Center's staff consists of a director, associate director, three evaluator/ counselors, one evaluator, one placement and financial assistance coordinator, one instructional coordinator, one secretary and one clerk typist. Those involved in counseling are certified counselors in Ohio as well as experienced in vocational, educational, and career planning. The associate director, along with other credentials, is certified by the Commission on Certification of Work Adjustment and Vocational Evaluation Specialists (CVE). Additional services are rendered by an adult education program supervisor, an adult basic education supervisor, and two displaced homemaker coordinators. Supportive services are provided by the more than 45 cooperating community social service agencies which often provide necessary financial aid, child care, transportation and medical assistance.

Delivering Career Counseling

Vocational education is effective in addressing the challenges of the present economy. It depends on its ability to assist individuals to identify and successfully match their relevant skills and aptitudes with their career goals and objectives. A human resource center provides an avenue for vocational education to deliver the necessary components, such as assessment, testing, guidance, counseling to adults in transition. It provides a viable and valuable service to individuals as well as the business community.

INDEX